CROSSING INTO MANHOOD

CROSSING INTO MANHOOD
A Men's Studies Curriculum

Christopher P. Mason

CAMBRIA
PRESS

YOUNGSTOWN, NEW YORK

Library of Congress Cataloging-in-Publication Data
Mason, Christopher P.
    Crossing into manhood: a men's studies curriculum / Christopher P. Mason.
        p.cm.
    Includes bibliographical references and index.
    ISBN-13: 978-1-934043-30-1 (alk. paper)
    ISBN-10: 1-934043-30-3 (alk. paper)
    1. Men—Identity. 2. Masculinity. 3. Boys—Education—Social aspects.
I. Title.

HQ1090.M382 2006
305.31—dc22

2006034624

*This book is dedicated to my wife, Jeanne,
and to the memory of my father,
Cecil Herbert Mason, Jr.*

TABLE OF CONTENTS

LIST OF DIAGRAMS, CHARTS, AND TABLES

FOREWORD

Chris Mason's deftly reasoned and inspiring book arrives at a propitious time for all those who care about boys and their education. It seems that for a long time "masculinity" has been besieged by criticism—at the extreme attacked as a toxic power. With good reason, the spotlight has been trained on gender equality, and on overcoming the social and educational barriers to women's and girls' achievement and success. While the journey is not yet complete and obstacles remain, gains for girls are among the most revolutionary of our time. It may well be, as some have said, that this was a necessary swing of the pendulum. But where has this left the boys?

Since the 1990s new research has uncovered mounting concern about boys' well-being and achievement. While the evidence is at times controversial, we now see clear signs and grave risk of underachievement among boys. There is growing concern that schools are not serving boys well. In higher education, young women outperform young men in admission and in academic performance. With so many factors at play, some claim that this "boy crisis" is exaggerated, but intuition and experience also tell us that all is not well—that we have failed the boys.

Writers have also dissected a crisis of masculinity and manhood, caught between ancient mythologies of what it means to be a man and the corrosive pressures of a decidedly complex world. "Masculinity" in all its complex meanings has emerged as a surprisingly rich and compelling topic—one that matters to how we educate boys everywhere.

And the astonishing if still fledgling research into the workings of the human brain has begun to tease out significant gender differences that will have a profound impact on how we educate boys and girls. While many have warned that the step from research to practice is still in its infancy, few can doubt that this science is set to revolutionize teaching and learning.

All of this comes at a time when single-sex education—why and how single-sex schools, divisions, grades or classes can serve the learning and maturation of boys and girls—has emerged as a significant stream in the contemporary debate. Many in the United States in particular are surprised to learn that single-sex schooling is a natural part of the educational scene in many parts of the world including the United Kingdom, Australia, and New Zealand. In the independent and parochial school sector of the United States, hundreds of single-sex schools are thriving and growing after a culling that quickened especially in and after the 1970s. Current evidence now lends renewed and powerful support to their mission and purpose. In 2006 the U.S. Department of Justice ruled in its Title IX decision in such a way as to remove any constitutional obstacles to the ability of public and charter schools to introduce single-sex schooling. In the wake of this announcement, we are witnessing an extraordinary outpouring of interest and action.

The arrival of Chris Mason's book is thus propitious because it comes at a time when our understanding of how boys learn and develop has grown profoundly, when our concern for their achievement and well-being has skyrocketed, and when interest in schools that can focus all their energy on boys and their needs is strong and buoyant. But what educators need and seek is an arsenal of programs and teaching practices that actually work.

The intellectual harvest of a seasoned and experienced educator with a deep wisdom about boys and schools, Chris Mason's book is an important contribution to that growing body of thinking about practice. It deserves close reading. First and foremost, he builds with infinite patience an inventory of writings on manhood, viewed from a wide range of theoretical and historical perspectives. He moves expertly across the continuum of that hot debate about the biological and cultural roots of masculinity. His project builds both a composite picture of the crisis within contemporary masculinity, and a warchest of sharp and useful tools with which to understand its many strands. There is a happy combination of critical and generous intellect at work here as he neatly shuffles and categorizes these perspectives and then coaxes from his survey a sound vision of what masculinity could mean.

While revealing this broad context, his special focus is the dynamic challenges of boys at the cusp of early adulthood. For Mason, late adolescence—that time of seemingly infinite power of body, mind and spirit—is the setting clay on the potter's wheel. This is the author's confident domain, and here he navigates controversial ground. For the adolescent male, universal and deeply embedded rites of passage enact notions of masculinity at their most personal and communal levels. For reasons that Mason unfolds, positive and life-affirming rites of passage to manhood have been negated or eroded in the modern age, and the energy directed along more destructive and pernicious channels.

As the progress of this book moves to the structure and content of a curriculum for these boys in passage to manhood, Mason distils and exploits the insights afforded by his careful review of a rich literature. What emerges is a powerful paradigm for a new masculinity for these young men—a masculinity that is humanistic, holistic, and vibrantly engaging.

The curricular program that Mason offers gives compelling content for the reconstruction of these rites of passage, a program led by caring adults and role models who want to help boys navigate to healthy and purposeful manhood. He advocates, with reason, that boys be "set apart" for this instruction in some way and at some point in their education. Here, he builds a well-rounded picture of one instructive ideal—what an all-boys' boarding school does at each stage in their progression through the school to provide a profoundly humane and engaging curriculum, one that simulates and re-works the experience of those rites of passage. (The Grail Legend will never quite look the same again!). Not surprisingly, the lengthy course outlines that close the book are designed to inspire boys' active encounter with the more accessible writings on masculinity reviewed in this study, spliced with imaginative resources from literature and movies.

Chris Mason's timely book is an important resource for practitioners who seek grounding in the literature of masculinity as a basis for teaching boys, and who need a wise and experienced guide through this rich and diverse world. His book helps—and indeed compels—those who teach and care about boys to create and share their own strategies for curriculum and school design, and to engage in this vital work with rigour and dedication, and with compassion and joy.

Bradley Adams
Executive Director
International Boys' Schools Coalition

PREFACE

I have been working with adolescents throughout my professional life, most of the time focusing on teenage boys in both educational and church settings. As an ordained Episcopal priest and educator, I have become increasingly concerned about the myopic angst many boys exhibit in their personal and social relations and view of life. In order to cope with their internal discomfort, boys will resort to hypermasculine posturing, cower in self-defeat, or retreat into narcissistic self-indulgence. These strategies reveal their inner weakness and need.

Boys' inner weakness and need are becoming increasingly evident in Western culture. On the one hand, the culture nurtures and glorifies dysfunctional masculinist ways and ideals, including an increasingly violent "boy code," while, on the other hand, failing to provide healthy and supportive initiation processes that can support boys in their growth and maturity. In short, boys are floundering, and only some kind of intervention and paradigm shift can help them cross over from boyhood into manhood.

Furthermore, the question increasingly being raised is who is going to do this important and life-saving work? I believe strongly that educational institutions must not only be engaged in the work of educating minds but also committed to the mission of supporting and nurturing adolescent boys as they make the crossing into manhood. The crossing is no automatic and easy task. Time, effort, sensitivity, and commitment are needed to make the crossing possible for our sons. I will argue that mature, initiated adult men need to stand up and assume this important task.

This book is a call to engagement with teenage boys in the work of forming men. My hope and prayer is that this book will foster commitment and action on the part of mature men to be initiatory elders for our sons during the critical transitional years from boyhood into manhood. My further hope is that this book will facilitate personal growth and understanding for our sons as they make their crossing into manhood.

ACKNOWLEDGMENTS

I wish to offer many thanks to the faculty and staff of the Blue Ridge School, and especially to former headmaster, Dr. Edward M. McFarlane, for eleven special years as a part of that educational community.

I also want to thank Adele Brinkley for her consummate editorial skills and Tommie Sargent, a colleague and fellow educator at Oak Hill Academy, for formatting this material.

I wish to express my thanks to the following: the American Psychological Association for permission to use a chart from an article in the *American Psychologist* (1997) by Halpern; to HarperCollins for permission use a chart from *Gods in Everyman* by Jean Shinoda Bolin; to Inner City Books for permission to use quoted material from *Under Saturn's Shadow* by James Hollis; Jossey-Bass for permission to use a table from *Boys and Girls Learn Differently* by Michael Gurian; to Lost Borders Press for permission to use quoted material from *The Four Shields: The Initiatory Seasons of Human Nature* by Steven Foster and Meredith Little; to McGraw-Hill for permission to use quoted materials from *Human Sexuality: Diversity in Contemporary America* by Strong, DeVault, Sayad, and Yarber; to Random House for permission to use a diagram from *Seasons of a Man's Life* by Daniel J. Levinson; to Routledge for permission to use a diagram from *On Jung* by Anthony Stevens; to Shambhala for permission to use a diagram found in *Ego and Archetype* by Edward Edinger; from Tiger Lily Publications for permission to use quoted material from *Where Were You When I Needed You, Dad?* by Jane Myers Drew; and from W.W. Norton and Company for permission to use a diagram from *Identity and the Life Cycle* by Erik Erikson.

CROSSING INTO MANHOOD

CHAPTER ONE

INTRODUCTION

BACKGROUND OF THE PROBLEM

The Greek playwright Aristophanes (448–330 B.C.) tells of a prehistorical period in which large round, roly-poly beings that had two faces, four hands, and four feet existed. Each being possessed both masculine and feminine genitalia and lived together peacefully in an idyllic world. However, hubris brought the wrath of the gods, and Zeus split humanity into two entities. Since then, humans have been engaged in a search for the missing half (Plato, *Symposium*). What man is searching for is a sense of the mirror self to complete the whole in a connection to another. This myth explains the beginning of the search for identity and provides the mythological background for the millennia-old struggle of attaining gender identity. It is a story prefigured in the psychological explanations of masculine development by Freud and Jung, and it is the untold theme of gender history.

For more than three thousand years, patriarchy has been the predominant social and relational paradigm of Western culture. At one level, patriarchy meant the authority a father had over the members of his own family, but at another level, it has come to signify the rule of men over society as well as male control of the economic, power, and decision-making structures of society. Because of patriarchy's ubiquity and influence over all of Western culture's history as a defining principle of gender roles and expectations, it is important to review briefly the historical development of patriarchy and its influence on masculine role models.

Doyle (1995) identified five different male models that have shaped Western masculine self-identity: the epic male, the spiritual male, the chivalric male, the renaissance male, and the bourgeois male. Although each model represented an exaggerated ideal impossible for any one man to attain completely, nevertheless, each model shaped the masculine identity and role expectations of males of the time and supported the patriarchal social order.

The first masculine model was the epic male of the Greek and Roman periods as depicted in the literature of Homer and Virgil. The epic male was characterized primarily as a man of action, a leader, and a fighter. Males who fulfilled this gender identity exhibited masterful skill in warfare and possessed great strength, courage, and loyalty to his comrades. A man's loyalty was hierarchically determined: first to king and leader, second to comrades in arms, and finally to clan and family. Homer's *The Iliad* and *The Odyssey* glorified the Greek heroes of the Trojan War as exemplars of the best of ideal manhood. Achilles and Odysseus take leading roles in Homer's epic tales depicting the best and brightest of the Greek nation's masculine role models. Achilles embodies the best in warrior manhood and loyalty to king and comrades. Not only does Odysseus exemplify these qualities, but also he models the manhood ideals of fierce loyalty to clan and family during his twenty-year odyssey to return home and retake his homeland. At the psychological level, *The Odyssey* represents the encounters Odysseus must face and successfully negotiate with his unconscious psyche in order to return home—a classic metaphor for the journey of self-discovery that all men must make in their lives in order to become authentic selves (Edinger, 1994).

In a similar manner, Virgil's *Aeneid* spotlights the Roman hero Aeneas as the warrior-adventurer who returns home to Italy from Troy and becomes the founder of Rome. Aeneas' adventures parallel those of Odysseus' exploits. Escaping from ruined Troy, Aeneas and his faithful crew wander for seven years before arriving in Italy. During that time Aeneas' courage and perseverance are tested as he endures hardships, subterfuges, the seductions of women, and fierce battles. The story of Aeneas has numerous psychological truths to tell about the journey men make through life, most notably the desire to reconnect with the long absent father and the issue of male loneliness (Baber, 1992). Throughout the epic, Aeneas is pictured as the ideal of Roman manhood, primarily that a man must face much suffering and hardship before he can reach his destination.

Along with the warrior-leader masculinity model presented in Greek and Roman societies was the widespread acceptance of homosexual and pederast sexual relations. Horace called homosexuality or *ephebic* love the "Greek vice," and though it was more prevalent and accepted in Greek society, it was practiced by the Romans too (Berardino, 1997). This practice did not seem problematic for most of society, and it certainly did not undermine the masculine ideal of the time. Rather, it was an acceptable part of an established role identity of the male gender and relations of the time.

The Christian era brought massive changes in values that profoundly influenced the course of Western culture and gender roles. Jesus' and the Christian church's emphasis on love and self-renunciation was a radical departure from classical ideals. Moreover, Jesus consorted with women during his ministry and exhorted a new paradigm for husbands and wives in the family (Ephesians 5:21–6:9). The Christian understanding of masculinity emerged from the writings of the early church fathers and from the fourth and fifth century monastic movement. Labeled the spiritual man, this masculine ideal "endorsed celibacy, or at least infrequent sexual experiences, as well as a turning away from earthly pursuit" (Doyle, p. 29). In short, the model spiritual male "was one in whom the spiritual was preeminent over the worldly" (Doyle, p. 29). He was motivated toward an afterlife above all else. St. Paul, the Christian missionary to the gentile world who helped establish the Christian church in the Roman Empire, and numerous saints, such as Benedict, founder of the monastic movement in Italy, and Francis of Assisi became objects of the spiritual male ideal.

Connected with the spiritual male model was the Christian church's stance against homosexuality. Although the Greek and Roman worlds accepted the practice of homosexuality, it was considered by early Christianity as evidence of the moral depravity of the pagan world. In contrast to the epic male's general acceptance of homosexuality, the spiritual male was expected to renounce sexual desires and practices and to adopt the celibate life. Celibacy was the ideal masculine gender role, but if a man could not follow the ideal, the only acceptable alternative was monogamous, heterosexual practices. From this period, the roots of antihomosexual thinking in Christian societies were established.

During the Middle Ages, the feudal system, with its emphasis on the soldier-knight class, ushered in a new masculine ideal, the chivalric male (Doyle, p. 30). Unlike the spiritual male ideal, the chivalric male ideal was akin to the epic male with its emphasis on the warrior-knight who possessed great physical strength, warfare skills, loyalty to his king or liege lord, and a chivalric devotion to his lady (Doyle). The knight was expected to idealize a woman to the point of adoration, much like the reverence accorded the Virgin Mary by Christians. The ideal of manhood found its fullest expression in the person of Lancelot of the Arthurian legend. Lancelot embodied all of the chivalric masculine ideals of physical strength, skill in war, devotion to king, and chivalric love of his lady. In most instances, this courtly love was not acted out sexually; however, it had a fantasized sensuality aspect to it.

Sixteenth century England saw the emergence of the Renaissance male model (Doyle). The Renaissance revitalized the virtues of learning, and the populace became increasingly independent in its thinking and inquisitive about the world around them. The model man "who sought intellectual goals that would free him from the restraints of a dogmatic church authority" (Doyle, p. 31) replaced the chivalric, warrior-knight masculine ideal. The quintessential Renaissance man was Michelangelo, an intellectual master in both the arts and sciences, who flourished under the patronage of the Catholic Church. Best known as a sculptor, he was famous for his painting of the ceiling of the Vatican's Cistine Chapel and for his experimental drawings of the human anatomy and bird wings that anticipated modern medicine and flight respectively.

According to Doyle, the Renaissance man had a dark side. Complex and introspective, he was a person who was sometimes beset with internal angst and conflict. William Shakespeare captured the tragedy of this masculine model in his literary characters of Hamlet, Macbeth, and Lear, dark, brooding protagonists who experienced great personal tragedy and degradation.

By the eighteenth century in England and the rest of Europe, a powerful and prominent middle class arose that prized and pursued money and social status. In this milieu evolved the bourgeois male ideal of manhood (Doyle). With money and prestige as the symbols of power, the ideal of the middle class man was the successful businessman and entrepreneur who dared to undertake adventurous and risky business enterprises in order to succeed in order to validate his sense of manhood. Mosse (1996) documents a resurgence in the Greek ideal of the masculine body as a symbol of manliness. The classical emphasis on outward harmony, control, and proportion was mirrored inwardly as indicative of manly will power and moral courage.

The sixteenth century enclosure movement contributed to the rise of the industrial age and significantly influenced the future development of masculine identity. The enclosure movement was the large-scale walling off of public lands by large landholders in order to preserve farming and animal management, but it effectively removed the land that the peasantry had traditionally been permitted to use for personal subsistence. The enclosure movement forced men and their families to migrate to the cities and to sell their labor to the mills and factories of the Industrial Revolution. Kimbrell (1995) called the enclosure of men a metaphor that explains the current masculine identity crisis. It began the economic process that ultimately removed men from a close connection with their families and finally with themselves. The result was that men were the victims of two enclosures:

> First, his land had been taken from him, enclosed for use by the large landowners for export crops. This enclosure violently cut him off from his traditional life, community, and work. Next he himself had been enclosed into the foreign environment of the industrial workplace, most often for six days a week, twelve to sixteen hours a day. Virtually all of his waking hours were spent away from his family and the natural world. This dual enclosure had a devastating impact on men working in the industrial workplace. Locked into their role as primary breadwinner in the new labor market,

> the majority of men became fully dispossessed. They were
> robbed of any usable property; they lost economic inde-
> pendence, now depending wholly on wages given by their
> employers; they lost spiritual independence as their fear of
> starvation and joblessness made them subservient to their
> bosses; and they had to forsake forever home employment
> and self-employment. (Kimbrell, 1995, pp. 38–39)

The enclosure of men became the first step in the transformation of masculine identity in the modern age. Men's bodies were enclosed; there-fore, their minds had to be enclosed as well in order to accommodate a new masculine mystique.

Kimbrell (1995) identified four archetypes of what he called the "mascu-line mystique," a term he coined for the "dysfunctional and reductionistic modern mythology about the nature of men" (p. xiv). This masculine mystique not only brought men into the modern crisis they are experiencing, but also it prevented them from doing something about their victimization, which has resulted in the "near-fatal undermining of their gender" (p. xiv). Kimbrell identified and discussed four archetypes of the masculine mystique: the machine man, the competition man, the profit man, and the power man.

The machine man is described as the robotic, mechanistic male who is not the result of hardwiring in the brain, but of the centuries-long encul-turation process of men for the specific economic and social imperatives of the industrial system. "Efficiency is the primary virtue of the modern male robopath" (Kimbrell, 1995, p. 62). The efficiency-driven man's overworked, mechanized life is responsible for two characteristics of the masculine mys-tique—lack of emotion and lack of caring. The result is that the machine man is crippled in his ability "to be a full and present, reflective and emo-tional human being for himself, his spouse, children, or friends" (Kimbrell, p. 64). Further negative results are that the machine man is "incapable of authentic emotional bonding with family, friends, or community" (Kimbrell, p. 64) and is unable to show care and concern for others or even for his own physical and mental health.

Kimbrell noted that the competition man is equally as dysfunctional as the machine man except in the workplace where he "thrives as an autonomous economic combatant" (Kimbrell, p. 83). The result is that the competition man has problems sharing honest thoughts or emotions as well as an inability to balance cooperation with competition. The most negative effect on the competition man is that "it profoundly undermines male friendship and bonding" (Kimbrell, p. 83).

Kimbrell described the profit man as one who is isolated and alienated because he is focused only on the sale. The profit man is also isolated from other men because they are potential competitors over whom he must triumph in order to earn a living. The striving for a profit causes the profit man to be isolated from the rest of humanity because collectively it is studied and viewed as a sales target. Furthermore, the profit man is isolated from his product because product morality, value, and worth are subsumed under the overarching need to make a profit. Self-interest, therefore, is the chief characteristic of the masculine mystique for which the profit man lives. One of the tragic victims of the profit man archetype is fatherhood. As industrialization has progressed, men have been systematically removed from the home for longer and longer hours to work removed from his family and from fathering his children. Choosing between fatherhood and making a living to support one's family creates a dilemma for men.

> Our society, still entranced by the masculine mystique, glorifies the successful professional man, frowns upon the man who picks his family over work, and virtually dismisses any man who would choose to be unemployed or a "househusband" in order to be a better father. Men know their place. They know that their principal defining role is to be the breadwinner, that their primary identity is their work, not being caring as fathers.... To be seen as adequate men, they must be "productive" citizens, able to support themselves and their families. They know that they must compete successfully and gain wealth and power if they are to be validated as men. And they know that failure in this central task, whether in the form of unemployment or low-level jobs (a near-certain fate for millions upon millions of men) will spell disaster both economically and for their masculine identity. (Kimbrell, pp. 179–180)

In describing the power man, Kimbrell asserted that dominance and power are basic characteristics of the masculine mystique and that men need to have power over such things as money, resources, and labor because of their masculinity. This definition of masculinity denies men their traditional, nutrient power and associates them with the shadow sides of power as manifested in rape, harassment, the destruction of the planet's ecological resources, and the exploitation of workers. The identification of men with technology and power has resulted in men becoming one-sided and dysfunctional, causing them to forsake participation in and relations with other men, women, and nature. The paradox of power contributes to sexual confusion and dysfunction in men. Kimbrell wrote,

> The power-man model demands that men be able to domi-
> nate women as part of their sexual role, that they penetrate
> women to control and conquer in true Baconian fashion.
> Men in our society face a difficult bind. While the growth
> of technology, with its identification with masculine power,
> swells in Priapus-like fashion, the average male faces the
> terror of the potential failure of his all-too-human personal
> power machine. If he is to be validated as a power man, he
> has to "get it up," keep it up, and use it in tireless pumping
> fashion so as to dominate and subdue his partner, preferably
> through her exhaustion from total sexual satiation. Any-
> thing less is seen as a failure of power by many men and
> women alike. So-called impotence (literally lack of power)
> or premature ejaculation then becomes the intimate sexual
> corollary to unemployment or technological illiteracy for
> men. It stigmatizes a man as a failure—demonstrates his
> inability to fulfill the dictates of the machine and power
> mythologies. (p. 128)

The result is that men are caught in the masculine mystique bind of male identity from which they cannot escape, which makes them a disposable gender, which subjects them to a system in which work is meaningless and endless, and which results in high incidents of physical and emotional maladies.

Keen (1991) used the metaphor of the "self-made man" to describe the eighteenth century American masculine gender model. Industrialization and westward expansion witnessed the elevation of scientists, inventors, and manufacturers who were masters of themselves and nature. Manhood was described as "muscular, pragmatic, and action-oriented" (Keen, p. 106). During the pioneer days, American men such as Daniel Boone were viewed as models of manhood. The nineteenth century saw a shift in the manhood ideal as the emphasis on "self" became focused on "self-improvement" (Keen, p. 107). Manhood became defined as "exercise, discipline, hard work, moderate habits, and true grit," (Keen, p. 107), with Teddy Roosevelt manifesting the most admired virtues of the age. The self-made man exhibited such characteristics as a powerful ego, strong character, and a larger-than-life social persona. However, beneath this extroverted façade was a repressed emotional world of dark desires. Rarely could men give voice to the shadow sides of their psyches, but Samuel Clements did in his diaries, especially in later life.

The twentieth century experienced two world wars and the Depression, which seriously challenged and exposed the American psyche and gave rise to the psychological man (Keen, p. 108). The post war period was a time when Freud and the psychoanalytical movement arose and asserted a new ideal for manhood. Freud opened up a psychological world of libido and desires, "cruel mothers, seducing fathers, and children who murdered their parents ... [where] incest was the rule and perversion the order of the day" (Keen, p. 109). Later, Freud's protégé, Carl Jung complemented and offered a counter point as men sought to understand themselves and their dreams that arose from the unconscious. Consequently, "modern psychology has given men back their inwardness, their subjectivity, their feelings, and the permission to pay attention to the stories of their lives" (Keen, p. 110).

The postmodern era, which began around 1960, is characterized by the information revolution, materialistic consumption, diverse lifestyles, and a lack of commitment to any single ideology. According to Keen, Postmodern man is a quintessential consumer.

> At best, postmodern man has gone for the gusto, done away with pleasure anxiety, and thrown off the old capitalist tyranny of scarcity-consciousness and postponed gratification. He is no longer trying to improve his soul, develop his willpower, or save himself for some future heaven. He has given up the quest for a single identity, a consistent point of view or triumph over tragedy .... His tastes, life-style, and

> convictions are formed by fashion .... His life is organized
> more around the idea of "taste" than of "right or wrong";
> his world is aesthetic rather than moral. (pp. 110–111)

Oscar Wilde and his character Dorian Gray prefigure the postmodern man perfectly with Gray's endless pursuit of the beautiful with a narcissistic desire for personal gratification coupled with materialistic consumption.

During the 1970s, the feminist movement's first critiques of masculine gender roles and expectations questioned and criticized traditional masculine gender explanations. Males have historically been the focal point of most psychological research, which viewed the male gender as representative of all humanity. However, feminist scholars who have revised the notions on women's psychological development have criticized and attacked this traditional assumption. Joseph Pleck's *The Myth of Masculinity* (1981) meticulously deconstructed the male sex role model with its representative empirical literature and concluded that the male sex role paradigm was an inadequate model of masculinity. He posited the following ten propositions in his "sex role strain" paradigm:

1. Sex roles are operationally defined by sex role stereotypes and norms.
2. Sex roles are contradictory and inconsistent.
3. The proportion of individuals who violate sex roles is high.
4. Violating sex roles leads to social condemnation.
5. Violating sex roles leads to negative psychological consequences.
6. Actual or imagined violation of sex roles leads individuals to over-conform to them.
7. Violating sex roles has more severe consequences for males than females.
8. Certain characteristics prescribed by sex roles are psychologically dysfunctional.
9. Each sex experiences sex role strain in its paid work and family roles.
10. Historical change causes sex role strain. (Pleck, pp. 135–152)

Pleck's view was that the Masculine Sex Role Identity (MSRI) paradigm has dominated the scientific and popular conceptions of sex roles since the 1930s and has been taken for granted. His sex role strain paradigm asserts that modern gender roles are contradictory and inconsistent and that there is no unifying structure for a monolithic gender role identity. In fact, pressuring males into a stereotypical male identity invites dysfunctionality and other psychological consequences. "The MSRI paradigm has helped to generate sex role strain," Pleck concluded (p. 160). He wrote,

> The concept of sex role identity prevents individuals who violate the traditional role for their sex from challenging it; instead, they feel personally inadequate and insecure—the subjective experience of sex role strain. The deeper the experience of the MSRI paradigm in the culture, the more widespread the experience of strain. Through this process the MSRI paradigm paradoxically sowed the seeds of its own demise. As sex role strain continued to build, the women's and men's liberation movements arose in response, providing individuals a way of understanding the strain they experience, analyzing its sources, and reducing it. (p. 160)

The Myth of Masculinity sounded the clarion call for the reexamination of masculine gender roles in every aspect of male life and identity. The unexamined ideology of patriarchal masculinity that defined men, as well as women and the institutions that nurtured them, came under attack by the scholars of the feminist movement (Kimmel and Messner, 2004).

By the 1970s, there had been a tremendous growth in women's studies programs, advocating a new model for the study of gender and rejecting the traditional assumption that masculinity was the norm by which both males and females were measured (Kimmel and Messner, 2004). Against this backdrop, the so-called "men's movement" emerged. Just as women began questioning their gender stereotyping, men started asking similar questions about masculine stereotypes. Erving Goffman (1963) made the following observation about an overarching, monolithic American male gender ideal:

> In an important sense there is only one complete unblushing male in America: a young, married, white, urban, northern, heterosexual Protestant father of college education, fully employed, of good complexion, weight, and height, and

> a recent record in sports. Every American male tends to look
> out upon the world from this perspective .... Any male who
> fails to qualify in any one of these ways is likely to view
> himself—during moments at least—as unworthy, incomplete,
> and inferior. (p. 128)

This gender ideal became the focus of questioning and critiquing on the part of both the women's and the men's movements. The term men's movement is somewhat of a misnomer because it is not a monolithic movement, but rather a number of different movements subsumed under one label (Clatterbaugh, 1997). The men's movement coalesced, however, around men's reactions to the anger the women's movement directed toward men (Williamson, 1997). While each strand has its distinctive characteristics and perspectives, "each has emerged and taken form in response to modern feminist movements as well as other components in the aggregate men's movement" (Clatterbaugh, p. 9).

Clatterbaugh (1997) identified eight major strands that make up the modern men's movement, each of which contributes a unique historical and ideological perspective. What all the strands have in common is that each starts by defining itself in respect to the feminist viewpoint and by finding some important connections between men and women. Additionally, each strand asserts that its platform is best for both men and women while seeking to address positively and support the specific issues and concerns of men (Clatterbaugh).

The conservative perspective affirms traditional social institutions and mores and the traditional roles for men as protectors and women as homemakers and caregivers (Clatterbaugh). This group contends that traditional notions of masculine and feminine roles are biologically and genetically determined in which men are naturally disposed to dominate in the public sphere of work and world, and women are naturally disposed to prevail in the private sphere of home and family (Clatterbaugh). The antecedents of the conservative perspective can be found in the writings of Edmund Burke (1809–1882), who affirmed the wisdom of societal traditions founded in such institutions as the family, the church, and the community. Burke and thinkers like him advocated a moral conservatism based on natural law that contains a set of absolute values upon which society is built and maintained. Charles Darwin (1809–1882) was a biological conservative whose evolutionary theory provided an explanation for the different social roles between the sexes (Clatterbaugh, p. 18). Because of the successful reproductive and survival strategies of certain individuals, their genes have been passed down through generations. At a collective level, societal human behavior molds men and women to be the way they are because "these behaviors have allowed them to be biologically successful" (Clatterbaugh, p. 18).

During the 1970s, the conservative perspective was passionately advocated by George Gilder in *Sexual Suicide* (1973) and later by David Blankenhorn in *Fatherless America* (1995). Blankenhorn incorporated the viewpoint held by Gilder and expanded it to include the disputes surrounding men's roles in the family (Clatterbaugh). The 1970s also witnessed the extension of the biological conservative perspective in a new discipline—sociobiology, a theory originated by Edward O. Wilson in *Sociobiology: The New Synthesis* (1975), which Wilson called "the systematic study of the biological basis of all social behavior" (Wilson, p. 2). During the 1990s, several new variations of the conservative perspective came to political power in Canada with the Reform Party and in the United States with the Republican Party (Clatterbaugh). These parties supported a pro-family anti-abortion platform, advocated the teaching of moral values in schools, and encouraged school prayer while taking an anti-interventionist approach to regulating economic matters. Frequently, the conservatives appealed to sociobiology to support their defense of traditional gender roles, such as in the famous remarks made by Newt Gingrich in opposition to equal roles for men and women in the military. According to Gingrich:

> If combat means being in a ditch, females have biological problems staying in a ditch for thirty days because they get infections, and they don't have upper body strength. I mean, some do, but they're relatively rare. On the other hand, men are basically little piglets, you drop them in the ditch, they roll around in it, doesn't matter, you know. These things are very real. (Clatterbaugh, p. 32. Quoted by Clarence Page, *Seattle Post-Intelligencer*, January 24, 1995)

These remarks are telling in that they indicate the conservative perspective's desire to maintain traditional gender roles. The conservatives contend that society will be happier and more civilized if males live in harmony with their natural roles. Substantial evidence exists, however, that the picture of reality as painted by the conservatives is not as they view it.

The profeminist perspective sides with the feminist position and rejects the assertion that the traditional masculinity ideal is biologically determined or a social necessity. Rather, patriarchy's oppression of women is sustained by male privilege and power, which is also detrimental to men (Clatterbaugh, pp. 10–11). This perspective emerged out of the feminist critique of masculinity in the 1960s as some men sought to identify with the concerns of feminists by aligning with the feminist position that American society was sexist. Women, according to this position, were victims of systemic discrimination and domination from men that prevented women access to the structures of power in society (Clatterbaugh, p. 41). Furthermore, this position argued that patriarchy harmed men in many ways (Clatterbaugh, p. 41).

Responding to these concerns, many men initiated consciousness-raising groups in the late 1960s and early 1970s. In 1970, the formation of the Men's Center in Berkeley, California, marked the beginning of the "feminist men's movement" (Williamson, 1997). Soon, men's centers formed around the country. Some groups were inspired by a growing number of feminist male authors, while other groups were outgrowths of local gatherings "inspired by a growing network of men who wanted to support women's causes and reexamine the masculine role's relationship to patriarchy" (Williamson, 1997, The Development of the Feminism Men's Movement, paragraph 3). While independent of each other, they all shared a common belief in the basic tenets of feminism and concerns about men's collusion in patriarchy (Clatterbaugh, p. 42). In the 1970s and early 1980s, several publications appeared, including *Brother: A Male Liberation Newspaper* and numerous pamphlets and journals such as "Unbecoming Men" (1971) and *M.: Gentle Men for Gender Justice,* later renamed *Changing Men: Issues in Gender, Sex, and Politics*, which still continues to be a significant organ of profeminist men's writings (Clatterbaugh, p. 43). During this time efforts were made to form a national organization with the First National Conference on the Masculine Mystique in 1974 and the first Men and Masculinity conference in 1975, both of which were strongly influenced by feminist groups (Clatterbaugh, p. 42). Held in Boston in 1981, the seventh Men and

Masculinities conference became a year later a national organization called The National Organization for Changing Men (NOCM). It changed its name again in 1990 to become the National Organization for Men Against Sexism (NOMAS). NOMAS continues to be the largest national profeminist men's organization (Clatterbaugh, p. 42).

During the 1990s men's studies as an academic discipline emerged with the formation of The Men's Studies Association (MSA) that was associated with NOMAS and the American Men's Studies Association (AMSA). Both groups take a scholarly approach to men's issues and masculinity and publish curricular materials for men's studies courses. In 1993, an interdisciplinary quarterly journal named *masculinities* appeared with a mission to be "an interdisciplinary quarterly, dedicated to publishing high quality scholarship in the broadly defined field of gender studies, with a particular focus on men and masculinity" (Clatterbaugh, p. 44). A second publication, *The Journal of Men's Studies*, which "publish(es) scholarly material in the field of men's studies, recognizing the varied influences of class, culture, race, and sexual orientation on defining men's experiences" (Clatterbaugh, p. 44) appeared.

The profeminist men's perspective rejects the moral and biological conservative perspective, arguing that masculinity is a cultural construct and not biologically determined. Furthermore, the profeminist perspective criticizes the traditional family as an institution highly valued by the moral conservatives because it continues to oppress women by locking them into prescribed housewife and caregiver roles and because it harms men's abilities to be caring, loving partners to women (Clatterbaugh, p. 66).

The earliest documented group that prefigures the men's rights position is the United States Divorce Reform, founded in Sacramento, California, by Ruben Kidd and George Partis in 1960 (Williamson, 1997, The Father's Rights Movement and the Development of a "Generalist" Outlook, paragraph 1). An early attempt to form a national men's movement, it soon had chapters in several states. The mission of the organization was to create a law in California establishing family arbitration centers, thereby removing divorce from the adversarial legal system (Williamson, 1997, The Father's Rights Movement and the Development of a "Generalist" Outlook, paragraph 10). The men's rights perspective emerged in the late 1970s with the merger of the father's rights movement and the men's rights political movement. Both movements shared the view that traditional masculinity roles are principally harmful to men, not women (Clatterbaugh, p. 69). The merged group blames women for advocating a new sexism that "thrives on male bashing and male blaming" (Clatterbaugh, p. 11). The primary agenda of this group is the establishment of laws to address the injustices suffered by men in such areas as divorce, child custody, domestic violence prosecution, and sexual harassment statutes (Clatterbaugh, p. 12).

One of the most important figures in the men's rights movement is Richard Doyle. As a member of America's Society of Divorced Men, he widened men's movement issues to include "not only divorce but also criminal justice, child abuse, biological gender issues, affirmative action, paternity court, and welfare for unwed mothers" (Williamson, 1997, The Father's Rights Movement and the Development of a "Generalist" Outlook, paragraph 12). Doyle wrote a highly controversial book entitled *The Rape of the Male* (1976), which viewed the legal system's treatment of men on issues of divorce, child custody, and marriage law as tantamount to rape. Doyle's tireless work brought unity to the men's movement. He was the first man "to broaden men's issues beyond the narrow confines of divorce ... [so that] for the first time, men could speak about a 'men's movement' rather than simply a 'divorce movement'" (Williamson, 1997, The Father's Rights Movement and the Development of a "Generalist" Outlook, paragraph 13). In 1970, Doyle helped form The Coalition of American Divorce Reform Elements (CADRE). Conceived of as an organization of organizations with the purpose of bringing unity to the leaders of many of the country's divorce reform groups, CADRE met with many problems, including disagreement over leadership roles and the strategic use of money. Three meetings were held before the group dissolved over differences in strategy and priorities (Williamson, 1997, The Father's Rights Movement and the Development of a "Generalist" Outlook, paragraph 14). Doyle later formed and became president of the Men's Rights Association (MRA) in May 1973.

The men's rights movement also has a number of small organizations devoted to men's rights issues. Initiated in the late 1970s, Free Men, later known as the Coalition of Free Men, publishes *Transitions* and is known as an important forum for men's rights issues. Men's Rights Incorporated, formed in 1977, issues news releases about men's rights issues and "challenges legal and policy discriminations against men" (Clatterbaugh, p. 71). In 1980, these two groups coalesced to establish the National Congress for Men and Children (NCMC), an umbrella organization whose motto is "Preserving the Promise of Fatherhood" (Clatterbaugh, p. 71).

During the 1990s the men's rights movement split into various factions. One group became explicitly a backlash movement that attacked feminism and adamantly stated that men are the victims in today's society. This wing of the movement publishes *The Backlash!* and the *Liberator*. The "gender reconciliation" wing of the men's rights movement and its organization known as the Movement for the Establishment of Real Gender Equality (MERGE) publishes *Balance,* whose mission is "to promote the vision of full equality and understanding between the 'sexes'" (Clatterbaugh, p. 73).

The men's rights perspective appeals to many men and women because it refuses to blame men for the problems of patriarchy, recognizing instead that gender role stereotypes harm both sexes. The modern masculine ideal is "not internally consistent and [it] often demands the impossible of men" (Clatterbaugh, p. 94).

The mythopoetic men's movement was first given its name by the mythologist Shepherd Bliss (Baber, 1992), who was dissatisfied with the then current term being applied and renamed it the New Age men's movement (See interview with Shepherd Bliss found in May 1995 M.E.N. Magazine [electronic version]). This perspective is based on the neo-Jungian understanding that masculinity arises from archetypal patterns hard-wired in the deep unconscious. Traditional stories, myths, and rituals of the ages reveal these patterns and proclaim that men and women are "essentially different kinds of beings who respond to different kinds of deep needs" (Clatterbaugh, p. 12). Robert Bly, author of *Iron John* (1992) and a widely acknowledged central figure in the mythopoetic men's movement, asserted that modern men are overly feminized and "soft," and that they need to tap into the deep resources in the chthonic story tradition in order to enliven and strengthen their gender (Bly, pp. 4–5). Bly and others, such as Robert Moore and Douglas Gillette (1990, 1992a, 1992b, 1993a, 1993b), Sam Keen (1992), and Michael Meade (1993), advocated for the rediscovery of deep masculine initiation processes.

The mythopoetic men's movement does not advocate a political agenda. Instead it is a "spiritual perspective" in which personal growth is a central tenet (Clatterbaugh, p. 95). The great popularity of this perspective is the result of a diverse assortment of workshops, retreats, and men's counseling groups, fueled by the enormous readership of Bly's book and other books, such as Moore and Gillette's *King, Warrior, Magician, Lover* (1991), Sam Keen's *Fire in the Belly* (1992), and Michael Meade's *Men and the Water of Life* (1993). These authors examine stories, myths, and images and are more symbolic and therapeutic than literal and theoretical in their perspective. The heart of the mythopoetic agenda is the recovery of missing or inadequate masculine initiation rites that facilitate men's growth into the mature masculine energies (Bly, 1992, p. 35; Clatterbaugh, p. 107; Moore and Gillette, 1990, p. 5).

The mythopoetic men's movement manifests itself most visibly in the hundreds of men's retreats held annually by the movement's authors and leaders. During these weekends, men are initiated into deep masculine archetypes, get in touch with and articulate their grief, and seek support from each other in reformulating a revitalized spiritual perspective for their own personal masculine story and identity. An offshoot of the mythopoetic movement is The New Warrior Adventure Training, a weekend focusing on drumming, dancing, and rituals as a means of recovering positive male energy (Clatterbaugh, p. 110). Overall, the mythopoetic perspective advocates therapeutic, individual, and spiritual changes in the lives of men rather than espousing a platform for political or social reform. It proffers yet another masculine ideal for individual male identity.

The socialist perspective views masculinities as products of "patriarchal capitalism ... [and] determined by who does what work, who controls the labor of others, and who controls the products of that labor" (Clatterbaugh, p. 13) There is little socialist perspective literature on masculinity. Adapting the thought of Karl Marx (1818–1883) and Friedrich Engels (1820–1895), this perspective is predicated on three basic tenets. The first is that masculinity is molded and created by the power and productivity alignments of labor inherent in a class-structured society. Secondly, the consequent cost to masculinity because of these alignments is alienation. Thirdly, there can be no alteration in masculinity until the power relations in class structures are changed (Clatterbaugh, p. 118).

Although they tend to be divided between the classical Marxist position, which says it is capitalism that causes the oppression of women and men, and that of the social feminist perspective, which states that masculinity and the oppression of women is shaped by patriarchal structures apart from capitalism, the adherents to this perspective come from the radical profeminist and New Left movements (Clatterbaugh, p. 120). Because of its ideological tenets, the socialist perspective tends not to seek incremental change by legal or educational means because a complete change in the material conditions of the capitalist society is required. In like manner, the social feminists of the movement disavow the patriarchal structures that comprise capitalist institutions (Clatterbaugh, p. 131). The socialists are also disinclined to support the modern men's movement because its agenda is principally a professional-managerial class orientation (Clatterbaugh, p. 131). The socialists' long-term goal "is to eradicate the owning class through implementation of worker control" (Clatterbaugh, p. 131). Unfortunately, the restricted human potential resulting from the capitalist and patriarchal system thwarts "attempts to educate men into a new masculinity or to unlearn the old masculinity" (Clatterbaugh, p. 135).

From the outset, the gay male perspective has been concerned with matters of liberation and security from oppression. This perspective has struggled with masculine identity questions by challenging what is truly masculine and what is truly feminine in gender role ideals and by questioning the viability and morality of hegemonic masculinities (Clatterbaugh, p. 13). The dominant patriarchal culture associates homosexuality with a lack of masculinity (Connell, 1995, p. 143). A corollary to the dominant patriarchal culture's view of homosexuality is homophobia. Coined in the 1970s, homophobia describes experiences of rejection and abuse that many gay men have incurred from heterosexual men (Connell, 1995, p. 40). It is a complex attitude heterosexual men have that begins with a "fascination with homosexuality ... [or] secret desire, driven out of consciousness and converted into hatred" (Connell, 1995, p. 40). However, homophobia has a social, discriminatory element that involves job discrimination, imprisonment, and even murder (Connell, 1995, p. 40; Clatterbaugh, p. 145).

The modern gay liberation movement began in 1969 with the four-day Stonewall Inn Rebellion in Greenwich Village. The result was the formation of a number of politically active gay liberation organizations such as the Mattachine Action Committee, the Gay Liberation Front, and the Gay Activist Alliance. Later, in the 1990s, Queer Nation and ACT-UP emerged as prominent activist pro-gay organizations. The early gay agenda undertook the re-visioning of traditional male role ideals in order to advocate other alternative masculinities. Another group called the "effeminists" were some of the first to espouse a clear feminist gay vision in their publication, *Double F: A Magazine of Effeminism*, which stated:

> This publication of the Revolutionary Effeminists... began ... in response to sexism within the gay male liberation movement. In 1970, three men formulated their concept of "flaming faggots," effeminate men fighting patriarchy with revolutionary means. (Snodgrass, 1977, p. 111)

The effeminists renounced the use of the term "gay" as a self-descriptor and criticized other men's liberation movements as alternate forms of patriarchal domination because of their lack of support of the radical feminist agenda (Clatterbaugh, p. 139). Later, the Radical Fairies advocated a gay spirituality and an independent gay culture in which men resided in "nonmonogamous collective living [arrangements] with nonhierarchical social structures and community spaces apart from heterosexist institutions and women" (Clatterbaugh, p. 139).

Despite its heterosexual bias, the profeminist men's movement attracted many gay men, who participated in many of the Men and Masculinity conferences because the National Organization for Men Against Sexism (NOMAS) identifies with the gay liberation agenda, which states that "homophobia contributes directly to the many injustices experienced by gay ... persons, and is a debilitating restriction for heterosexual men. We call for an end to all forms of discrimination based on sexual-affectional orientation, and the creation of a gay-affirmative society" (National Organization for Changing Men. Quoted from Clatterbaugh, p. 140). The gay men's movement also has a continuing involvement with the men's rights movements because both groups share a common concern about divorce and child custody reform.

The March on Washington for Lesbian, Gay, and Bi Equal Rights and Liberation on April 25, 1993, by hundreds of thousands of gay men and women and other sexual minorities was a significant event in the gay movement. The concerns of the sexual minorities were clearly stated in the march's demands:

1. We demand passage of a Lesbian, Gay, Bisexual, and Transgender civil rights bill and an end to discrimination by state and federal governments including the military; repeal of all sodomy laws and other laws that criminalize private sexual expression between consenting adults.
2. We demand massive increase in funding for AIDS education, research, and patient care; universal access to health care including alternative therapies; and an end to sexism in medical research and health care.
3. We demand legislation to prevent discrimination against Lesbians, Gays, Bisexuals and Transgendered people in the areas of family diversity, custody, adoption and foster care and that the definition of family includes the full diversity of all family structures.
4. We demand full and equal inclusion of Lesbians, Gays, Bisexuals and Transgendered people in the educational system, and inclusion of Lesbian, Gay, Bisexual and Transgender studies in multicultural curricula.
5. We demand the right to reproductive freedom and choice, to control our own bodies, and an end to sexist discrimination.
6. We demand an end to racial and ethnic discrimination in all forms.
7. We demand an end to discrimination and violent oppression based on actual or perceived sexual orientation / identification, race, religion, identity, sex and gender expression, disability, age, class AIDS / HIV infection. (A Simple Matter of Justice, *Program Guide*, p. 16. Quoted from Clatterbaugh, pp. 152–153.)

The list of demands clearly reflects the gay movement's desire to align itself with other liberation movements and recognizes that a number of different sexual minorities suffer from oppression from the dominant masculinity.

In the past year, the gay men's movement has gained considerable ground because of two events that have been and are currently transpiring. The first was the passage of a resolution by the Episcopal Church USA at its triennial convention in 2003 affirming the ordination to the Episcopate of the Church's first openly practicing homosexual. Though met with much dissent, the move to validate the ordination of Bishop Eugene Robinson of New Hampshire signaled a new era of religious tolerance and acceptance of the homosexual male ideal. Additionally, the marriage of more than 2000 gay and lesbian couples in San Francisco, California, during February 2004 opened the door to legitimating the gay lifestyle and family role ideals of homosexual men. Clearly, the national debate on the homosexual agenda and the consequent impact it has on masculine identity ideals is one of the most significant developments of the new century.

The African American men's perspective warns that African American men are becoming an endangered species because of "a unique set of difficulties that derive from history and societal racism" (Clatterbaugh, p. 13). According to Marable, the entire history of African American men can be characterized as a constant struggle to survive and forge an identity against the dominant white class and racism (Kimmel and Messner, p. 21). The history of African American men began with enforced slavery and transplantation to the Americas, where, in most instances, he was treated no better than a farm animal, a cog in the wheel of the agrarian economy (Kimmel and Messner, p. 22).

The Civil War literally and symbolically became the watershed event of the African American man's emancipation, but they would have to continue to assert their manhood throughout the rest of American history (Kimmel, 1997, p. 74). One former slave summed up his new status as a man by saying, "When God made me I wasn't much, [b]ut I's a man now" (Kimmel, 1997, p. 75). White racism reacted by projecting their emasculation fears on African American men and disciplined them by castration and lynchings (Kimmel, 1997, p. 95). In his book, *The Fire Next Time* (1962), James Baldwin gave voice to the rage African American men felt as victims of the projected fears of white racism when he wrote that the African American man was "forced each day to snatch his manhood, his identity, out of the fire of human cruelty that rages to destroy it" (Baldwin, p. 132).

The Civil Rights movement of the 1960s called attention to African American liberation by challenging America to give African American people their full humanity. The more militant Black Panther party had a stronger and more violent appeal. Eldridge Cleaver in *Soul on Ice* (1968) said,

"We shall have our manhood. We shall have it or the earth will be leveled by our attempts to gain it" (Cleaver, 1968, quoted from Kimmel, p. 271). The African American male experience has been characterized as living in the tension of the opposites between seeking liberation peacefully while dealing with feelings of anger toward the dominant white patriarchal system.

A significant event in the African American men's movement occurred on October 16, 1995, with the Million Man March in Washington, DC. Sponsored and directed by the Nation of Islam leader, Louis Farrakhan, the event called the nation's attention to the social and moral crisis facing African Americans in America (Clatterbaugh, p. 170). Farrakhan's essentially conservative moral message was for African American men to be better husbands, fathers, providers, and ideals of manhood for their families and for their community (Clatterbaugh, pp. 170–171).

Farrakhan is but one voice among many to address the African American male's identity. A significant portion of the African American liberation movement owes its foundation to the Reverends Martin Luther King, Jr., Ralph Abernathy, and Jesse Jackson as well as the Promise Keepers' spokespersons, Tony Evans and Crawford Loritts. Farrakhan, Huey P. Newton, and Bobby Seale represent the militant and separatist wing, and W.E.B. DuBois, Richard Wright, and Manning Marable represent the black socialist wing. Clarence Thomas, Thomas Sowell, and J.C. Watts are important conservative thinkers (Clatterbaugh, p. 160). Many other voices and messages in the African American community also claim to speak for the African American male experience.

Clyde W. Franklin, II (1994) identified the following five different Black masculinities who characterize African American men: conforming masculinity, ritualistic masculinity, innovative masculinity, retreatist masculinity, and rebellious masculinity (pp. 280–281). Conforming masculinity accepts mainstream society's heterosexual standards of masculinity. African American males conform "despite the fact that, when society teaches men to work hard, set high goals, and strive for success, it does not teach Black men simultaneously that their probability of failure is high because blocked opportunities for Black males are endemic to American society" (Franklin, p. 280). Ritualistic masculinity describes African American men who conform to and obey society's standards of masculinity while not believing in its rules and institutions. For this group, it is a matter of "playing the game" (Franklin, pp. 180–181). In innovative masculinity, African American men have forsaken conformity from society's standards while exaggerating some of its traits in the pursuit of material success, as evidenced by black-on-black homicide, drug dealings, and theft (Franklin, p. 281). Retreatist masculinity abandons any hope of success, and men in this category typically become drug addicted, alcoholics, and homeless. This group has forsaken searching for work or for any meaningful existence (Franklin, pp. 281–282). Franklin's final group is rebellious masculinity as symbolized by the Black Panthers of the 1960s or in any activist group committed to African American liberation (Franklin, pp. 281–282).

Finally, the Evangelical Christian men's movement perspective, also known as Promise Keepers, advocate a Biblically-based platform whereby men of all races assume their God-given roles as fathers, providers, and heads of their families. This group acknowledges that there is a moral crisis "in part because men have abdicated their responsibilities and in part because women, influenced by feminism, have taken on the man's role" (Clatterbaugh, p. 14). Bill McCartney, the former football head coach at the University of Colorado, began the Promise Keepers in 1990. Having begun in Denver, Colorado, with seventy men, the movement has grown phenomenally with rallies attracted 4200 in 1991; 22,000 in 1992; 50,000 in 1993; 278,000 in 1994; and 725,000 in 1995 (The Nation, 1996, quoted from Center for Democracy Studies [electronic version]). Promise Keepers' peak yearly attendance was in 1996 with 1.1 million men in attendance at 22 events, followed in 1997 with the million man "Stand in the Gap" meeting on the Mall in Washington, DC (Statistics quoted from Promise Keepers History).

Following in the footsteps of Billy Sunday in the 1920s, Jerry Falwell's Moral Majority and Pat Robertson's Christian Coalition, Promise Keepers is the latest organizational attempt of the Christian right to motivate men religiously. The following Seven Promises are the core tenets of Promise Keepers:

1. A Promise Keeper is committed to honoring Jesus Christ through worship, prayer and obedience to God's Word in the power of the Holy Spirit.

2. A Promise Keeper is committed to pursuing vital relationships with a few other men, understanding that he needs brothers to help him keep his promises.
3. A Promise Keeper is committed to practicing spiritual, moral, ethical, and sexual purity.
4. A Promise Keeper is committed to building strong marriages and families through love, protection and biblical values.
5. A Promise Keeper is committed to supporting the mission of his church by honoring and praying for his pastor, and by actively giving his time and resources.
6. A Promise Keeper is committed to reaching beyond any racial and denominational barriers to demonstrate the power of biblical unity.
7. A Promise Keeper is committed to influencing his world, being obedient to the Great Commandment (see Mark 12:30–31) and the Great Commission (see Matthew 28:19–20).

Men attending the 1993 men's conference also received a copy of *The Masculine Journey* by Robert Hicks (1993). According to Promise Keepers, masculine identity is based on three basic premises. First, men are sinners possessed with free will and exposed to all kinds of sinfulness, as characterized by the use of such phrases as "the savagery of the soul" and the "insanity in our hearts" (Hicks, 1993, pp. 41, 43). Hence, the third promise of spiritual, moral, ethical, and sexual purity is the religious antidote to the view that men are naturally promiscuous and craven by nature (Clatterbaugh, p. 180). The second premise of Promise Keepers is that it is extremely difficult to be a Christian man in today's permissive society that is hostile to Christian values (McCartney, 1992, p. 13). Men are embroiled in a culture war fighting against moral decay and collapse (Hicks, p. 57). The third premise of Promise Keepers is that men are called and created differently from women in order to exercise masculine leadership. "Made in God's image, His representatives on earth, and His vice-regents," men are in the image of God and Jesus, who are the models of ideal masculinity (Hicks, p. 18).

Promise Keepers claims to be a strictly spiritual movement without a political agenda. Spiritual renewal is the prescription for the renewal of men's identity and for reclaiming their rightful role in the institutions of the family and society. However, many secular and religious critics view Promise Keepers as a reassertion of patriarchal dominance.

It is easy to conclude from this brief historical sketch of masculinity that the once unitary and bonding masculine ideals have in modern times fragmented into a myriad of vastly different and competing images. Each masculine ideal emerged in response to a number of diverse historical, sociological, and cultural factors that shaped it and which in turn shaped men's self-understandings and roles. Today, a cacophony of competing and very diverse masculinities calls out for attention and for emulation. The former consensus of what it meant to be a man is gone and may never reappear. Diversity and difference seem to be the order of the day.

STATEMENT OF THE PROBLEM

Traditional maxims of manhood have been attacked from a number of quarters, forcing men to explain themselves, to change, or to become something else than what they are. In an article entitled "Guns and Dolls" (1990), *Newsweek* summarized the current manhood problem as the following:

> Perhaps the time has come for a new agenda. Women, after all, are not a big problem. Our society does not suffer from burdensome amounts of empathy and altruism, or a plague of nurturance. The problem is men—or more accurately, maleness... Men are killing themselves doing all the things that our society wants them to do. At every age they're dying in accidents, they're being shot, they drive cars badly, they ride the tops of elevators, they're two-fisted drinkers. And violence against women is incredibly pervasive. Maybe it's men's raging hormones, [or] ... because they're trying to be a *man*. (Keen, pp. 5–6, quoted from *Newsweek*, May 3, 1990)

For the past two decades, men have been questioning much of what they have learned about being a man. Given the rapid cultural changes that have taken place in gender ideals, the conventional assumption that males are more privileged than their female counterparts seems spurious. More and more men are experiencing gender role strain as they attempt to live up to traditional masculine ideals. Moreover, they are expressing the pain they have experienced as men in attempting to heal the wounds they incurred while attempting to live up to an image of masculinity that has little or no relation to their real feelings or experiences as men. In his book *Knights without Armor: A Practical Guide for Men in Quest of Masculine Soul* (1991), Aaron Kipnis sums up the modern male dilemma in the following rather confessional terms:

> We're angry and confused about the double standards we encounter in many arenas, the reverse sexism and rigid gender-role expectations. Many of us are isolated, and uncertain about how to break out of old male stereotypes. Some are simply numb. We lack elders, positive role models, or leaders with vision. In the past we have often turned to women for solutions, which can create different sorts of problems such as dependency and isolation from other men. (p. 11)

Today men are seeking new and meaningful masculine ideals that will permit and nurture an authentic male reconnection to his feelings, to his body, to his family and children, to his women, to other men, and to nature.

In their book, *In a Time of Fallen Heroes: The Re-Creation of Masculinity* (1993), Betcher and Pollack echo in more strident words those of Kipnis, describing the times in which men live as "a time of fallen heroes:"

> The monuments built of men, by men, and for men have tumbled. Men have not just been brought to earth, their strengths put in perspective by their flaws. Even their virtues are suspect vices: power has turned out to be oppression, strength rigidity, and self-sufficiency an inability to be emotionally close... . Women—the most oppressed majority—have made incursions into men's traditional prerogatives and even more inroads into their confidence. If men still appear in control, their smug certainty is gone. It is a difficult time to be proud of being a man. (p. 1)

Betcher and Pollack call men back to their roots and to a heroic inward journey of self-discovery and reevaluation of masculine ideals, an examination of their own identity in relation to others and to their work, play, and parenting and to their wives and children (Betcher and Pollack, p. 22).

In his book *Under Saturn's Shadow: The Wounding and Healing of Men* (1995), James Hollis described men as laboring under an oppressive weight of the shadow of dysfunctional masculine ideologies, which he terms saturnine. Saturn was the Roman equivalent of the Greek mythological figure, Cronus, the son of Uranus, the male sky god, and Gaia, the feminine Mother Earth. Uranus hated and feared his children and had them put away, but Cronus with the help of his mother fashioned an adamantine sickle and castrated his father. From his severed phallus sprang both fearsome giants and Aphrodite, the goddess of love and beauty. Later, Cronus dethroned his father, but he became a tyrant like his father had been. In similar fashion, whenever Cronus and Rhea produced children, Cronus swallowed all of them, except for his son Zeus, who led a revolt of the gods against Cronus. Nevertheless, like the male leaders before him, Zeus also became tyrannical. This myth by Hesiod (ca. 700 B.C.) is the archetypal story of patriarchy and the power complex coupled with jealousy and insecurity, and it characterizes what Hollis describes as the "Saturnian legacy" (Hollis, p. 11). Hollis summarizes this oppressive masculine ideology as "the eight secrets men carry within:"

1. Men's lives are as much governed by restrictive role expectations as are the lives of women.
2. Men's lives are essentially governed by fear.
3. The power of the feminine is immerse in the psychic economy of men.
4. Men collude in a conspiracy of silence whose aim is to suppress their emotional truth.
5. Because men must leave the Mother, and transcend the mother complex, wounding is necessary.
6. Men's lives are violent because their souls have been violated.
7. Every man carries a deep longing for his father and for his tribal Fathers.
8. If men are to heal, they must activate within what they did not receive from without. (Hollis, p. 11)

Together these messages wound men terribly because they become the life scripts by which men are compelled to live and by which men are driven to seek power at the expense of others. However, they are always driven by fear, which in turn wounds themselves and others (Hollis). Kimbrell (1995) labeled the maladjustment of men under the weight of destructive and dysfunctional masculine expectations the "masculine mystique." This manhood code has "become omnipresent in the lives of men ... [and] not only did it help bring men into their current crisis but it has also kept men from protesting their victimization, and even led them to support a system that has meant a near-fatal undermining of their gender" (Kimbrell, p. xiv).

While the male wound can be crushing and oppressive to men, it can also prompt men to grow up (Hollis, p. 64). This process has been a traditional feature of masculine development for millennia and finds its expression in male initiation rites (Hollis, p. 66; Moore and Gillette, 1990, pp. 3–4). These wounding rites were inflicted in a ritual manner with deep care and concern in order "to help both the youth and the society he must sustain. As he encounters pain, with all its immediacy, he learns in the rigors of his flesh the message that he can't go home again. He is granted an ecstatic vision, crosses the divide, and enters the adult world" (Hollis, p. 67). The modern male problem is the lack of rituals of initiation "into the deep structures of manhood" (Moore and Gillette, 1990, p. 3). Instead, today's rites of initiation are "pseudo-rituals ... [that] initiate the boy into a kind of masculinity that is skewed, stunted, and false. It is a patriarchal 'manhood,' one that is abusive of others, and often of self" (Moore and Gillette, 1990, p. 5). Moore and Gillette identified two essential elements to authentic initiation rituals: the need for sacred space and the presence of a ritual elder (Moore and Gillette, 1990, p. 6). The problem is that there is a scarcity of ritual elders in modern culture; hence, "pseudo-initiations remain skewed toward the reinforcement of Boy psychology rather than allowing for movement toward Man psychology, even if some sort of ritual process exists, and even if a kind of sacred space has been set up" (Moore and Gillette, 1990, p. 7).

What is problematic for men is even worse for boys. In his book *Real Boys: Rescuing Our Sons from the Myths of Boyhood* (1999), William Pollack sounds the alarm about males in American culture:

> Today's boys are in serious trouble, including many who seem "normal" and to be doing just fine. Confused by society's mixed messages about what's expected of them as boys, ... many feel a sadness and disconnection they cannot even name.

> New research shows that boys are faring less well in school
> than they did in the past and in comparison to girls, that
> many boys have remarkably fragile self-esteem, and that
> the rates of both depression and suicide in boys are frighteningly
> on the rise. Many of our sons are currently in a desperate
> crisis (p. xxi).

Statistically, boys are categorized as "learning disabled" twice as often
as girls are and comprise two-thirds of the nation's special education classes
(Pollack, p. xxiii). Moreover, boys are having serious problems outside of
the school building, too. They are the victims of violent crime three times
more often than girls and are likely to commit suicide four to six times more
frequently (Pollack, p. xxiii).

In American society today, boys do face serious gender-specific obstacles.
Aaron Kipnis (1999) and Michael Gurian (1999a) document a number of
disturbing statistics about our nation's sons. According to Kipnis, in 1999
American boys were responsible for the following:

- The majority of children abused, neglected, and murdered
- The bulk of children in foster care and juvenile institutions
- 70 to 75 percent of student suspensions, expulsions, grade failures,
  special education referrals, school violence casualties, and all other
  assault victims (Kipnis, 1999, p. x)

Kipnis attributes these alarming statistics to a number of contributing
factors that include physical and sexual abuse, inadequate male mentoring
and father absence, shaming, poverty and neglect, inadequate and inappropriate education, spiritual impoverishment, gender role stereotyping and
anti-boy bias, substance abuse, access to weapons, racism, and a number of
other influences that Kipnis believed are relatively preventable and treatable
in the early years of boys' lives (Kipnis, 1999, pp. x-xi). Gurian's statistics
suggest that the "moral emergency that is gradually ... becoming an everyday
part of male life" as illustrated in the following:

- More of our children are arrested for crimes than in any other country.
  Ninety percent of arrestees are boys.

- Our young males make up 80 percent of drug-addicted and alcoholic youth.
- Our rate of mental disorders in the male population per capita is one of the highest in the world.... Approximately 3,000,000 kids are on Ritalin in the U.S.; 90 percent of them are boys.
- The child suicide rate has escalated over the last decade with an increasing acceleration, mainly among adolescent boys.

Gurian stated emphatically that boys are in trouble because of a number of factors. In particular, he stressed the moral and character crisis in American boys (Gurian, 1999a, pp. 5–6). Citing such factors as boys' lack of impulse control, conscience, the inability to discern between right and wrong, and the culture's neglect of boys' issues and concerns, Gurian stated, "Our culture directly poisons the character development of its males and neglects essential building blocks for that character development" (1999a, p. 6).

In *Lost Boys: Why Our Sons Turn Violent and How We Can Save Them* (1999), James Garbarino documented in shocking detail the violence in which boys are immersed in their daily lives at home, at school, and in the neighborhood. He identified a number of risk factors that cause or contribute to juvenile violence. The first is the geographic influence of which those most affected by youth violence have roots in the Old South where a "code of honor that is passed on from generation to generation through childrearing that accounts for this cultural susceptibility to homicide" (pp. 11–12). Other risk factors contributing to youth violence include child abuse, gang membership, substance abuse, weapons possession, arrest record, neurological disorders that include Attention Deficit Disorder, and difficulties at school (Garbarino).

The problems boys face are caused by premature separation from their mothers. The developmental transition from a primary identification with mother toward an identification with father often results in boys feeling vulnerable and inadequate (Pollack, pp. 26–27). The need to consolidate his gender role identity and self-identity necessitate the boy's distancing himself from his mother and much that is associated with her (Pollack, p. 12). To protect himself from unresolved, dependent yearning for mother, males frequently use strategies of masking and avoiding. These characteristics result in boys feeling ashamed, vulnerable, and disconnected from their true emotions (Pollack).

Males live in an unfortunate double bind. On the one hand, they must be prepared to fight and protect and deal with all the fears and anxieties these masculine role ideals require. On the other hand, they are expected to be interpersonally connected and nurturing to their wives and families. One response requires inflexible, shame-based defenses to ward off fear, and the other response requires flexibility and tolerance toward shame in daily life. Consequently, boys tend to erect rigid internal and external defenses against shame experiences. They tend to identify with superheroes that embody invulnerability of one kind or another. Male culture pushes boys toward and rewards them for aggressive competition with each other. For those males who can live up to these expectations, they are rewarded with a high sense of self-esteem. Those who fail are left feeling humiliated and isolated (Pollack, p. xxv).

Boys absorb all of these expectations through society's promulgation of the unwritten Boy Code, a set of expectations, behaviors, and rules of conduct boys learn as they grow up about how to act. David and Brannon (1976) identified four stereotypical male ideals of manhood. The first is the Steady Oak, which teaches boys the stoic rejection of pain or grief. The second is the Give 'em Hell mask of false bravado, daring, and violence. The Big Wheel emphasizes the need to achieve status and power no matter the cost. Finally, the No Sissy Stuff is the traumatizing social role that condemns boys for having warm, dependent feelings that could be construed as feminine. These false and dysfunctional standards are traumatizing to boys, who are given cultural messages to endure them without complaint and on their own.

Coupled with the Boy Code is the inability of boys to express their emotions adequately. In part, this is the result of the way boys are raised in modern society, which leaves them without the use of an emotional vocabulary to express themselves other than through anger and aggression (Kindlon & Thompson, 1999). When asked how something makes him feel, a boy will frequently not know how to respond. This inability to associate with and name feelings in oneself and in others is called "emotional illiteracy" (Kindlon and Thompson, 1999, p. 5). Because boys are not encouraged to express and reflect upon their feelings, "they act with careless disregard for the feelings of others at home, at school, or on the playground" (Kindlon & Thompson, 1999, p. 5). According to Kindlon & Thompson,

> Lacking an emotional education, a boy meets the pressures of adolescence and that singularly cruel peer culture with the only responses he has learned and practiced—and that he knows are socially acceptable—the typically "manly" responses of anger, aggression, and emotional withdrawal. (p. 5)

Therefore, boys suffer deeply from the wounds of our modern cultural masculine stereotypes and from ideals with their dysfunctional expectations and scripts for masculine behavior.

It is hoped that the foregoing has established a predicate for a succinct statement of the problem to be addressed in this study. What has been labeled the Boy Code as well as traditional masculine gender norms is dysfunctional and oppressive. The preponderant literature about masculine gender identity advocates a re-conceptualization of masculine gender to account for a greater diversity of understanding and a more flexible construction of masculinity. Furthermore, the often-invisible agenda of masculine gender formation needs restructuring and re-articulation. Next to the family, the educational system is arguably the most influential institution upon the construction of masculine gender identity, yet very little has been done to address the specific and unique needs of boys during the critical years in which their gender identity is formed. A new approach to teaching young men and to supporting their masculine identity formation is necessary.

PURPOSE OF THE STUDY

The purpose of this study was to examine the literature addressing masculine gender matters and to articulate a curriculum that addresses the gender formation issues and needs of late adolescent boys. The research questions that this study addresses in the process of formulating this curriculum framework include the following:

- What are the key conceptual components of each of the three major schools of thought in masculine gender studies: the psychoanalytic, the social constructionist, and the essentialist?

- Based on current theory and research, what components might be included in a model masculine gender studies curriculum for late adolescent young men?

While addressing these questions, this study articulates a framework and conceptual outline for a future gender studies curriculum for late adolescent young men. In the process, a new paradigm is articulated that is a synthesis of the three major theoretical approaches to masculine gender identity. This paradigm will be a masculinity that affirms individual uniqueness and acknowledges the diversity of cultural manifestations of masculinity. This masculinity will consciously integrate the cultural, social, and psychological components of male gender dynamics in a healthy and functional way that nourishes and enhances individual expression and social responsibility. It will be a masculinity that honors the unique brain and hormonal structures of males and that permits the nurturing of the male Self.

Principally, the following three schools of thought shape the professional literature on masculine gender studies: the psychoanalytic, the social constructionist, and the essentialist. The following section summarizes the major approaches of each of the three theoretical approaches.

The Psychoanalytic Viewpoint

The psychoanalytic view of masculinity draws upon the work of Sigmund Freud (1856–1939) and his theory of psychosexual development during which children pass through a series of stages he termed the oral, anal, phallic, latency, and genital. According to Freud, boys have a particularly challenging Oedipus complex to negotiate. The Oedipus myth relates the story of King Laius who learns of a prophecy that tells of a son of his who will one day kill him. Fearing for his life, Laius orders his young son, Oedipus, to be taken into the countryside and killed, but a well-meaning servant spares the boy and gives him to a sheepherder to raise. Years later, a chance encounter of the now-grown Oedipus with his stranger-father, King Laius, on the road ensues in an argument in which Oedipus kills the king thus fulfilling the prophecy. Oedipus becomes the king in another city where he unwittingly marries his mother. He eventually learns of the truth of his life, blinds himself, and abdicates the throne to his sons. Freud interpreted the myth as a paradigm for a boy's unconscious striving to possess his mother sexually by overthrowing and usurping his father's position (1905/1962). The psychoanalytic tradition has placed great emphasis on this Oedipal dynamic, which has great impact upon a boy's psychosexual development, including the ability to function in the areas of love and work. According to the psychoanalytic viewpoint, the resolution of the Oedipal complex is the foundation upon which a man's sense of masculinity is constructed (Kupfersmid, 1995).

Another instructive Greek myth about contemporary masculinity is the myth of Narcissus. This myth suggests that men are frequently viewed as engaged in a type of self-involvement and self-love that appears "narcissistic" to their female partners. Ovid tells the story of Narcissus, a beautiful youth who is the son of the river god Cephisus and the nymph Liriope. The blind prophet Tiresias foretells that Narcissus will live a long life, but only if he never comes to know himself. Echo falls in love with him, but he rebuffs her. He experiences her desire for connection as imprisoning. One day, when Narcissus bends over a pool of water to drink, the god Nemesis causes him to fall in love with his reflection. Transfixed by the image, he is unable to bring the image to himself in order to achieve union. Accompanying Narcissus to the end is Echo, a nymph who can only repeat his last words, "Farewell … farewell." This myth emphasizes the modern-day dilemma of men and women who cannot understand each other and are thereby condemned to painful isolation.

The myth illustrates the modern-day problem that men are overly autonomous and women are overly dependent on connection. The need to hold on to independence has its psychological antecedents in boyhood during which boys are expected to disidentify from their mothers and become different in order to become masculine. For boys to define themselves as masculine they must separate from the mother—intrapsychically and interpersonally. This separation requires "more of a defensive hardening of the self and ego boundaries of little boys, and later of adult males, on both a conscious and an unconscious level" (Pollack, p. 39; Connell, p. 20). Little boys and grown men need to repel their earlier sense of oneness with their mothers because it tends to threaten their autonomy and their identities as males.

Consequently, core masculine identity emerges at an early stage in life with the boy's disidentification with the mother. It is a "process that requires separation from the most cherished, admired, and loved object in his life—at what would be a phase-inappropriate time from the point of view of girls' development" (Pollack, p. 40). Furthermore, because there is gender difference between mother and son in addition to the psychological disidentification process, boys are likely to be pushed out of the mother-son relationship. The consequence of this process becomes that males are more vulnerable to traumatic and premature actual separations, known as *traumatic abrogation* of the early holding environment (Pollack, p. 41). Later in life, this life cycle loss and fracture in masculine development leaves many men fearful of intimate connection. According to Pollack, men are "doomed to search endlessly, as in Aristophanes' myth, and yet, as in the tale of Narcissus, fend women off because of their fear of retraumatization" (p. 41).

A second critical component is the role shame plays in men's lives. Shame indicates that a man is vulnerable, different, exposed, or out-of-control (Krugman, 1995). When the shaming process is adaptive, boys learn appropriate interactions with authority figures and peers. However, when it is disrupted by developmental and gender role pressures or trauma, integration of shame experiences can be maladaptive. Krugman (1995) points out that "(a) shame is an innate response tendency that (b) has the adaptive function of sensitizing the individual to his or her status / connection with others; that (c) shame functions in normal and pathological development; and that (d) shame plays a formidable and problematic role in normative male development" (p. 93). Even the normative male shame process that shapes appropriate masculine attitudes and behavior leaves many boys shame-sensitive, and unable to grow and integrate shame responses.

The core shame experience consists of three components. First, there is a strong psychophysiological component that includes autonomic arousal such a sweating and blushing as well as a "shame signature" sequence of body movements that include eyes turned away, head lowering, and upper body being turned away. Together, these actions initiate the flight-fight response (Krugman, 1995). The second component is negative self-appraisal that results in lowered self-esteem. (Krugman, 1995) Finally, the third component is the resultant heightened self-consciousness with an impaired sequence of smooth, uninterrupted memory, speech, and motor coordination processes (Krugman, 1995, p. 96). In short, shame is a painful self-awareness with the feeling of being negatively evaluated by others and resulting in the desire to hide.

Males have difficulty integrating and responding to shame experiences; therefore, they react with avoidance, compensatory behaviors, and the fight-flight response. Males will also react with immature defense mechanisms, such as denial, projection, splitting, and acting out (Valliant, 1977 from Krugman, 1995, p. 100). Feelings of vulnerability and other appropriate and necessary affects are minimized or denied in lieu of some other hyper-masculine stance. Finally, when verbal rebuffs are ineffective, shame initiates feelings of rage that result in violent action (Krugman, 1995, p. 100).

Block Lewis (1971) has differentiated two types of the shame processes. The first she calls "overt undifferentiated shame," the typical uncomfortably intense self-consciousness that causes a person to want to hide and thwarts the ability to think and speak coherently. A second shame process she calls "by-passed shame," a condition in which the feeling processes are removed or reduced to a twinge of discomfort and the thought process is amplified. Men in today's culture tend to manifest this by-passed shame process more often than the former. Shame manifests itself in other ways, such as in contempt (Morrison, 1983), externalization (Cicchetti and Toth, 1991), and objectification (Kinston, 1983).

When boys handle shame and integrate it appropriately, they learn modesty and tact and develop the capacity to respond to both internal and external affective signals. On the other hand, when shame is amplified rather than diminished, and the male feels threatened, a series of various types of immature reactions can be triggered, such as splitting, denial, projection, impulsivity, and depression. As a result, males seek to avoid situations and relations that reveal their inner sense of inadequacy. Typically, males gravitate from externalization and action solutions to emotional situations, thereby deflecting attention away from the emotion to the action. Consequently, males are doers and problem-solvers rather than talkers.

Male inability to integrate shame experiences has a number of unfortunate effects. For example, males can be deeply conflicted about intimacy, sexuality, and their feelings toward women, and these feelings can easily become projected as humiliated rage at women who are perceived as controlling and withholding (Krugman, 1995, p. 113). Additionally, unresolved, narcissistic dilemmas leave many men unable to handle failure and can result in such feelings and behaviors as self-involvement, self-importance, and emotional distance, with an inability to consider the needs of others, problems with intimacy and parenting, and social and emotional isolation (Krugman, 1995, p. 113). Furthermore, to the extent that a boy has experienced appropriate family socialization, he will be able to venture into the world secure that he can stand on his own and remain in control without humiliation and isolation (Krugman, 1995). When internal and external boundaries are not firmly established in boyhood, inadequate self-regulation results, and boys can become vulnerable to extreme emotional expressions on the one hand or to isolation and distance on the other. Well-integrated shame also assists boys in dealing with conflict without resorting to violence. The shame process assists the development of words and non-threatening gestures that promote the mediation of issues of dominance and competition (Krugman, 1995, p. 115).

When shame experiences remain unintegrated in men's lives, their lives can become severely dysfunctional and lead to a number of character pathologies of malignant narcissism and sociopathology (Krugman, 1995, p. 115). Narcissistic personality traits can manifest themselves as character defenses in which the adult male exhibits patterns of extreme self-centeredness, grandiosity, and contempt for others. Krugman describes this process as "the inferior self, demeaned and helpless, is either deeply hidden or projected onto the other, who, in turn, feels devalued or denigrated" (p. 116). A second dissociated type of narcissistic disorder results in the self being projected outward onto an idealized other while the individual consciously experiences the inferior shamed self (Krugman, 1995). Another dysfunctional state results when boys grow up in abusive environments and develop uncontrolled volatile emotional states with poor self-concepts. These males typically split their identification with their parents, a scenario that frequently results in depression and mood instability as well as the tendency to become drug and alcohol involved.

A third, critical component in the psychoanalytic view concerns male sexuality. Males are created inside women's bodies and are dependent on their mothers for physical and emotional nurturance. During these early, vulnerable years, males experience intense physical and emotional pleasure and security from the ministrations of their mothers. Chodorow (1978) and Pollack (1990) viewed this as creating a problematic dilemma for traditional male development. According to this view the mother's emotional comfort is transient as the child quickly experiences conflict between attachment and autonomy (Brooks and Gilbert, 1995, p. 253). Young boys need to differentiate themselves from their mothers if they are to define themselves successfully as masculine. Consequently, the young boy's earliest female associations are full of conflict. "Drawn to, yet fearful of, mother's love and nurturance, the young boy develops 'defensive autonomy' or 'pseudo-self-sufficiency,' as well as 'fear of being engulfed'" (Brooks and Gilbert, 1995, p. 253). Unfortunately, in many instances, this situation is exacerbated by the physical and psychological absence of the father, who the young boy views as rejecting and disinterested (Osherson, 1986, p. 6). Further complicating the developmental dilemma of boys is the extensive gender socialization that requires boys to be competitive, aggressive and possessive of a general "insensitivity to the influence of girls" (Maccoby, 1990, p. 515). This hypermasculinity often defies clear definition except by what it is not—not feminine. Numerous research documents the "No Sissy Stuff" (David and Brannon, 1976) and the "antifeminine element in the male role" (Doyle, 1995, p. 135), also known as "femiphobia" (O'Donovan, 1988).

Given this context, the fundamental challenge of adolescence is to transit from an all-boy gender-segregated social environment to a male-female, inter-gender, adult social context. In short, in adolescence, boys discover girls, but unfortunately they lack early positive female interactions in addition to receiving early conflicting information about sexuality. The literature about men reinforces the idea that men possess a hidden confusion in the area of sexuality. Solomon (1982) identified sexual dysfunction as one of the six major defining issues for men. Kanin (1967) noted that men's sexual preoccupation is the result of intense social pressures to validate their masculinity. Moreover, adolescent boys and girls have manifestly different agendas, such as:

> The young male ... pushes for more sexual activity when
> dating ... conversely, many young females ... spend a good

> deal of time preventing sexual intimacy. Therefore, because
> of early differences in learning how to be sexual, males com-
> mitted to sexuality, but less trained in affection and love,
> may interact with females who are committed to love but
> relatively untrained in sexuality. (Gagnon and Henderson,
> 1975, 38)

As a result, males and females have differing viewpoints on sexuality and relations. Peplau, Rubin, and Hill (1977) studied dating couples and found that "virtually every male in the study was highly interested in having sexual intercourse ... women exercised 'negative control,' responding to the male's initiative by either granting or denying his request" (p. 105). According to Farrell (1987) this pattern fosters women's enormous sexual leverage power over men, resulting in men's efforts to win women's attention and sexual favors. Adolescence, according to Farrell, is the time when males learn the male primary fantasy that the most desirable types of women are the beautiful centerfold models. On the other hand, women learn to seek out men who fit the success image. Farrell argued that because many young women fit the centerfold model image but very few young men live up to the success image, the first sexual encounters between men and women result in feelings of sexual inadequacy and powerlessness. Consequently, young men learn to earn women's sexual attention through a commitment to achievement, while craving and resenting the sexual gifts of women (Brooks &s Gilbert, 1995).

Consequently, males are set up to encounter significant problems with sexuality. Hormonal and social pressures impel men to conquer women, who are, in turn, simultaneously programmed to control sexual activity negatively. The result is psychic distress that contributes to the resentful feelings young males have toward young women, who are perceived as inhibiting pleasurable sexual feelings and preventing males from validating their masculinity (Brooks and Gilbert, 1995).

The Social Constructionist View

According to Kimmel and Messner (2004), the social constructionist view, states "that the important fact of men's lives is not that they are biological males, but that they become men. Our sex may be male, but our identity is developed through a complex process of interaction with the culture in which we both learn the gender scripts appropriate to our culture and attempt to modify those scripts to make them more palatable" (p. xv). The social constructionist view rejects any monolithic, universal masculinity ideal. Instead, it affirms that masculinity is constructed in interaction with culture in particular places and at particular times. Moreover, depending on the composition of cultural subgroups within the culture, varieties of masculinity exist within cultures (Kimmel & Messner, 2004). Kimmel & Messner asserted that "in the contemporary United States, masculinity is constructed differently by class culture, by race and ethnicity, and by age." Hence, social constructionists use the term masculinities (Kimmel). Kimmel emphatically summarizes the social constructionist viewpoint as the following:

> Manhood is neither static nor timeless. Manhood does not bubble up to consciousness from our biological constitution; it is created in our culture.... What it means to be a man in America depends heavily on one's class, race, ethnicity, age, sexuality, region of the country. (1997, p. 5)

Social constructionists say there is no one overarching, masculinity ideal, but a number of different masculinities arise when men interact within the social context in which they find themselves and in conjunction with their unique personality traits and social experiences.

R. W. Connell in *Masculinities* (1995) posited that a three-part structure of gender paradigm is needed that distinguishes the relations of "(a) power, (b) production, and (c) cathexis" (Connell, 1995, p. 74). Power relations in Western society refer to the overall dominance of men and to the subordination of women. Despite the occasional exception to the norm by which women function in contradiction to the established rule of male dominance, these reversals, according to Connell, "define a problem of legitimacy" to patriarchal power (p. 74). Connell described production relations as the gender divisions of labor by which tasks and jobs in society are distributed to men and women as well as consideration for "the economic consequences of gender divisions of labor" (p. 74). Therefore, social constructionists stress the inequality of economic power between men and women with men dominating because of the gendered accumulation process (Connell, 1995). The third prong of Connell's gender model is cathexis, which is defined as "desire in Freudian terms, [an] emotional energy ... attached to an object" (Connell, 1995, p. 74). From this viewpoint, both heterosexual and homosexual relations can be included in a masculine gender paradigm as well as a number of other possible variations.

Connell (1995) further argued that gender also interacts with race and class as well as with nationality and status in the world order. Messerschmidt (2004) distinguished the construction of masculinity by its labor, power, and sexual components as they impact young men on the street, in the workplace, and in the family. Other writers, such as Manning Marable (2004), examined the conditions that influence and denote the Black man, while Alfredo Mirande (2004) described the macho of Mexican or Latino masculinity. These kinds of social constructionist analyses abound and provide a rich depth and complexity to the understanding of masculine gender as it manifests itself throughout world cultures.

The Essentialist Viewpoint

A third school of thought focusing on masculinity is the essentialist viewpoint. This approach stresses that men are intrinsically different from women because of some internal biological or physic essence. Socio-biology, the scientific discipline that seeks to identify the biological and genetic sources of social behavior in humans and other animals, is a form of essentialism that asserts that male behavior patterns are encoded in the genes. The foundational essentialist psychological work belongs to Carl Jung, who emphasized the existence of the *anima* and *animus* archetypes in the psyche as determinative of masculinity and femininity. Jung postulated that the *anima* was the unconscious feminine principle that resided in the man and that the *animus* was the unconscious masculine principle in the female. In this respect, every person has qualities that are both masculine and feminine. Furthermore, these archetypes are universal in as much as everyone inherits these psychic structures (Hall and Nordby, 1999). The *anima* was Jung's pivotal concept in masculine psychology because it helped a man become empathically involved in life, and its integration into a man's consciousness was a necessity in order for him to become fully individuated—Jung's term for the process of attaining a fully conscious self-understanding and wholeness (p. 34). The integration of the *anima* into the masculine psyche, according to Jung, was an initiatory experience, analogous to innumerable primitive and religious initiation rites throughout time and across cultures (Jung, *Psychology and Alchemy*, paragraph 249 as cited from Jacobi, 1973, p. 141; Henderson, 1979; Gilmore, 1990).

Jung and the neo-Jungians postulated their own psychodynamic stage theory of masculine development. The first stage is childhood, which lasts until puberty and in which consciousness is governed by instinct and mediated through his parents, particularly the mother (Hall & Nordby, 1999). The second stage is youth and young adulthood, lasting to age 35 or 40, which Jung characterized as a period when "the demands of life which harshly put an end to the dream of childhood ... that gives rise to ... inner, psychic difficulties [characterized by] a more or less patent clinging to the childhood level of consciousness, a resistance to the fateful forces in and around us which would involve us in the world" (Jung, 1991, pp. 26–27). During this stage, the young man is expected to make his way in the world by adopting a functioning *persona* and to assume a responsible role as a man. A related developmental task of this stage is for the boy to "achieve a healthy separation from the original bond with his personal mother [while he] develop[s] an awareness of the importance of the image of the archetypal mother in his psyche" (Pederson, 1991, p. 74). The third stage is midlife occurring between the ages of 40 and 55, during which a man re-encounters the feminine *anima* because the archetype challenges a man to make the transition "from a persona-orientation to a Self-orientation" (Stein, 1983, p. 27). The *anima* serves to reconnect the man in midlife with the neglected feminine side of his psyche in order to "unite a pair of essential opposites" (Stein, 1983, p. 94). It is out of the union of the man's *persona* with the *anima* that the man's *self* is born. Stein summarizes the goal of this developmental stage by saying that

> the optimal outcome of the midlife transition ... is the cre-
> ation of a reworked, more psychologically inclusive, and
> consequently more complex conscious sense of identity: one

that does not take the form of a lithic personality monument, however, but of a uniquely and firmly channeled flow of libido, that still allows room for the play of floating in liminality (Stein, 1983, p. 139).

The essentialist school of thought highlights the need for some kind of rite of initiation to usher young men from immature masculinity into mature masculinity as a critical factor in a young man's development. Robert Moore did a great deal of work on the archetype of initiation and asserted that it is part of the psychic make-up of the psyche (Havlick, 2001). Furthermore, Gilmore (1990) stressed in the following passage the universality of initiation rites:

There is a constantly recurring notion that real manhood is different from simple anatomical maleness, that it is not a natural condition that comes about spontaneously through biological maturation but rather is a precarious or artificial state that boys must win against powerful odds. This recurrent notion that manhood is problematic, a critical threshold that boys must pass through testing, is found at all levels of sociocultural development regardless of what other alternative roles are recognized. (p. 11)

Bly (1991) amplified Gilmore's assertion by stating, "Boys need a second birth, this time a birth from men" (p. 16) while Henderson described masculine initiation as "a process of transition between Mother and Father, or between inner and outer worlds of experience" (Henderson, 1979, p. 76). Pederson (1991) saw a three-fold function for rites of initiation:

The first is an exogenous need to achieve separation and differentiation from the mother and to align his identity more with the father, which is accomplished in the symbolic death and rebirth aspect of the ritual. The second is the endogenous need to define his place within the group—to identify his role, obligations, and responsibilities. And third, these rites fulfill both an endogenous and exogenous need to incorporate the feminine within himself, in a way that allows him to be separate from his mother, sisters, and other females in his group. (p. 93)

Initiation and initiation experiences, therefore, are essential to the development of mature masculinity. When done with loving care by male ritual elders, these experiences can affirm life as well as help the young man make the difficult transition from youth into manhood.

A related concept to initiation is the notion of "male wounding." In his book, *Under Saturn's Shadow: The Wounding and Healing of Men*, James Hollis (1994) insightfully wrote about the "oppressive weight on the soul" the masculine ideologies men bear that wound males, which he summarizes in "the eight secrets men carry within" (pp. 10–11). Hollis expounded on the implications and consequences to men's lives of the Saturnian burden, noting that there is a "double-edged sword of wounding. There are wounds that crush the soul, distort and misdirect the energy of life, and those that prompt us to grow up" (p. 65). Hollis continued by discussing the "necessary wounds" that are found in male initiation rites. In this respect, Hollis echoed the insights of Eliade (1958), Keen (1992), Bly (1992), and others who see initiation wounding as vital and necessary. Although real, the initiatory wounds are symbolic and filled with archetypal significance in order to provide a young male with "an introduction to the world's wounding, the experience of which would henceforth become one's daily experience" (Hollis, 1994, p. 105).

Hollis, Moore and Gillette (1990), Bly (1992), and Keen (1992) decried the lack of viable and life-enhancing initiation experiences in today's culture. Rather, the existence of immature and destructive pseudo-initiation rituals serves only to reinforce puerile narcissistic notions and to inhibit the transition into adulthood.

Following the thinking of Carl Jung, Moore and Gillette stressed that deep within the masculine psyche are "blueprints, what we can also call 'hard wiring,' for the calm and positive mature masculine [that] Jungians refer to ... as archetypes, or 'primordial images'" (Moore and Gillette, 1990, p. 9). Moore said, "this Great Code is, in fact, [our] two million year old DNA" (Moore, The Great Code, http://www.robertmoore-phd.com/The_Great_Code.cfm). Moore and Gillette proceed to elaborate on the crystalline structure of the deep masculine as a quaternity composed of four principal archetypes that they name the King, the Warrior, the Magician, and the Lover (Moore and Gillette, 1990; 1992a; 1992b; 1993a; 1993b).

As energy flows, the archetypes constellate certain qualities within a man. The King archetype manifests first as an ordering and centering function and secondly as an offering for fertility and blessing (Moore and Gillette, 1992a, pp. 114–146). The Warrior archetype manifests as appropriately controlled aggression and assertiveness; helps with providing personal boundaries, enables goal-oriented living, and self-discipline and faithfulness in service to larger goals (Moore and Gillette, 1992b, pp. 98–117). The Magician archetype appears as "the archetype of introversion and reflection ... who quickly gets to the heart of problems others can't fathom [and who] often ... will understand people better than they understand themselves" (Moore & Gillette, 1993b, p. 188). The fourth masculine archetype is the Lover that is constellated as sexuality, desire, relationship, expressiveness, incarnation, and joy (Moore and Gillette, 1993a). Together, these four archetypes comprise the mature masculine structure, which, when accessed and integrated, can be transformative by assisting men in making the transition from boyhood to adult manhood.

Finally, Michael Gurian is a pioneer in the area of neurobiological differences between males and females. Gurian, "utilizes a reliance on religion and social ideology, but also elevates hard science into equal partnership with religion and ideology in human identity development" (Michael Gurian Homepage, A New Social Theory (www.michael-gurian.com). Gurian (1999a) developed the idea of the male emotional system as composed of testosterone, a male brain structure, and biology, all of which have certain effects that influence the way males think, feel, act, and relate to the world. For instance, testosterone enhances aggression as well as a quick release of tension and emotion. Gurian noted that the male brain "is hardwired to be better at spatial relationships than emotional ones ... [because there is a] smaller corpus callosum in the male brain" (1999a, p. 38). The corpus callosum is a bundle of nerves that connects the brain's right and left hemispheres, allowing for a crossing of information from one side to the other. Gurian also cited the slower developing frontal lobes in males, which also inhibit the handling of many social and cognitive functions dealing with emotional relations. Gurian concluded that male brains are better suited for spatial activities and other object-oriented activities (Gurian, 1999a). Employing nature-based neurobiological principles, Gurian argued that there are male-specific strategies and processes that adolescent boys experience that nurture a healthy development from boyhood through adolescence into adulthood.

In his insightful book about the moral development of boys, *The Good Son* (1999b), Gurian used a similar approach. He wrote,

> Males undoubtedly enjoy certain advantages in our culture. But they do not have the advantage of being born with an inherent path to self worth. Their early brain development pushes their lives more outward into the surrounding world than inward into their emotional development.... A male born into a human society starts out with a longer biological road toward respect than a female.... And so it is to be a boy and to be a man. Nature does not provide him with a blueprint for worth. The boy and the man must be raised to see the possibility of self-worth, then meet a few others who provide the vision of a road toward it, and then spend a lifetime pursuing that worth through action and relationship. (Gurian, 1999b, pp. 29–30)

Gurian asserted that boys need more structure, discipline, guidance, and training than is commonly provided to girls in parenting and child rearing. Gurian elaborated on the contents of a values-laden program that nurtures the core of manhood (Gurian, 1999b, pp. 229–275). The plan addresses the values of compassion, honor, loyalty, duty, fairness, virtue, decency, dignity, character, discipline, responsibility, and enterprise. A final chapter addresses ten integrities which Gurian urged educators, parents, and mentors to convey to adolescent boys as prerequisites to becoming a man (Gurian, 1999b, p. 256). The ten integrities are ancestral integrity, psychological integrity, social integrity, spiritual integrity, moral integrity, emotional integrity, sexual integrity, marital (or gender) integrity, physical integrity, and intellectual integrity.

Summary

Given the foregoing, what is now needed is the development of a new paradigm of masculinity. Pollack and Levant (1995) called for a "bio-psycho-social model of the construction of gender" that accounts for individual and group dynamics in a depth psychology of unconscious processes (Pollack and Levant, 1995, p. 386). This psychology must negotiate the crisis of connection between males and females and promote empathic dialogue (Pollack and Levant, 1995). This study articulated a blending of the various competing points of view by utilizing key elements from each as needed in an attempt to address the emerging mature masculine consciousness of late-adolescent boys. As Shepherd Bliss said, "It is not either-or, that you either believe in archetypes or the social construction of reality; you can have both-and, unless you are a fundamentalist" (Bliss, 1995, p. 301). Therefore, this work proposes an eclectic approach to fostering gender consciousness and sensitivity in an age appropriate manner.

LIMITATIONS OF THE STUDY

This work narrowly focused on late-adolescent boys and their developmental, psychological, and educational issues. As a result, much ancillary material that relates to men in other developmental stages was glossed over or ignored. Issues and concepts apropos to the masculine life cycle in its entirety were included to the extent it was necessary to provide context and clarity to the overall conceptual presentation of the work.

CHAPTER TWO

MASCULINE BIOLOGY

> Males and females are equal in their common membership of
> the same species, humankind, but to maintain that they are the
> same in aptitude, skill or behavior is to build a society based on
> a biological and scientific lie. (Moir & Jessel, 1990, *Brain Sex*)

Until recently, science has regarded men and women as both different and
yet similar extensions of nature's plan. Charles Darwin (1871) was the first to
question this notion seriously. For Darwin, a central tenet of his evolutionary
theory was that sex differences were of paramount importance. Sigmund
Freud (1925; 1953) focused on sex differences in humans by linking a person's
genital anatomy to his or her psychosexual development. According to Freud,
male and female intellectual and behavioral development, though different,
was the same until the emergence of the awareness of the phallus. Female
analysts, such as Karen Horney challenged Freud, arguing that women's
attitudinal differences stemmed from a distinct developmental path for
women. Margaret Meade also stressed cultural determination in influencing
sex differences. During the 1950s and 1960s, ethologists, using Darwin
as a starting point, attributed sex differences to evolutionary processes of
adaptation and ecology. The zoologist, Jean Piaget, observed children and

concluded that the key to adaptation was the individual's cognitive and intellectual development, which was influenced by sex differences. Over the past twenty years, the question has become not if there are differences between males and females but what to make of them (Blustain, 2000).

This debate is being waged by two general groups of researchers: sociobiologists / evolutionary psychologists and social constructionists, the former claiming that evolution and biology are prime determinants of gender behavior, and the latter that claim that there is more variation in gender behavior caused by societal influences. In essence, the nature versus nurture question is a debate between essentialists and social constructionists.

The unwritten rule in the social sciences has been Durkheim's maxim that social events need to be explained in relation to other social data; therefore, matters concerning behavior are social constructions. Biological dicta, such as genetic influences, are ruled out in favor of societal and human-interaction constructions. The social constructionists take the side of nurture in the nature versus nurture debate.

In her book, *Paradoxes of Gender* (1994), feminist and sociologist, Judith Lorber takes issue with the sociobiologists and the evolutionary psychologists who contend that behavior is influenced by the genes. She sees gender as a social institution with its origin in human culture. Lorber contends, "Gender (is) an institution that establishes patterns of expectations for individuals, orders the social processes of everyday life, is built into the major social organizations of society, such as the economy, ideology, the family, politics, and is also an entity in an of itself" (p. 1). As a human invention, gender structures and organizes human social and cultural life and reinforces individuals' experience of gender, and "the social reproduction of gender in individuals reproduces the gendered societal structure; as individuals act out gender norms and expectations in face-to-face interaction, they are constructing gendered systems of dominance and power" (Lorber, p. 6).

With specific reference to sex differences, Lorber acknowledged physiological differences between males and females but said these differences "are completely transformed by social practices to fit the salient categories of a society, the most pervasive of which are 'female' and 'male' and 'women' and 'men'" (p. 18). However, neither sex nor gender are distinct categories *sui generis*: "Combinations of incongruous genes, genitalia, and hormonal input are ignored in sex categorization, just as combinations of incongruous identity, sexuality, appearance, and behavior are ignored in the social construction of gender statuses" (Lorber, pp. 38–39). Lorber criticized sociobiology as offering inadequate evidence that biological phenomenon produces gendered behavior. Gendering begins from the time the sex of a fetus is known in the womb and continues throughout life as the individual interacts in society, receiving and transmitting gendered behaviors and reinforcement. Lorber cited the example of sports organization and healthcare as "the ways bodies are gendered by social practices and how the female body is socially constructed to be inferior" (p. 41). She concluded her examination of sex differences as a social construction by quoting Catherine MacKinnon (1987), who wrote that in Western society the male is the standard of universal humanness because

> virtually every quality that distinguishes men from women is already affirmatively compensated in this society. Men's physiology defines most sports, their needs define auto and health insurance coverage, their socially defined biographies define workplace expectations and successful career patterns, their perspectives and concerns define quality in scholarship, their experiences and obsessions define merit, their objectification of art defines art, their military service defines citizenship, their presence defines family, their inability to get along with each other—their wars and relationships—define history, their image defines god, and their genitals define sex. For each of their differences from women, what amounts to an affirmative action plan is in effect, otherwise known as the structure and values of American society. (quoted in Lorber, pp. 53–54)

The social constructionist viewpoint has increasingly come under attack as evidence accumulates which demonstrates that human behavior is strongly influenced by the genes. Scientists like David Buss stress that biology and culture interact in complex ways. "People think it's genetic determinism but it's not; they think human behavior is intractable or unchangeable, whereas the opposite is true, the more knowledge you have the more you'll be able to change it" (Buss, 2004). The preponderance of the evidence, however, led Christina Hoff Summers (2000) to conclude that "the characteristically different interests, preferences, and behaviors of males and females are expressions of innate 'hardwired' biological differences" (p. 152).

CURRENT SCIENTIFIC RESEARCH

Developmental psychologist, David Geary (1998) and evolutionary psychologist, David Buss (2003) argued that gender differences do exist and are the result of the Darwinian principle of sexual selection. Over time, these sex differences are encoded in the genes. While there are some exceptions, generally the pattern emerges that women invest more of themselves in their offspring than men do, and men tend to be more promiscuous with multiple sexual partners than do women. Evolutionary biologist, Bobbi Low, in her book *Why Sex Matters: A Darwinian Look at Human Behavior* (2000), reiterated the evolutionary theory of human behavior through the strategies of sexual selection, reciprocity, and kin selection. She wrote,

> Mating effort, typical of males in most species, has what economists call a large "fixed cost"; that is, much effort must be invested to get any return whatsoever, but after some level, great additional gains come from just a little more investment. So specializing in pure mating effort has great impact on a male's life. A male must grow large if physical combat is any part of competition; he may have to range far; perhaps he must grow weapons or decorations, like a moose or a peacock; he may have to fight—all these have costs. (p. 43)

Throughout her book, Low asserted that the essentialist argument that human physiology and behavior are directed by genetics while acknowledging the influence of social environment. She said, "There is no doubt that genes influence not only our physical structure and physiology, but our behavior; there is no doubt that historical accident often plays a role; nor is there any doubt that cultural and social pressures can influence behavior" (Low, p. 4).

Geary's extensively documented treatise on human sex differences highlighted a number of specific differences caused by sexual selection. He asserted that childhood is the time when the cognitive, social, and behavioral skills and competencies necessary for survival and reproduction consistent with the local environment are developed (Geary, 1998, p. 256). During the course of human evolution, the length of this developmental period has grown extensively because of the increased complexity of human social systems as they relate to reproduction. Thus, according to Geary, "one important function of childhood is to provide the experiences needed to refine those competencies that are associated with intrasexual competition and other reproductive activities in adulthood" (p. 256). The different pattern of male physical development, play interests, exploratory behavior and styles, social behaviors such as coalition-formation for dominance, aggression, and motives "can be readily understood in terms of sexual selection in general and intrasexual competition in particular" (Geary, p. 256). For Geary, male sex differences and behaviors "have almost certainly been shaped by sexual selection, and the majority of these differences have resulted from male-male competition over access to mates" (p. 257). Behaviors, such as risk-taking in order to achieve social status and social dominance in groups are more evident in boys than girls (Geary, 1998, pp. 245–246). Because of the different sexual reproductive strategies adopted by males and females, a distinctive "pattern of cognitive competencies in the structure and functioning of many of the brain systems" (Geary, p. 301) evolved in males and females. Generally, the result is that females demonstrate greater "cognitive competencies associated with one-on-one social relationships," (Geary, p. 301) including a greater facility in the use of verbal and written language than males, while males generally exhibit "cognitive competencies associated with representing and acting on the large-scale physical environment" (Geary, p. 302). Those cognitive competencies include solving three-dimensional geometry problems (Geary). Geary noted that there is more variability in cognitive performance among males than among females and attributes this variability to the fragility of boys as a learning group. According to him,

> In difficult contexts (e.g. poor health care, inadequate nutrition, and so forth), the prediction is that more boys will be adversely affected than girls, which, in turn, will result in an overrepresentation of boys among the lowest scoring individuals and an underrepresentation of boys among the highest scoring individuals. (Geary, p. 316; Halpern, 1997)

Consequently, boys are more susceptible to stress related factors and environmental conditions in modern society than females are (Geary, 1998).

In the past decade, there has been dramatic growth in the development of the biological sciences as they relate to providing a foundation for understanding much gender-based behavior, causing some observers to label this "a revolutionary age in biology" (Fukuyama, 1997). These developments have had enormous influences on the social sciences, too. Evolutionary psychologist, David Buss (2004), in an interview with *The Evolutionist*, an Internet-based magazine made the following comment:

> Five years ago, none of these texts had anything about evolution. There's been a massive change; an acceptance of at least certain aspects of evolutionary psychology that have never been accepted before. Psychologists in general tend to be very empirically minded and so they want to see the data, and at least the more reasonable ones are persuaded by data. There are still people that, despite the evidence, will claim that the sexes are identical... . That position is getting harder because these results have now been replicated by independent investigators. But I've been pleased with the overall speed with which these things have been accepted. I thought it would take a lot longer. (www.1se.ac.uk/Depts/cpnss/darwin/evo/buss.htm)

In his book, *The Evolution of Desire: Strategies of Human Mating* (2003), Buss used a 37-country cross-cultural study to prove that men and women have markedly different mate-selection strategies: males seek young, attractive women who will be sexually faithful, but females prefer males who have material and financial resources, power and high social status. This difference in mate-selection strategy, according to Buss, is the result of innate psychological mechanisms that have become hardwired in the human species as the species has adapted to its environment over the course of human evolution. Furthermore, Buss (2000) contended that jealousy is an adaptive emotional behavior that facilitates the human species in coping with reproductive threats. Research by molecular biologists and neuroanatomists, focusing on the chemical and neuronal wiring in the brain, has localized in the brain such psychological phenomena as lust or fear, in addition to the ability to appreciate music or the facility to make choices (Fukuyama, 1997). Neuroanatomist, Laura Allen wrote the following about her research on the human brain: "As I began to look at the human brain, I kept finding differences. Seven or eight of the ten structures we measured turned out to be different between men and women" (Sommers, p. 89). In the future, as the human genome is decoded and understood, more biological determinants for human behavior are likely to be elicited.

CURRENT NEUROBIOLOGICAL RESEARCH

Perhaps the best known advocate for neurobiological differences in males and females is Michael Gurian (*The Wonder of Boys: What Parents, Mentors and Educators Can Do to Shape Boys into Exceptional Men*, 1996; *Boys and Girls Learn Differently: A Guide for Teachers and Parents*, 2001; *What Could He Be Thinking?: How a Man's Mind Really Works*, 2003). In his research, Gurian asserted that although there are some socialized differences between the sexes, "there is a primal nature to 'man' and 'woman' on which culture has only a minor effect" (2003, p. xxii). While all human brains possess three similar parts called the brain stem, the limbic system, and the neocortex, the difference between the male and female brain lies in the size of particular parts of the brain and how these parts are connected and function together (Gurian, 2003).

Gurian & Blum (1998) cite current neurobiological research for their assertions, two of which will be highlighted in this work. The first is the work of Drs. Ruben and Raquel Gur of the University of Pennsylvania School of Medicine, who use modern technologies of Positron Emission Technology (PET) scanning and Magnetic Resonance Imaging (MRI) to measure how and to what extent males and females use their brains for certain tasks. One of the findings they discovered is that females use more parts of their brain than males (Blum, p. 53; Gur, et al. 1995). In another study, the Gurs did MRI scans on 116 healthy men and women and found evidence that women have relatively larger brain sections that control aggression and monitor behavior, while men have relatively larger sections of the brain that promote aggression. According to Dr. Ruben Gur, "This study provides neurobiological evidence that women have more brain tissue that's used censoring aggressive and angry responses, while men have more brain tissue of the type that initiates aggression and impulsive, angry responses" (VanScoy, 2004, www.hon.ch/News/HSN/509404.html).

Another husband and wife research team, Sally E. and Bennett A. Shaywitz of the Yale University School of Medicine also used MRI imaging while giving 19 males and 19 females a rhyming task to complete. According to their findings published in *Nature* (1995)

> We find significant sex differences in activation patterns during phonological tasks: in males, brain activation is localized to left inferior gyrus (IFG) regions; in females the pattern of activation is very different, engaging more diffuse neural systems involving both left and right IFG regions. These data provide the first clear evidence of sex differences in the functional organization of the brain for language and indicate that these differences exist at the level of phonological processing. (pp. 607–609)

This research confirmed the findings of the Gur research team, indicating that females use both sides of their brain hemispheres more readily than males. Scientific evidence continues to amass that points to male and female brain differences that influence behavior and cognition (Halpern, 1997). For a more complete list of cognitive sex differences, see Appendix B.

MALE BRAIN STRUCTURE

A considerable amount of scientific research has been conducted comparing male and female brain structures. Pulitzer prize-winning science journalist, Deborah Blum, in her book *Sex on the Brain: The Biological Differences between Men and Women* (1998), discussed the differences between male and female brain structures. From a size perspective, male brains are generally 15 percent larger than female brains, which have an impact on intelligence, with males being more adept at spatial reasoning (Blum, pp. 38–39). Another size differential noted by Blum is that the anterior commissure, a narrow strip of nerve fibers that connect the two hemispheres together, tends to be slightly larger in women than in men. Hence, the designation that men's brain functioning is more "lateralized," that is, more brain activity tends to take place in one hemisphere than the other while undertaking a task (Blum, p. 46). A third difference between the male and female brain is that the male brain tends to shrink faster with age with the most visible difference occurring in the frontal lobe (Blum, p. 51). According to Dr. Reuben Gur, "Men lose tissue in the frontal lobe at such a rate that by the time they reach middle age, even though they start with larger brains, their frontal lobe is the same size as the frontal lobe of women" (Blum, p. 52).

Michael Gurian (1996; 1999a; 2001; 2004) cites a number of brain structure differences between the male and female brain. In males the corpus callosum, the nerve structure that connects the right hemisphere of the brain with the left and that facilitates communication between the two hemispheres, is approximately 25% smaller in males than in females (Gurian, 1999a, p. 39; 2003, pp. 11–12). The result is that males have a more difficult time connecting feelings and thoughts to words, thereby causing males to "have a more difficult time making language out of experience than women do" (Gurian, 2003, p. 12). A second brain structural difference is that the frontal lobes, which are responsible for "many social and cognitive functions related to emotional relationships," (Gurian, 1999a, p. 39) are smaller in males and develop at a slower rate in male than in female brains. Because the corpus callosum and frontal lobe brain structures are smaller, males are more attuned to and adept at spatial activities, such as hunting and tracking "objects moving through space" as well as a proclivity for other complex skills involving spatial abilities such as "mechanical design, measurement, direction, abstraction, and manipulation of physical objects" (Gurian, 1999a, pp. 38–39; 2003, p. 11; Halpern, 1997, p. 1094) than women. A third structural difference is in the amygdala, a brain structure deep within the limbic system that regulates emotional reactions and aggressive responses. This structure is larger in males, thereby helping males be aggressive. Furthermore, there are fewer synaptic linkages from the amygdala to other brain structures such as the frontal lobe that controls emotions, resulting in "less impulse control and moral decision making" (Gurian, 2003, p. 14). Another structural difference is the memory center, known as the hippocampus, which is larger in the female brain than in the male brain (Gurian, 2003). Additionally, the female brain possesses more synaptic linkages between the hippocampus and the other emotive centers than the male brain does, resulting in females having better memory capacities for physical and emotional details than males (Gurian, 2003, pp. 14–15). Finally, the cingulate gyrus, a feeling and emotion structure within the limbic system, is used more extensively by the female brain at rest, while the male brain at rest has greater synaptic transmissions to the fight-or-flight brain stem (Gurian, 2003, p. 15). Consequently, women think things out before engaging in action, whereas males tend to react impulsively when the fight-or-flight mechanism is triggered (Gurian, 2003, p. 16).

Chemical composition is different between the male and female brains. The hypothalamus secrets two brain chemicals: *serotonin*, which regulates mood and emotion among other things, and *oxytocin*, which influences the capacity to bond and maintain healthy interpersonal relations. Studies have shown that males have less of these two brain chemicals than females; consequently, males tend to act more impulsively and engage in less bonding (Gurian, 2003, p. 12; George, 1997, p. 302). For a more complete list and explanation of Gurian's gender brain differences with their effects, see Appendix A.

The Role of Testosterone

The hypothalamus also secrets testosterone, a powerful hormone that influences male aggression and sexual behavior. In addition to causing increased aggression conditioned on the need for asserting or maintaining dominance or control (Geary, 1998; Clare, 2000), testosterone influences the size and formation of many brain structures, including the corpus callosum (Gurian, 2003, p. 8) as well as an influence on "sex-typical patterns of cognitive performance" (Halpern, p. 1095), such as significantly improving visual-spatial skills. The biological difference between males and females is caused in large part by the large infusions of testosterone secreted by the hypothalamus prenatally, at puberty, and throughout life. In males, testosterone has a virilizing effect that includes the development of the penis and the scrotum, the deepening of the male vocal chords, and the growth of facial and body hair. It also promotes the development of male muscle mass and strength, greater bone density, and overall height. According to Clare (2000)

> The normal woman produces about 200 micrograms of testosterone and 120 micrograms of estrogen each day, a testosterone / estrogen ratio of about 1.6 to 1. The normal male produces about the same amount of estrogen daily (100 micrograms) but

a comparatively huge amount of testosterone—5100 micrograms per day—giving a testosterone/estrogen ratio of 51 to 1. Not only do men have very much higher levels of testosterone than women, they have them at their highest just after puberty and in the early and mid-twenties—when male antisocial activity and aggression is at its peak. (p. 20)

Gurian emphasized that adolescent males experience testosterone surges five to seven times a day, making the hormone a prime mover in the male's biology and brain structures (Gurian, 1999a, p. 93).

Coupled with the unique male brain structures and the influence of testosterone, the following three principal behavior patterns exhibited by males were identified by Gurian:

1. the search for instant or quick gratification, whether in eating quickly, jumping from activity to activity, or quick sexual conquest;
2. the tendency to move quickly to problem-solving, even in emotionally complex experiences;
3. the tendency to find activities through which his body will build physical tension—like sports or other concentrated, single-task experiences—then release the tension with an "Ahhh." (Gurian, 1996, p. 11)

Additionally, Gurian identified other testosterone-driven effects. These include the male proclivity toward dominance patterns, less inclination to consider and evaluate the consequences of physical and social aggression toward others, a delayed reaction and response to emotions, a tendency toward exhibiting mechanistic, most efficient, behaviors, and uniquely male structures such as sports and games to prompt emotional development and expression (Gurian, 1996, pp. 33–36).

IMPLICATIONS FOR THINKING, FEELING, AND ACTING

Based on the foregoing discussion, several implications can be drawn regarding the construction of a gender studies curriculum for late adolescent boys. The growing scientific data documenting the sex differences between males and females as they relate to behavior, learning, and cognition make it clear that there is a need to address positively the distinctive needs of boys. Like girls, boys have a unique and distinctive learning style that is predicated on their male-specific brain structures and on their chemical, hormonal, and social needs. Educators who work with males need to understand and appreciate boys' distinctive ways of acting, thinking, and behaving. Additionally, Michael Gurian stated that there is a need for more gender education to help students learn about themselves and how they tick (2001).

This conclusion flies in the face of the current gender-equity movement which disapproves and seeks to eliminate typical, healthy male behaviors, such as rough-and-tumble play and natural boy-type aggressiveness, and replace it with feminine activities and a feminized educational curriculum (Sommers, 2000). According to Sommers, those educators who embrace the ideology of the gender equity movement state that these healthy male behaviors "are not natural but are artifacts of culture," and they "embrace the belief that gender-fair schools will require a new pedagogy that upsets and neutralizes many behavioral conventions associated with being a boy or a girl" (Sommers, p. 85). Anthony Pellegrini, an early-childhood education professor at the University of Minnesota, saw the elimination of rough-and-tumble play and recess as profound insensitivity to boys' biologically driven natural play needs (Pellegrini et al., 1995). A revisioning and a rethinking of the manner in which the educational and social needs of boys are addressed in the school setting is needed.

The first implication for a gender studies curriculum is the need to address boys' unique male biological, hormonal, and brain structures. Such a curriculum can take the brain structures and hormones listed in Appendix B as a starting point to address with boys their distinctive biological heritage and make up. By educating boys about their distinctive male biology and making them aware of how their own internal processes work, teachers can assist boys in becoming more self-regulating of their hormones and biologically-driven behaviors.

Advocating a male-friendly focus on the biological uniqueness and differences between males and females, however, does not mean that one sex is smarter or better than the other. Such valuations have no place in a masculine gender studies curriculum. Halpern (1997) researched this issue and concluded with the following:

> Some of the differences favor females and some favor males.
> It is about as meaningful to ask "Which is the smarter sex?"
> or "Which has the better brain?" as it is to ask "Which has the
> better genitals?" Bigotry does not stem from the fact that
> there are group differences; it arises in the evaluation of the
> differences, when group members decide that the traits and
> abilities associated with other groups are inferior to the ones
> found in their own group. (Halpern, 1997)

The use of biological differences in an attempt to advance a political agenda or to be politically correct is an abuse of the information itself and an abuse on the gender on which the data are used (Halpern, p. 1098).

A second implication for a gender studies curriculum is the context in which such a curriculum is to be taught. Halpern (1997) suggested that there may be social reasons for considering single-sex education classes. Sommers (2000) cited a 1998 report by British headmasters entitled "Can Boys Do Better?" that advocates for one-sex classrooms among other gender-specific strategies. Stephen Webb (Webb, 2001) called for a reconsideration of all-male education as one viable alternative to educating boys. Because adolescence is such "an emotionally-charged period of transition and transformation ... (f)or some people, this passage is best navigated apart (somewhat) from the other sex" (Webb, pp. 601+). A masculine gender studies curriculum seems the perfect setting for an all-male grouping of late adolescent boys. Webb expressed the rationale for single-sex classrooms by saying, "separation also creates and encourages a special bonding between members of the same sex. This is especially important today, when males are often not encouraged to articulate and express the full range of their human emotions and needs" (Webb, pp. 601+). Therefore, all male classrooms permit an honesty that might not otherwise be forthcoming in a mixed sex classroom setting. The Haverford School in Philadelphia, Pennsylvania, a private, all-male school, understands and values the unique needs of boys. In 1994, the school created a resource center for discussing and thinking about boys' lives. Called The Men's Studies Project, it employs careful research and scholarship to help parents, educators, and communities effectively raise, educate, understand, and support boys. Dr. Michael Reichert, the project's director, sponsors and conducts school-based research and seminars and forums on raising boys and conducts programs for boys on gender-based issues. As a result, his work has inaugurated a school-wide dialogue on assumptions and practices concerning the educating and raising of boys.

Current research on masculine biology is focusing on the unique differences that males possess which impact their thinking, behaving, and feeling. Schools need to take this body of information seriously as they address the needs of all their students. A masculine gender studies curriculum that addresses the unique brain and biological make-up of males is urgently needed to help males make the transition from adolescence into adulthood. A masculine gender studies course curriculum seems best suited in an all-male setting. Furthermore, such a curriculum needs to appreciate the special needs and challenges males have in navigating the road to responsible manhood.

CHAPTER THREE

MASCULINE DEVELOPMENT THROUGH THE LIFE CYCLE

The information necessary to create a male is encoded in our DNA, but it takes all the institutions of a culture to produce a man.
                                                                    Sandor McNab

To every thing there is a season, and a time to every purpose under the heaven.
                              The Bible, King James Version, Ecclesiastes 3: 1

Since time immemorial, humans have tacitly recognized that human beings undergo stages and periods of human development that qualitatively affect their thinking, feeling, behavior, and fundamental orientation toward the world. There are many metaphors to express the growth and transformation of the male child into the adult male and from the adult male to the elder male. Carl Jung used the metaphor of the hero to describe the notion of longing for consciousness, a deep sense of connection and union within one's self and with the created order (Jung, 1991, p. 6). Joseph Campbell (1973) termed it the "call to adventure" (p. 58): the intentional decision or the accidental and haphazard occurrence that impels the individual to seek his destiny, fraught with promise and danger, in order to become whomever or whatever his life may make him (Campbell, p. 58). Mythology is much more expressive and indicative of the depth and meaning of human development with its nuances of "journey," "danger," and "mystery" as metaphors for human physical and psychological development. Ancient myths, such as Homer's *The Odyssey*, and modern myths, such as Tolkein's *The Lord of the Rings* trilogy, trumpet the hero's quest as he seeks to fulfill his destiny and life's meaning against the backdrop of titanic forces that seek to overwhelm and destroy him. During the battles, the hero courageously overcomes his inner fears and uncertainties in order to continue onward into the unknown.

In a similar manner, masculine development is very much a problematic journey as the male individual seeks to find his own self-fulfillment in the world of other persons. Jung called this journey "the process of individuation which ... has its own dangers [as] there is nothing in nature that does not contain as much evil as good" (Jung, 1989, p. 55). Furthermore, it is a journey within a social context that includes the personal interactions and experiences with significant others as well as the cultural milieu of transmitted values of the society in which a person lives. Erik Erikson (1950) summarized this duality in his explanation for his epigenetic chart of his eight ages of man:

> The underlying assumptions ... are (1) that the human personality in principle develops according to steps predetermined in the growing person's readiness to be driven toward, to be aware of, and to interact with, a widening social radius; and (2) that society, in principle, tends to be so constituted as to meet and invite this succession of potentialities for interaction and attempts to safeguard and to encourage the proper rate and the proper sequence of their enfolding. This is the "maintenance of the human world." (Erikson, p. 270)

Hence, an analysis of the various masculine developmental models cannot minimize the challenges and dangers the growing male encounters as he matures into a man. The problematic nature of these challenges and dangers, moreover, must be faced and resolved satisfactorily intrapsychically and socially.

Stage development theory provides a kind of life map from which to interpret and understand the dynamic issues and "critical steps ... characteristic of turning points" (Erikson, 1950, p. 270) that the male encounters over the course of a lifetime. This study addressed three models, each somewhat different, with a view toward discovering what insights they offer to an understanding of male gender development and awareness. Additionally, the masculine developmental theory provides a cognitive-affective-behavioral matrix by which to establish a proposed gender studies curriculum for late adolescent young men.

THE PSYCHOANALYTIC MODEL

The psychoanalytic approach to individual development is embodied in the work of Erik Erikson (*Childhood and Society*, 1950; *Identity: Youth and Crisis*, 1968; *Identity and the Life Cycle*, 1980), who reformulated Freud's four-stage psychosexual development of the oral, anal, phallic, and latency phases. Erikson expanded and adapted Freud's view that individual development follows biological maturation in an epigenetic pattern as the individual is inserted in the social and cultural institutions of his own particular society (Erikson, 1950, p. 246). Erikson's model posited eight sequential stages, which the ego must confront and integrate as a fundamental conflict inherent in that particular stage of development (Erikson, 1950, pp. 247–274). In order to progress to the next stage, the critical issue confronting the individual in that developmental stage must be resolved through "progress and regression, integration and retardation" (Erikson, 1950, p. 271). If the central developmental issue of a particular stage is not resolved successfully, the individual's development will be thwarted because he will not be able to negotiate successfully the issues confronting him in successive stages (Erikson, 1950, p. 271). The ultimate goal of epigenetic development is a "'healthy' personality in an adult," which Erikson defined in terms of Marie Johada's constructs of "a healthy personality [that] *actively masters* his environment, shows a certain *unity of personality*, and is able to *perceive* the world and himself *correctly*" (Erikson, 1968, p. 92).

Because this study focused on a particular period of time known as late adolescence, Erikson's stage development schema will concentrate on how the first four stages of his eight ages of man (Erikson, 1950), with each stage's conflict, danger, and promise, impact the adolescent's sense of identity. Finally, the sixth stage with its anticipated prospects and challenges for adolescents will be discussed.

The central task of adolescence is "the final establishment of a dominant positive ego identity," said Erikson (1950, p. 306). However, in order to accomplish this goal, the individual male must have successfully negotiated the first four developmental phases. In stage one, the *oral / sensory* phase, during the first year of his life, the young male infant is utterly dependent upon everyone, especially his mother, for his basic needs getting met. If his needs are consistently and reliably met, the infant male will develop a healthy personality consisting of trust.

> The general state of trust ... implies not only that one has learned to rely on the sameness and consistency of outer providers, but also that one may trust oneself and the capacity of one's own organs to cope with urges; and that one is able to consider oneself trustworthy enough so that the providers will not need to be on guard lest they be nipped... . This forms the basis in the child for a sense of identity which will later combine a sense of being 'all right,' of being oneself, and of becoming what other people trust one will become. (Erikson, 1950, pp. 248–249)

If this basic trust is not established, the male child will fail to develop in later years a positive attitude toward others, resulting in an attitude of mistrust with a consequent deficiency of "hope: the enduring predisposition to believe in the attainability of primal wishes in spite of the anarchic urges and rages of dependency" (Erikson, 1968, p. 106). The identity gain from the first stage of development is summarized in the statement: "I am what hope I have and give" (Erikson, 1968, p. 107).

In stage two, called by Erikson the *muscular-anal* stage, during the second and third years of life, the male child faces the issue of toilet training and the control of his physical bodily functions, resulting in the young male's experience of autonomy. Erikson labeled this stage, "This sudden violent wish to have a choice, to appropriate demandingly, and to eliminate stubbornly" (1950, p. 252). To navigate this stage successfully, the male child needs to have the experience of making choices. Hence, the struggle of this stage of development is for autonomy as the child learns to master his physical bodily functions, when "to hold" and when "to let go" (Erikson, 1968, p. 109). Furthermore, according to Erikson, "A sense of self-control without loss of self-esteem is the ontogenetic source of *free will*. From an unavoidable sense of loss of self-control and of parental overcontrol comes a lasting propensity for *doubt* and *shame* (1968, pp. 109–110)." A number of maladjustments in adolescence can result from shaming and doubt induced in childhood, including the proclivity to evade interaction with others or by engaging in defiant autonomy, such as gang involvement (Erikson, 1968, pp. 111–112). The identity gain from the successful negotiation of this stage of development is summed up as "I am what I can will freely" (Erikson, 1968, p. 114).

The third stage of childhood starts around the age of four, when the child begins to distance himself from his parents and orient more toward the outer world, developing a sense of initiative by being more intrusive into the surrounding environment. Erikson made much of the fact that this stage corresponds with Freud's phallic stage of psychosexual development, in which "infantile genitality" begins to impact the way which "the child ... develops the prerequisites for masculine or feminine initiative and, above all, some sexual self-images which will become essential ingredients in the positive and negative aspects of his future identity" (1968, p. 118). At this stage, "a deep sense of guilt is awakened" and conscience, the governor of initiative emerges as a powerful "inner voice of self-observation, self-guidance, and self-punishment, which divides him radically within himself" (Erikson, 1968, p. 119). The danger is that parents will punish a child too strictly or harshly, causing the child to develop too rigid a conscience that inhibits initiative by inducing feelings of guilt. A successful navigation of the childhood stage results in "freeing the child's initiative and sense of purpose for adult tasks which promise ... a fulfillment of one's range of capacities" (Erikson, 1968, p. 122). This process of maturity can be summarized as a growing guilt-free conviction that "I am what I can imagine I will be" (Erikson, 1968, p. 122).

Erikson called the fourth stage the school age during which children are in elementary school, and each child must learn to work and acquire the skills of literacy and the basic technology of his culture, such as reading, writing, and arithmetic. Indispensable to this stage is the sense of industry whereby "he now learns to win recognition by producing things" (Erikson, 1968, pp. 123–124). The danger is that the child may experience a sense of inferiority or "the sense that one will never be 'any good'" (Erikson, 1968, p. 125). The strength a child earns as a result of a successful experience of this stage is that of competence, a feeling that he can perform well. The contribution from the school age to the sense of identity is that "I am what I can learn and make work" (Erikson, 1968, p. 127).

The fifth stage in Erikson's epigenetic development is adolescence, which presents the problem of a sense of ego identity with its consequent danger of identity confusion. This stage is characterized by the need of youths to consolidate their social roles as well as a bewildering range of choices and decisions that youth must make, such as those regarding occupational identity, intimacy including sexuality and relationships, and political ideologies (Erikson, 1968). Ego identity, then, is the culmination "of a gradual integration of all identifications" from the previous developmental stages, and a permanent ego identity that

> cannot begin to exist without the trust of the first oral stage; it cannot be completed without a promise of fulfillment which from the dominant image of adulthood reaches down into the baby's beginning and which creates at every step an accruing sense of ego strength. (Erikson, 1980, p. 96)

Erikson reiterated that it is essential that the maturing child successfully negotiate the crises presented at each stage of development in order that the healthy adult can emerge.

Erikson called the sixth through eighth stages the "three stages of adulthood" (Erikson, 1980). The sixth stage poses the crisis of intimacy and distantiation versus self-absorption, whereby the individual must be able to form intimate relationships with oneself and others and where sexual intimacy is only part of the issue, or the counterpart which is "distantiation: the readiness to repudiate, to isolate, and, if necessary, to destroy those forces and people whose essence seems dangerous to one's own" (Erikson, 1980, p. 101). The seventh stage presents the crisis of generativity versus stagnation.

Erikson defined generativity as "the interest in establishing and guiding the next generation" or "where such enrichment fails, together, regression from generativity to an obsessive need for pseudo intimacy takes place, often with a pervading sense of stagnation and interpersonal impoverishment" (1980, p. 103). The eighth stage of old age poses the crisis of integrity versus despair and disgust. Integrity has the qualities of acceptance of one's life and history, including the influence of those significant others in one's life, taking responsibility for one's life, and accepting of the individuality and differences of others while affirming one's own lifestyle (Erikson, 1980, p. 104). Integrity's counterpart is despair, which is characterized by "an unconscious fear of death, … often hidden behind a show of disgust, a misanthropy, or a chronic contemptuous displeasure with particular institutions and particular people" (Erikson, 1980, p. 105).

Erikson's eight-stage epigenetic theory of development is important for establishing a link with and expanding Freud's psychosexual developmental theory and for taking into account the social components of individual development. The result is to inaugurate an interdisciplinary theory of social interaction in which individual and social dimensions of development are interwoven.

THE JUNGIAN MASCULINE DEVELOPMENT MODEL

Carl Jung (1875–1961) never wrote a single published work devoted exclusively to masculine developmental psychology. Therefore, one has to extract Jung's masculine developmental thinking from the myriad of his collected works. Fortunately, John Beebe (*Aspects of the Masculine*, 1991) has done this from which the primary source material of Jung's writings will be taken. However, there is a corpus of Jungian writers who have contributed much to the Jungian model of masculine development, including Murray Stein (*Stages of Masculine Development,* Lectures delivered at the C.G. Jung Institute of Chicago, 1987) and Anthony Stevens (*On Jung,* 1990; *Archetype: An Updated Natural History of the Self,* 2003), whose works will be cited in this study as well.

Jung called the developing ego's process of becoming conscious the "hero … (who) is first and foremost a self-representation of the longing of the unconscious, of its unquenched and unquenchable desire for the light of consciousness" (Jung, 1991, p. 6). The heroic journey of becoming conscious requires that the ego overcome its dependency upon the unconscious as symbolized by the mother. "Whenever some great work is to be accomplished, before which a man recoils, doubtful of this strength, his libido streams back to the fountainhead—and that is the dangerous moment when the issue hangs between annihilation and new life" (Jung, 1991, p. 13). The first task of development is the necessity of the son separating from the mother, who represents the regression to unconsciousness, "a shrinking back, and this leads to infantilism and finally 'into the mother'" (Jung, 1990, p. 17). However, one separates from the unconscious at great loss and peril because "it is as much a vital necessity for the unconscious to be joined to the conscious as it is for the latter not to lose contact with the unconscious" (Jung, 1990, p. 18). Jung wrote the following about the feminine principle that he called the anima:

> The anima is a factor of utmost importance in the psychology of a man wherever emotions and affects are at work. She intensifies, exaggerates, falsifies, and mythologizes all emotional relations with his work and with other people of both sexes .... After the middle of life, however, permanent loss of the anima means a diminution of vitality, of flexibility, and of human kindness. (1990, pp. 120–121)

The heroic victory over the mother is only temporary because in the second part of life one must reintegrate the feminine, a process that Jung calls "the individuation process" (Jung, 1990, p. 21).

Jung talked about masculine development in terms of psychological consciousness. According to him, the goal of the first half of life is to develop an ego structure, to make one's place in the world, and to gain mastery over one's inner house and outer environment: "to win for oneself a place in society and to transform one's nature so that it is more or less fitted to this kind of existence" (Jung, 1990, p. 29). The goal of the second half of life is individuation, the process of becoming as much of an individual personality as possible. Individuation is not adaptation to the norms of society. Instead it is the emergence and enhancement of one's own inner potentials for personality development. In order to accomplish this goal, the following series of integrations are necessary: shadow integration, the integration of the anima and the animus, contact with the Self, and the development of an ego / self axis (Stevens, 1991, pp. 65–68).

To illustrate the parabola of development from birth to death, Jung employed the metaphor of the sun's transit from dawn to sunset.

> In the morning it rises from the nocturnal sea of unconsciousness and looks upon the wide, bright world which lies before it in an expanse that steadily widens the higher it climbs in the firmament. In this extension of its field of action caused by its own rising, the sun will discover its significance; it will see the attainment of the greatest possible height, and the widest possible dissemination of its blessings, as its goal. In this conviction the sun pursues its course to the unforeseen zenith—unforeseen, because its career is unique and individual, and the culminating point could not be calculated in advance. At the stroke of noon the descent begins. And the descent means the reversal of all the ideals and values that were cherished in the morning. The sun falls into contradiction with itself. It is as though it should draw in its rays instead of emitting them. Light and warmth decline and are at last extinguished.... Fortunately we are not rising and setting suns ... but there is something sunlike within us, and to speak of the morning and spring, of the evening and autumn of life is not mere sentimental jargon.... The one hundred and eighty degrees of the arc of life are divisible into four parts. The first quarter, lying to the east, is childhood, that state in which we are a problem for others but are not yet conscious of any problems of our own. Conscious problems fill out the second and third quarters; while in the last, in extreme old age, we descend again into that condition where, regardless of our state of consciousness, we once more become something of a problem for others. Childhood and extreme old age are, of course, utterly different, and yet they have one thing in common: submersion in unconscious psychic happenings. (Jung, 1990, p. 31 and 36)

These life transitions are fraught with problems and yet possess promises for the developing personality, which finds its highest expression in what Jung termed the *mysterium coinunctionis*, the union of the opposites, a process reserved for the second half of life. The mysterium coinunctionis is an alchemical process of extracting gold from lead that Jung psychologized as the process of individuation. Jolande Jacobi (1973) summarized the broad outline of the individuation process as the following:

> The task of the first half is "initiation into outward reality." Through consolidation of the ego, differentiation of the main function and of the dominant attitude type, and development of an appropriate persona, it aims at the adaptation of the individual to the demands of his environment. The task of the second half of life is a so-called "initiation into the inner reality," a deeper self-knowledge of humanity, a "turning back" (*reflection*) to the traits of one's nature that have hitherto remained unconscious or become so. By raising these traits to consciousness the individual achieves an inward and outward bond with the world and the cosmic order. (1973, pp. 108–109)

Like Freud and Erikson, Jung envisioned masculine development as progressing through epigenetic life stages. In his lectures, Stein (1987) identified five stages of masculine development. Stage one involves childhood and the mother. The mother is the first significant person a man confronts in his life. The relationship with the mother is fundamental and provides the ground for the way the infant relates to the objective world. Jung's qualities of introversion / extroversion are connected with how the mother receives the infant. If the mother is warm, the child will be extroverted; if the mother's reception is cold, the child will be introverted (Stevens, 2003, pp. 106–107). His first identity, then, is as a son of a mother. Although, the male infant must have a relationship with his mother, he must separate from her in a certain way in order to progress to the next stage of development.

The second stage, during adolescence and young adulthood, is called the hero stage. In this stage the young man must establish an identity with a father spirit or have a strong connection to his own inner masculinity. In the natural progression of development, the mother introduces the child to the father and includes him in the relationship between mother and son, changing the dyadic relationship to a triadic one. This transition assists the son in identifying with his father and seeking to be like him. Later, in his early teens, the son will outgrow his father and view him as deficient in some ways, paving the way for the boy to identify with other adult males who become male mentors. This process of disidentification-identification helps the son to break free from the father. The father's role in a son's life is twofold: to assist the son in initiation into manhood and to permit himself to be idealized by the son. Through the two roles, the father helps the son to build a positive father complex of masculine qualities (Stevens, 2003, p. 131). Identity for a young man in this stage is as a father's son, the time when he begins to assume young adulthood roles as a father himself. The father imago will reemerge later in life, often at midlife and in the dreams of men as the Self figure.

The third stage, which involves midlife and the confrontation with the anima, generally begins around the age of forty. At this point in his development, a man must return to the anima, but this time as the inner feminine. During this stage, a man's identity is as a hero who must separate the inner feminine (*anima*) from the outer mother, and with the man becoming a warrior who carries the soul of the anima. Stage four, which takes a man through retirement to about age 75, is characterized as the Odysseus stage and involves the finding and living out of a sense of mission in life (Stein, 1983, p. 124). In order to accomplish this task, the man must have adequately moved through the previous developmental stages. This stage focuses on the issue of the Self and a man's identity as a prophet or a missionary. The fifth and final stage is old age and involves confronting and dealing with the God question, life's ultimate meaning for a man personally as well as metaphysically and spiritually (Stevens, 1990, p. 224). At this stage a man's identity is a sage or a wise old man.

LEVINSON'S DEVELOPMENTAL MODEL

By their own admission, Daniel Levinson et al. (*Seasons of a Man's Life*, 1978) acknowledged that their model of adult development emerges from the tradition of Freud, Jung, and Erikson (Levinson, 1978, p. 5). Unlike Erikson's model, theirs does not include the early years of development but instead concentrates on the adult life cycle using resources from psychology, biology, and sociology (Levinson, p. 5). The basis of this developmental model is the idea of the "individual life structure" composed of four eras lasting approximately 25 years each and emerging through an alternating pattern of "a relatively stable, structure-building period ... followed by a transitional, structure-changing period" (Levinson, p. 317).

During the structure-building period there are a number of critical choices that a man must make. The first task is to construct a "life structure: a man must make certain key choices, form a structure around them, and pursue his goals and values within this structure" (Levinson, p. 49). Other tasks specific to the stages of a man are also a part of the developmental agenda. These stable periods last six to ten years.

A transitional period that lasts approximately four to five years follows, brings to an end the current life structure, and thereby promotes the emergence of a new one (Levinson, p. 49). During transitional periods, the principal tasks are "to question and reappraise the existing structure, to explore various possibilities for change in self and world, and to move toward commitment to the crucial choices that form the basis for a new life structure in the ensuing stable period" (Levinson, p. 49).

The most crucial turning points are the cross-era transitions because they are "bridge(s), or a boundary zone, between two states of greater stability" (Levinson, pp. 49–50). Transitional periods end when a man stops questioning and exploring and is ready to make critical commitments that inaugurate a "building, living within and enhancing a new life structure" (Levinson, p. 52).

With the foregoing in mind, we now turn to Levinson's life structure stages, composed of the following four eras: Childhood and Adolescence, Early Adulthood, Middle Adulthood, and Late Adulthood. Within each era, developmental periods give nuance and meaning to the life structure eras.

The first is the Early Adult Transition, beginning around age 17 and ending around age 22, during which the life tasks are to end childhood and adolescence and to begin entering the pre-adult world. This transition begins by a young man's questioning his existing place and status in the pre-adult world and by changing or ending his existing primary individual, group, and institutional relations (Levinson, p. 56). A second task involves making and testing important initial choices about living in the adult world and forming a personal, nascent adult identity.

The next period is Entering the Adult World, which occurs between ages 22 and 28 with the principal task of constructing a "provisional structure that provides a workable link between the valued self and the adult society" (Levinson, p. 57). During this period, the young man must explore and experiment with adult possibilities in an open way that allows for maximum flexibility and movement. At the same time, the young man must develop a "stable life structure ... by becom(ing) more responsible (for his own life affairs) and (by) 'making something of (his own) life'" (Levinson, p. 58). These two tasks must be balanced in a young man's life, for any extremes in one direction or the other will lead either to a rootless life or to becoming over-committed to a life structure prematurely (Levinson, p. 58).

The Age Thirty Transition follows and is an occasion for the young man to modify the previous life structure or to recreate a new one on a more satisfactory basis. Levinson terms this transition a "crisis" because a man may encounter great difficulty dealing with the challenges of this period, wherein "he finds his present life structure intolerable, yet seems unable to form a better one... (resulting) in the danger of chaos and dissolution, the loss of hope for the future" (Levinson, p. 58).

Beginning around age 33 and lasting to around age 40, the next stage is called the Settling Down period, during which a man builds a second life structure. During this time a man has major goals: "(a) to establish a niche in society: to anchor his life more firmly, develop competence in a chosen craft, and become a valued member of a valued world ... (b) He works at making it: striving to advance, to progress on a timetable" (Levinson, p. 59). During this time, the metaphor of the ladder becomes a central concept in a man's life as he seeks to advance himself personally and professionally and to receive the affirmation for his efforts from society and from his peers (Levinson, p. 59).

The Midlife Transition, occurring from age 40 to 45, follows and offers new challenges during which a man's life structure comes into question. At this point a man questions what he has done with his life. This period is a time of great struggle for men both inwardly and with the outer world (Levinson, p. 60).

Middle Adulthood from age 45 to age 50 follows and is characterized by forming a new life structure. At times, this period is marked by significant events in a person's personal or professional life, such as a divorce, serious illness, death, or a change in job or career (Levinson, p. 61). For many, however, there is no significant change, and this period is the "fullest and most creative season in the life cycle" (Levinson, p. 62). Levinson termed the major developmental task of midlife as that of "individuation" wherein a man must "confront and reintegrate a polarity—that is, a pair of tendencies or states that are usually experienced as polar opposites, as if a man must be one or the other and cannot be both" (Levinson, pp. 196–197). These polarities are identified as Young / Old, Destruction / Creation, Masculine / Feminine, and Attachment / Separateness.

Although they did not study men beyond the midlife period, Levinson et al. theorized that the sequence of transition-stable periods of development continues throughout the life cycle (Levinson, p. 62) The later life periods begin with the Age 50 Transition period, similar to the Age 30 Transition, during which a man assesses and modifies the life structure he has built. The Culmination of Middle Adulthood period, between ages 55 and 60, is a stable period during which a man may build a second middle adult life structure and is characterized as potentially a "time of great fulfillment" (Levinson, p. 62). Between ages 60 and 65 is the Late Adult Transition, which ends middle adulthood and initiates late adulthood. During the Late Adulthood period after age 65, a man must create a life structure that deals with physical issues of health and psychological issues of no longer being young (Levinson, pp. 34–35). Connected with these issues is the issue of confronting one's own mortality and creating a legacy which "defines to a large degree the ultimate value of his life—and his claim to immortality" (Levinson, pp. 217–218).

IMPLICATIONS FOR EDUCATING LATE-ADOLESCENT BOYS

A number of important implications for a male gender curriculum can be drawn based on the developmental theories of Erikson, Jung, and Levinson. First and foremost, the problematic nature of masculine development must again be stressed. All of the male developmental models emphasize that there are dangers and challenges to becoming a fully mature male in psychological, behavioral, and social terms. Using Jung's and Levinson's terminology of individuation, the process of becoming fully conscious by integrating the polar opposites within one's psyche and life structure is a risk because the individual might regress and fall back to a more immature and less aware state. Also, the project of constructing a life structure might fail and necessitate additional attempts to form a lasting and meaningful structure. Erikson emphasized this notion by stressing that the negotiation of each psychosocial stage is dependent upon the successful navigation of the prior stages. If a man is unsuccessful in his life project, his development is stunted and thwarted.

Jung was correct in labeling male development as the call to heroic adventure. An immense amount of courage is needed to move from the mother world to the father world and finally to become individuated as a unique person. The forces of regression and unconsciousness are strong indeed, and an indomitable will and a tenacious spirit are required to maximize what destiny our human developmental capacities call us to become. The call to heroic adventure is the first message to late-adolescent boys in a male gender curriculum. Although the clarion call to become what a person can fully be is a heroic quest that will require utmost strength, perseverance, and courage, maturation will evoke unimaginable benefits as an individual grows and develops into the fullness of being.

Despite the risks, male developmental processes have positive aspects. There is a comfort in knowing that there is a road map, a purposive developmental track that males are on. The road is not entirely uncharted, and while each person's life is unique, there is some common ground. Erikson's model is the strongest in identifying the early stages of development from childhood through adolescence, but Levinson is particularly insightful for charting the adult stages. Jung's model provides the overview of the entire journey. Each developmental model stresses that a series of separations and integrations are necessary in order for growth to progress. Jung calls masculine maturation the reconciliation of the opposites, while Levinson calls it the integration of polarities. To become fully mature and conscious, the dualities and complexities of a person's life and experiences must be reconciled and integrated into a meaningful unity. Generally, all three developmental models concur that the first half of a man's life is spent in forging an external personality in order to make a place in the world, including establishing an occupation and a family. The forties are an especially problematic time, even a crisis, during which a man must question and confront the meaning of his life and what he has accomplished heretofore. The second half of life is spent engaging the inner Self and forging a life structure that provides meaning and purpose in his declining years.

Erikson's, Jung's, and Levinson's masculine developmental models are helpful and insightful in articulating the life maps and developmental issues inherent in becoming a fully aware and mature man. These maps provide the markers for the male journey toward wholeness. James Hollis (1994) summarized this process of discovery when he said, "To live the journey of the soul is to serve nature, to serve others and to serve that mystery of which we are the experiment" (p. 133).

CHAPTER FOUR

UNIQUELY MASCULINE ISSUES: THE MASCULINE WOUND

Healing
I am not a mechanism, an assembly of various sections.
And it is not because the mechanism is working wrongly, that I am ill.
I am ill because of wounds to the soul, to the deep emotional self—
And the wounds to the soul take a long, long time, and only time can help
and patience, and a certain difficult repentance
long difficult repentance, realization of life's mistake,
and the freeing oneself from the endless repetition of the mistake
which mankind at large has chosen to sanctify.

D. H. Lawrence

The hero's journey is one of adventure, but it is also one of depth. While the hero confronts outer reality with all its physical dangers and challenges, a similar process takes place inwardly, as a search for inner sources of ultimate value. Such is the story of Odysseus as told by Homer in *The Odyssey*. The conquering hero of Troy, Odysseus is inflated with *hubris*, the Greek word for excessive, arrogant pride, and journeys for ten long years throughout the Mediterranean Sea in an attempt to return to his home of

Ithaca. Angered by the blinding of his Cyclops son, Polyphemus, and Odysseus' subsequent boast that it was he, Odysseus, who had cunningly done the blinding, Poseidon, the god of the sea, thwarts Odysseus' journey home. Odysseus is doomed to wander the sea, suffering at the hands of elemental forces at Poseidon's instigation. Finally, Odysseus learns from Circe that he must go to the Underworld to seek the wisdom of the blind prophet Tiresias in order to find his way safely home. The Underworld is the fearsome, dismal, and dark world of the joyless dead. However, it is also a source of saving knowledge to the hero who is courageous enough to undertake the journey.

Odysseus' initial reaction is one of despair: "At this I felt a weight like stone within me, and, moaning, pressed my length against the bed with no desire to see the daylight more. (Finally) I had wept and tossed and had my fill of this despair..." (Homer, p. 180). It is absolutely essential that Odysseus make this descent into the nether regions of the Underworld in order to learn vital information about himself and his destiny. It is not a pretty task. Robert Bly calls this masculine descent "katabasis" a situation that "makes him (a man) aware of a depression that may have been living unnoticed in him for years. A mean life of ordinariness, heaviness, silences, cracks in the road, weightiness, and soberness begins" (Bly, 1992, p. 70). Tiresias reveals to Odysseus his destiny, why he is unable to return home, and the goal of his journey. In other words, Tiresias helps Odysseus to gain a greater perspective on his own life and to look with more depth into his strengths and weaknesses. The journey into the Underworld, then, is an inner journey of self-knowledge to gain insights into himself that he was blinded from seeing because of his heroic pride.

After speaking with Tiresias, Odysseus sadly discovers his own mother's spirit in the Underworld and learns that she died from grief over his absence, giving confirmation to Odysseus that true to the meaning of his name is "trouble," for he has brought trouble to all who he loves (Houston, p. 189). Finally, before leaving the Underworld, Odysseus encounters the other male Greek heroes, each of who recounts his life's tale of tragedy and pain. Jean Houston summarized Odysseus' insight as the following:

> (W)hat Odysseus finds, over and over again, is the pain given to others by his own heroic identity and the pain and futility shared by all the heroic Fathers. There is no way to

be a hero that is not etched in the acid bath of anguish and meaningless. (Houston, p. 190)

The descent into the Underworld is a painful yet necessary journey of inner awareness and enlightenment. After Odysseus makes the journey into the Underworld, he is transformed and understands the larger and deeper meaning of his own life and destiny.

In one way of another, the story of Odysseus is the story of everyman. He inaugurates the dawning of western consciousness as he becomes conscious of the mysteries of life and the meaning and significance of his inner psychic and external physical journey. Like Odysseus, man must now embark on an analysis and treatment of the inner dynamics and meaning of the masculine wound.

SHAMING AS WOUNDING

Shame plays a significant role in men's lives. It indicates that a man is vulnerable, different, exposed, or out-of-control. When the shaming process is adaptive, boys learn appropriate interactions with authority figures and peers. However, when it is disrupted by developmental and gender role pressures or trauma, integration of shame experiences can be maladaptive. Krugman (1995) pointed out that "(a) shame is an innate response tendency that (b) has the adaptive function of sensitizing the individual to his or her status/connection with others; that (c) shame functions in normal and pathological development; and that (d) shame plays a formidable and problematic role in normative male development" (p. 93). Even the normative male shame process that shapes appropriate masculine attitudes and behavior leaves many boys especially shame-sensitive and unable to grow and integrate shame responses.

The core shame experience consists of three components. First, there is a strong psychophysiological component that includes autonomic arousal such a sweating and blushing as well as a "shame signature" sequence of body movements that include eyes turned away, head lowering, and upper body turned away. Together, these actions initiate the flight-fight response. The second component is negative self-appraisal that results in lowered self-esteem. Finally, the third component is the resultant heightened self-consciousness with an impaired sequence of smooth, uninterrupted memory, speech, and motor coordination processes. In short, shame is a painful self-awareness with the feeling that one is being negatively evaluated by others that result in the desire to hide (Krugman, p. 96).

Everingham (1995a) identified the following ten rules of habitual human interaction that causes shaming:

1. *Control.* Be in control of all behavior, interactions, and feelings. Control is basic to these rules.
2. *Blame.* If something goes wrong, blame somebody, even yourself. Don't blame the shame-generating system, or these rules.
3. *Perfectionism.* Always be, do, and feel "right." Don't try if you might make a mistake. Justify everything.
4. *Incompleteness.* Don't resolve disagreements or complete transactions. Keep feuds and resentments going. Don't confront.
5. *Denial.* Deny feelings, needs, desires—your own and others', especially "inappropriate" ones. Deny—even the obvious.
6. *No Talk.* Hide secrets with a strict code of silence, among ourselves and others. Hold your breath, look away, shut up.
7. *Disqualification.* Deny by disguising. Spin the shameful episode around; call it something else; distort it. Look away from the shameful part and focus attention on the positive or truthful part.
8. *Unreliability.* Don't be reliable or trustworthy, or act in a predictable way. Keep 'em guessing. Expect the same from others.
9. *Not Allowing The Five Freedoms.* Don't let folks perceive, think and interpret, feel, desire, or imagine *in their own way.* Especially not children, clients, subordinates, or yourself.
10. *Moral Intimidation.* Assume the right to decide what—and therefore, who—is right, appropriate, humane, enlightened, professional, mature, or politically correct. Enforce moral authority with shaming threats, rhetorical questions, subtle or overt name-calling. (Everingham, 1995a, p. 229)

Together these rules of interaction dehumanize and devalue one's personhood. Oftentimes, males are left feeling confused, threatened, and angry.

Males have difficulty integrating and responding to shame experiences; therefore, they react with avoidance, compensatory behaviors, and the fight-flight response (Krugman, p. 100). Males will also react with immature defense mechanisms such as denial, projection, splitting, and acting out. Feelings of vulnerability and other appropriate and necessary affects are minimized or denied in lieu of some other hypermasculine stance (Krugman, p. 100). Finally, when verbal rebuffs are ineffective, shame initiates feelings of rage that result in violent action (Krugman, p. 100).

Block Lewis (1971) differentiated two types of shame processes. The first she called "overt undifferentiated shame" the typical uncomfortably intense self-consciousness that causes one to want to hide as well as exhibit the inability to think and speak coherently (Krugman, p. 101). A second shame process she called "by-passed shame" in which the feeling processes are removed or reduced to a twinge of discomfort while the thought process is amplified (Krugman, p. 101). Men in today's culture tend to manifest this by-passed shame process. Shame manifests itself in other ways, such as in contempt (Morrison 1983), externalization (Cicchetti and Toth, 1991), and objectification (Kinston, 1983).

When shame is handled and integrated appropriately in boys, they will learn modesty and tact as well as develop the capacity to respond to both internal and external affective signals (Krugman, p. 105). On the other hand, when shame is amplified rather than diminished, and the male feels threatened, a series of various types of immature reactions can be triggered such as splitting, denial, projection, impulsivity, and depression (Krugman, p. 105).

The developmental transition from a primary identification with mother toward an identification with father often results in boys feeling vulnerable and inadequate. The need to consolidate his gender role identity and self-identity necessitate a boy's distancing himself from mother and much that is associated with her. To protect himself from unresolved dependent yearnings for mother, males frequently use strategies of masking and avoiding (Krugman, p. 107). The presence of a "good-enough" male in the boy's life at this time can help a boy make the transition from mother to father identification more of a natural shift of interest than a fearful leap. Without a secure male identification, boys gravitate toward stereotypical gender role signs and symbols and even violent actions as alternatives to a secure male identity (Krugman, p. 109).

Males have an unfortunate double bind with which they must live. On the one hand, they must be prepared to fight, protect, and deal with all the fears and anxieties these roles require; on the other hand, they are expected to be connected interpersonally and nurturing to their wives and families. One requires inflexible shame-based defenses to ward off fear, and the other requires flexibility and tolerance toward shame in daily life. Consequently, boys tend to erect rigid internal and external defenses against shame experiences (Krugman, p. 110). They tend to identify with superheroes that embody invulnerability of one kind or another. Male culture pushes and rewards boys toward aggressive competition with each other. For those males who can live up to these expectations, they are rewarded with a higher sense of self-esteem; for those who fail, they are left feeling humiliated and isolated (Krugman, pp. 110–111).

No wonder that males seek to avoid situations and relations that reveal their inner sense of inadequacy. Typically, males gravitate to externalization and action solutions to emotional situations, thereby deflecting attention away from the emotion to the action. Therefore, males are doers and problem-solvers rather than talkers (Krugman, p. 112).

Male inability to integrate shame experiences has a number of unfortunate effects. Males can be deeply conflicted about intimacy, sexuality, and their feeling toward women, and these feelings can easily become projected as humiliated rage at women who are perceived as controlling and withholding (Krugman, p. 113). As a result, unresolved narcissistic dilemmas leave many men unable to handle failure, resulting in such feelings and behaviors as self-involvement, self-importance, and emotional distance, joined to an inability to consider the needs of others, problems with intimacy and parenting, and social and emotional isolation (Krugman, p. 113). Furthermore, to the extent that a boy has experienced appropriate family socialization, he will be able to venture into the world secure that he can stand on his own and remain in control without humiliation and isolation. When internal and external boundaries are not firmly established in boyhood, inadequate self-regulation results, and boys can become vulnerable to extreme emotional expressions or to isolation and distance (Krugman, p. 114).

Well-integrated shame also assists boys in dealing with conflict without resorting to violence. The shame process assists the development of words and non-threatening gestures that promote the mediation of issues of dominance and competition (Krugman, pp. 114–115).

When shame experiences remain unintegrated in men's lives, males can become severely dysfunctional, leading to a number of character pathologies of malignant narcissism and sociopathology (Krugman, p. 115). Narcissistic personality traits can manifest themselves as character defenses through which the adult male exhibits patterns of extreme self-centeredness, grandiosity, and contempt for others. Krugman (1995) described this process as "the inferior self, demeaned and helpless, is either deeply hidden or projected onto the other, who, in turn, feels devalued or denigrated" (p. 116). A second dissociated type of narcissistic disorder results in the self being projected outward onto an idealized other while the individual consciously experiences the inferior shamed self (Krugman, p. 116). Another dysfunctional state results when boys grow up in abusive environments and develop uncontrolled volatile emotional states with poor self-concepts. These males typically split their identification with their parents, frequently resulting in depression and mood instability. These adult males tend to become drug and alcohol involved and lead impulse-driven lives (Krugman, pp. 116–117).

The most extreme dysfunctionalities in men are those in which men are overly dependent on others, especially women, and become enraged because shame is either a "signal of danger to meaningful bonding ... [or] ... the breakdown of the capacity to bond" (Lansky, p. 208). Spouse battering and physical or sexual abuse of a child frequently arises from these kinds of shame-anxiety sequences (Krugman, p. 117). Additionally, fratricidal behavior that results from insults perceived as "disses" (disrespecting), often provokes impulsive violence in response to the shaming experience as a way of fending off "fragmentation and depression by discharging rage and fear" (Krugman, p. 118). Other antisocial personality disorders exhibit extreme defensive efforts to deal with helplessness and dependency that leave men with a chronic sense of emptiness and being alone (Kernberg, 1992, p. 222). Another variation is that of the "super-ego pathology" (Kernberg, 1992, p. 222) in which men are extremely devaluing of others, manipulative, and riddled with envy. These men often avoid discomforting feelings by going into action and exhibiting such behaviors as lying, stealing, swindling, sexual promiscuity, assaulting, and even murdering (Krugman, p. 118). Male depression is the result of the "traumatic abrogation of the holding environment" as well as a reaction to gender role failure (Krugman, p. 119). Lansky (1992) stated that "suicidal crises ... reflect narcissistic breakdown, collapse, and exposure" (1992, p. 199). When faced with unbearable shame, males go into action to relieve the tension and escape the pain of despair by transforming it through suicide (Krugman, p. 120).

A related disability is that of *alexithymia*, which is characterized by "the inability to identify and describe one's feelings in words" (Daly et al., 1999, p. 161). Men who cannot recognize emotions may have a physiological sensation called a "buzz" consisting of "tightness in the throat, constriction in the chest, clenching in the gut, antsy feeling in the legs, constriction in the face, difficulty concentrating, and gritting of teeth" (Daly, p. 161). According to Daly et al. (1999) there are four typical male responses to the buzz:

> (1) Distraction, which serves as a "circuit breaker," allowing men to disengage from the buzz; (2) the Rubber Band Syndrome, in which the buzz builds and builds until it erupts in an explosion of anger; (3) the Tin Man approach, which requires locking the buzz up tighter than a drum so that the man no longer feels anything; or (4) the Mixed Messenger, in which the buzz oozes out through the man's nonverbal behavior. (Daly et al., p. 161)

This lack of emotional expression in many men is caused by a number of factors, namely their early socialization to be emotionally stoic and the many Boy Code messages not to cry or to express pain. Additionally, Pollock (1995) attributed male inability to express emotions to boys' early separation from their mothers, which he terms as a traumatic abrogation of the holding environment (1995, p. 41). Pollock further declared, "This traumatic experience of abandonment occurs so early in the life course that the shameful memory of the loss is likely to be deeply repressed" (p. 41).

Furthermore, boys must disidentify with mother and identify with the father, who may himself be physically and emotionally absent. If he is available to the son, he will be very demanding of his son. This problematic father-son relationship leaves a deep impression on males, called in the men's studies literature "the wound."

MASCULINE WOUNDING IN THE LITERATURE

The masculine wound—characterized by Robert Bly (1992) as that vague feeling of unhappiness coupled with a lack of vital energy and life force in men (p. 3)—has been described variously in the men's studies literature. In myth, Johnson (1989) termed the masculine wound as the "Fisher King wound" found in the Holy Grail myth (p. 1). The Fisher King was wounded in his thigh, indicating a "wound in his generative ability, in his capacity for relationship" (Johnson, p. 7). It manifests itself in men as a nagging sense of suffering, injury, and incompleteness (Johnson, pp. 7–8). Furthermore, it is a wound that seems to defy cure (Pollock, 1995b). William Pollock identified Aristophanes' prehistoric roly-poly double creatures that were split in half and forever doomed to search for their mirror halves (1995b, pp. 36–37). The myth celebrates man's original wholeness and his desire to reunite with his missing half lost in his earlier developmental history (Pollock, 1995b, p. 37). A third myth is that of Narcissus, who flees from the amorous advances of Echo and ends up amorously transfixed over his own refection in a pool of water. The myth highlights men's narcissistic self-love because "(he) is frightened by what he is not taught—love, intimacy, and object relations—(so) he chooses self again and again" (Blazina, p. 289).

The Oedipus myth highlights father-son competition and conflict, as does the "Laius complex" that focuses on the fear fathers have of their sons taking their power (Blazina, p. 287). The Greek Cronos-Zeus myth also trumpets the power, jealousy, and insecurity inherent in the father-son relationship that repeats from one generation to the next. James Hollis (Hollis, 1994) called this pattern the "Saturnian legacy" whereby "(men) have suffered from the corruption of empowerment, driven by fear, wounding themselves and others" (p. 11). He also spoke of the three W's of the Saturnian legacy, namely work, war, and worry (p. 15). According to Hollis, a man is "meant to work always, any work which supported those for whom one was responsible… (and) that personal satisfaction was set aside before fidelity to that enormous responsibility (Hollis, p. 14). The second Saturnian legacy is war, which is "(Man's) fate... was to grow up and become a soldier, to go to some foreign place and kill or be killed, or come home tortured and maimed" (Hollis, p. 15). The third Saturnian legacy is worry: "It was not all paranoia; there was something to worry about and as a man I was expected to be responsive and responsible" (Hollis, p. 24). Therefore, according to Hollis, men's lives are characterized by fear (Hollis, p. 24). This fear is of not only of measuring up when manhood is measured by winning and losing and in producing. It is compounded by silence because he is "unable to admit this to himself lest his hold on things slip, unable to share with his comrades lest he be shamed" (Hollis, p. 24). A tragic double bind results when wounding is not transformed into meaningful suffering and a deepened consciousness:

> So the double bind is: be a man and prove it, but the rules shift constantly so you don't even know how to play the game. And once you have "arrived," the rules will change again and someone else will be better than you. (Hollis, p. 77)

Consequently, men live shallow lives defined by possessions and social status, but inwardly they are filled with rage (Hollis, p. 79).

> His rage was the anger accumulated from a life lost, given to others, given to Saturn. And yet he had obeyed cultural values: take care of your parents, provide for your family, pass on a better life to your children. He did everything he was supposed to do except live his own life (Hollis, p. 80).

Further exacerbating the wound is that men cannot speak honestly about their rage because it is shaming, so they increasingly isolate themselves and internalize their rage (Hollis, p. 81). This internalization manifests itself as depression, or somatic illness, or it is projected outward onto others, such as women and children or subordinates.

Guy Corneau (1991) described the masculine wound as "the fragility of masculine identity" (p. 13). He contended that males have difficulty advancing into mature manhood because of the absence of a father, regardless if the father's absence is psychological or physical. Father absence can take the form of fathers who are physically present in the son's life but who behave in unacceptable and inappropriate ways, such as authoritarian styles and who are "oppressive and jealous of their sons' talents and smother their sons' attempts at creativity or self affirmation" (Corneau, p. 13). According to Corneau, this lack of emotional connection between father and son inhibits the son's ability to establish his own masculine identity and progress into manhood (p. 13). Therefore, sons have fragile sexual identities (Corneau, pp. 13–15) and are unable to establish an internal structure (Corneau, p. 17). Corneau concluded rather strongly with the following summary of what the research shows regarding inadequate fathering:

> … in their teenage years (males) experience confusion about their sexual identity and adopt feminine types of behavior; their sense of self-esteem is unsteady; they repress their aggressivity (and consequently, their need for self-affirmation), their ambition, and their inquisitiveness. Some of them may suffer inhibitions with regard to their sexuality. They may also exhibit learning problems. They have trouble respecting moral values and accepting responsibilities; they have little sense of duty or obligation toward others. The absence of limits also makes it difficult for them to act with authority or to respect the authority of others. Their insufficient internal structure results in a certain laxity, a lack of rigor, a general inability to organize their lives effectively… . Inadequately fathered sons are also more apt to develop psychological problems that manifest as juvenile delinquency and abuse of drugs and alcohol. (1991, p. 20)

The fragility of the male self is echoed over and over again in the literature (Blum, p. 84; Horne and Kiselica, p. 23; Osherson, p. 10; Pollock, 1998, p. 42; Schenk and Everingham, p. 3). However, Gurian (1999) made an even stronger statement about male vulnerability and fragility by associating it with posttraumatic stress disorder. He said

> They are unable to internally and adequately process the traumas because of poor personal emotional development and / or inadequate time and energy spent with them by caregivers and community. Like soldiers traumatized in wartime, these males act out, experience heightened levels of psychiatric illness and disability, use drugs and alcohol, and / or become violent. (Gurian, 1999, p. 24)

It is no wonder, then, that males suffer and behave dysfunctionally under the heavy weight of shaming and wounding. The fact is that males fear not being loved and that they have to earn love by being successful or by projecting a certain image (Heuer, p. 259). The drive to earn love and affirmation leads to a denial of males' basic physical and emotional needs (Krugman, p. 117). Some men escape through self-inflation to help them feel good about themselves (Kaufman, p. 35), while other men escape through depression (Krugman, p. 119). Both avenues lead to anger and rage, control, and an unquenchable pursuit of perfection. Sadly, at the same time, men find themselves isolated from each other (Hollis, p. 73), and sons are deprived of the male role models they need in order to develop into mature, healthy men themselves, thereby perpetuating the cycle of male woundedness (Osherson, pp. 5–6). Exacerbating the wound is the fact that males have a difficult time admitting that they have wounds, so they cover them up and / or look for quick fixes to heal their wounds. Only when males are willing to enter their woundedness, take the road to kata-basis, and descend into the metaphorical Underworld, can there be hope for healing.

IMPLICATIONS FOR EDUCATING LATE-ADOLESCENT BOYS

Just as D. H. Lawrence in his poem "Healing" laments, males suffer under a terrible burden of cultural and personal expectations that make them machine-like, expendable in the game of progress and profit. In order to achieve these false standards of success, men have been taught to deny their psychic and physical pain and view themselves as "mechanisms," cutting themselves off from their true selves and causing deep wounding. This wounding is not only assumed by individual males to be the normative way to live, but also it is culturally and institutionally endorsed for all males. Though the process is long and difficult, there is hope for healing. In D. H. Lawrence's words, the hope is in a "long, difficult repentance, realization of life's mistake, and the freeing of oneself from the endless repetition of the mistake which man-kind at large has chosen to sanctify" (Lawrence, 1971). The long, difficult repentance, which is healing, necessitates that males, following Odysseus, descend into the Underworld and confront their shame and their wounding.

It is a fearsome and painful task, but it is, nevertheless, a necessary journey of self-discovery and acknowledgment.

The confrontation and acknowledgment of the process of shaming and wounding is a central construct in a male gender curriculum for late adolescent boys. John Everingham (1995b) called for facing shaming and wounding directly in order to understand its effects on a person's life (p. 95). He offered the following eighteen tools to help a male confront and heal shaming and wounding: Knowing and Breaking the Rules of Shaming, Recognize Shame (its emotional, physical, and mental keys), Naming It, Feeling It, Talking About It, Hit The Wall, Integrate Healing into Your Body, Establish and Maintain Boundaries, Confronting Shaming Behavior, Build and Repair Interpersonal Bridges, Eat the Shadow, Experience the Orphan, Acknowledge Your Wounds, Let Go of Victim, Forgive, Embrace Paradox, Dance the Four Quarters, and Go Beyond Shame. Everingham also established 12-step group therapy programs, such as AA, men's groups, study groups, and other Anonymous organizations, as healing methods of shaming and wounding (1995b, pp. 94–119). A male gender-sensitive cur-riculum will make use of these tools to help educate late adolescent boys about becoming comfortable dealing with the shaming and wounding in their lives.

Boys need a safe place in which to gather and express their vulnerable emotions. These "guy spaces" (Pollock, 1998, pp. 269–270) can be places where boys gather to reconnect with each other without recourse to justifica-tion or vilification. These spaces will permit both physical and emotional expressions of authentic male action-oriented behaviors (Pollock, 1998, p. 270).

Boys also need connection to other male adults who care and who will help them express the full gamut of their fears and feelings safely. It is important that males learn to be in the company of each other. Dougherty (1995) asserted that only in the company of men can men reconnect to intimacy and their feelings (p. 264). Behind the anger and the rage will be the restorative feeling of grief. Hollis (1994) called grief honest: "It values what was lost or was never there ... (and as) open remembering ... it may not feel very good at the moment, it is (nevertheless) cleansing and healing in its honesty" (p. 117).

Hollis (1994) outlined the following seven-step process for male self-healing that can be used as a model for a gender-sensitive curriculum:

1. Remember the loss of the fathers.
2. Tell the secrets.
3. Seek mentors and mentor others.
4. Risk loving men.
5. Heal thyself.
6. Recover your soul's journey.
7. Join the revolution.

Much has already been said about this process; however, a few more words in way of explanation of the self-healing process may be necessary. The first step toward healing is that males must acknowledge that they have lost their relatedness to their families, to their work, and to their inner lives. Appropriately, anger and grief will emerge toward their shaming and wounding (Hollis, p. 116). Males need to be honest in relating the essential male secrets, "that they feel themselves failures as men, ... that they are torn between fear and rage, and that they are emotionally dependent but resentful" (Hollis, p. 121). Men need the company of other men for guidance and support, especially older men who have already made the journey (Hollis, pp. 122–123). Male intimacy and genuine male expressions of caring and love are okay. Males need to take responsibility for caring for themselves: "Being a man means knowing what you want and then mobilizing the inner resources to achieve it" (Hollis, p. 128). Male healing is possible by acknowledging the soul's journey by "see(ing) himself in a larger context, in the context of the eternal" (Hollis, p. 132). The revolution among males begins when they become conscious of their shaming and woundedness and start taking responsibility for their healing. While this process is not a panacea, Hollis hoped that individual men would achieve consciousness and healing of their masculine shaming and woundedness while helping others to do so (p. 116).

CHAPTER FIVE

UNIQUELY MASCULINE ISSUES: MASCULINE INITIATION

The impulse to be initiated into manhood may be archetypal, but *how* that longing is defined, is socially constructed.

David J. Tacey (1997)

Nobody was born a man; you earned manhood provided you were good enough, bold enough.

Norman Mailer

The initiation experience is deeply embedded within human experience (Eliade, 1958, p. 3). The Paleolithic cave paintings of Lascaux, dated between 11,000 and 18,000 years ago, were sacred initiatory sites. "They are the original men's rite sanctuaries where the boys became no longer their mothers' sons but their fathers' sons (Campbell, p. 101). Eliade (1958) stated that initiation is "one of the most significant spiritual phenomena in the history of humanity" (p. 3). Given its ubiquitous and timeless existence, initiation has been described by Gilmore (1990) as a "deep structure of masculinity" (1990, p. 3) and Henderson (1967) called it "the archetype of initiation" (1967, p. 19).

Initiation is a collection of ceremonies and instructions intended to effect a significant change in an individual initiate's religious and social status (Eliade, p. x). Referred to as rites of passage (Van Gennep, 1960), these ritual processes and teachings are intended to be transformative: an inherent existential change transpires in the one initiated (Eliade, p. x; Campbell, p. 10) with a concomitant deepening of understanding and maturity about what it means to be a man and a responsible member of his community (Eliade, p. x). Furthermore, initiation functions to terminate one stage of the individual's life cycle and to inaugurate the next (Stevens, 1990, p. 185).

THE NEED FOR INITIATION

Steinberg (1993) referred to initiation as that process that helps and guides males through significant developmental transitions (p. 163). As a cycle of death-rebirth, initiation assists in the young male's death to childhood with its mother attachment in order to be reborn into manhood (Steinberg, p. 163; Stevens, p. 187; Gilmore, p. 27). Initiation, then, is a necessary action to prevent regression and to prod males into growth (Erikson, 1968, p. 114; Stevens, p. 201; Gilmore, p. 228). Furthermore, it is an attempt to replace the maternal "pleasure principle" with the paternal "reality principle" of work (Gilmore, p. 229). Gilmore (1990) cites numerous examples of cultures in which initiation processes require an abrupt removal of the boy from the mother to be placed in a new and totally different setting with other boy initiates and men. Generally speaking, the harsher the environment and the scarcer of resources, the more rigidly structured the male initiation processes become in stressing manhood ideals (Gilmore, p. 224). Western industrial cultures are more diffuse and ambiguous, resulting in a more problematic resolution of the developmental growth process into manhood (Gilmore, p. 124).

Despite the disuse and disappearance of initiation rituals in Western culture, the archetypal need to be initiated exists in all persons (Stevens, p. 196). Henderson (1967) noted that archetypal symbols of initiation emerge in dreams during critical periods throughout the life cycle. Without initiation rituals adolescents exhibit "initiation hunger," which is described by Erikson (1980) as a longing for intimacy. "Young persons often indicate in rather pathetic ways a feeling that only a merging with a 'leader' can save them—an adult who is able and willing to offer himself as a safe object for experimental surrender and as a guide" (Erikson, 1980, pp. 125–126). Initiation hunger is expressed in many ways, such as gang membership, Gothic dress and tattooing, and self-mutilation and piercing. Initiation hunger in late-adolescents is the symbolic expression of the need for initiation and the pull toward maturity. The importance of initiation rites is that they fulfill initiation hunger in socially acceptable ways (Stevens, 1990, pp. 203–204).

The growing number of uninitiated boy-men in Western culture has become increasingly problematic (Stevens, p. 189; Moore and Gillette, 1990, p. xvi). Stevens cited Tiger and Fox (1972) who lamented the loss of initiatory practices in schools, universities, and apprenticeship programs. The result is uninitiated males who seek a pseudo-initiation in their peer group such as gangs:

> The outcome was that contemporary educational trends were fostering contemporary social ills: instead of producing mature males inspired with the common ideals of the community, our educational system was loosing upon the world whole generations of morally and sexually ambivalent 'Tricksters.' (Tiger and Fox, p. 189)

The trickster has a long anthropological history as "an impulsive, self-centered character that is controlled by his appetites and makes absolutely no contribution to the common good" (Stevens, p. 155). The trickster is also characterized as the detached manipulator, who is unable to feel connected to people or to the larger world and consequently becomes exploitative and deceiving (Moore and Gillette, 1993, pp. 167–168). There are a great many immature men who cannot get their lives together because they have never experienced initiation into mature manhood. Instead, they are eternal adolescents, called by Jungians the *"puer aeternus,"* boys who never attain nor are they able to attain mature manhood (Von Franz, 1970). They are generally fixated with an intense mother-bond and tend in the sexual sphere to be homosexual or Don Juans (Stevens, p. 154). Such eternal youth are "narcissistic … with (a) failure to achieve a mature social adaptation together with a compensatory arrogance and false individualism" (Stevens, p. 154).

The necessary transition from the mother world to the father world is fraught with emotional dangers. Initiation ritual processes are meant to complement and assist the natural biological developmental process by providing a culture-created ritual drama by which boys can be ushered into manhood. In the absence of vital initiation processes, uninitiated or pseudo-initiated youth are unable to make the transition into mature manhood and unable to experience the transformation needed for heroic consciousness to develop.

THE PREREQUISITES OF INITIATION

Initiation does not occur haphazardly. Certain conditions must exist in order for ritual initiation to take place efficaciously. The first condition is a sense of sacred space. Eliade (1958) referred to the "heterogeneity of space" as categories of sacred and profane space. Sacred space is qualitatively different from profane or ordinary space in that it has a fixed center (*axis mundi*), a cosmic tree leading into the heavens and connecting with divine or supernatural beings, from which humans can gain an orientation to the world. In this way, then, initiation is a supremely spiritual process:

> Initiation ... is an act that involves not only the religious life of the individual, in the modern meaning of the word "religion"; it involves his *entire* life. It is through initiation that ... man becomes what he is and what he should be—a being open to the life of the spirit, hence one who participates in the culture into which he was born. (Eliade, 1958, p. 3)

Sacred space, then, is a place set apart from the mundane, ordinary world of places. Historically, these have been places where primitive people removed their tribes' boys from the world of the mothers to a place in the bush, such as contemporary cathedrals and monasteries and retreat centers where initiatory process can be experienced, intensified, and focused without distraction. According to Eliade, this sacred space or "ground is at once an image of the world (*imago mundi*) and a world sanctified by the presence of the Divine Being" (Eliade, 1958, p. 6). Sacred space is extraordinary space with tremendous archetypal energies present, so it must be contained in order for it to be transformative (Moore and Gillette, 1993, p. 109; Moore, 2001, p. 147).

Containment is the psychosocial process by which deep structural changes in a person's psyche takes place. It is the framing of a holding environment in which individuals and groups can confront and assimilate the unsettling dynamics of personal change with its accompanying truths and emotions (Moore, 2001, p. 147). Without adequate containment, initiates will find the process of initiation overwhelming and devastating—literally making one crazy (Moore & Gillette, 1993, p. 108; Moore, p. 147). Containment is the establishment of boundaries, the structuring of space and time in order to channel the archetypal energies of initiation as well as providing an *axis mundi*, an ordering conduit, through which these energies flow (Moore and Gillette, 1993, p. 146).

The second indispensable component of initiation process is the presence of (a) ritual elder(s). Eliade (1958) describes the essential presence of the old men at puberty rites of passage as they serve to assist young initiates through the various parts of initiation rituals. These men form the community of initiators who guide and instruct the boys in the ways of manhood, tell the ancient, important stories about the community's history and identity, perform faithfully the rituals and ceremonies fraught with symbolic importance, and finally reinstate the young men back into the community (Eliade, 1958, p. 39). Therefore, the initiation process cannot take place without the presence of a community of men who are themselves initiated and who know the ritual roadmap and the potential dangers and terrors (Eliade, 1958, p. xii). The ritual elders, the caretakers of the ritual space, recognize how fragile and uncontrollable the passage can be (Moore, 2001, p. 59). As stewards of archetypal power, ritual elders access and disseminate these initiatory symbols in order to promote transformation within the wider community (Moore and Gillette, 1993, p. 202).

The Process of Initiation

Eliade characterized the initiatory process as "metacultural and transhistorical" and conforming to a basic pattern that is relatively consistent throughout world cultures (1958, p. 130). The root meaning and process of initiation is that of death and rebirth. The ritual death, especially in puberty rites, is symbolized as a death to childhood, and the rebirth is symbolized as a rebirth into initiated manhood. Arnold Van Gennep in *The Rites of Passage* (1909/1960) was the first to introduce the idea of a three-part initiation process which he termed separation, transition, and incorporation. Joseph Campbell (1973) echoed Van Gennep's conceptual framework and viewed the mythology of the hero as analogous to that of the rites of passage, which he labeled the "monomyth" that encompasses "separation-initiation-return" as its central paradigm (p. 30). According to Campbell,

> A hero ventures forth from the world of common day into a region of supernatural wonder: fabulous forces are there encountered and a decisive victory is won; the hero comes back from this mysterious adventure with the power to bestow boons on his fellow men. (p. 30)

This mythic pattern is recapitulated in most of the world's puberty rites of passage. Henderson (1968) identifies this pattern as the archetype of initiation.

Moore (2001) labeled the threefold initiation process as Phase One: Ordinary Consciousness Challenged, Phase Two: Ordinary Consciousness Transcended, and Phase Three: Ordinary Consciousness Reconstituted (pp. 184–186). Phase One is the way in which a person presently experiences and makes sense of the world. In Erickson's words, it is the state of having a psychosocial identity connected to a particular place and time, while Levinson (1978) located this state in the Early Adult Transition period. During this phase the young initiate is separated from his mother and from the opposite sex in general and sleeps in a special domicile with the other initiates. According to Weisfeld (1999), who examined puberty rites of passage from a functional viewpoint, "Physical separation lends an air of significance to the process" and "the solemnity of training usually is underscored by the observance of food taboos or other restrictions; adoption of special garb, hairstyle, or bodily markings; or subjection to an ordeal" (p. 113). Separation by sex helps the initiate to master sex-specific tasks such as instruction in social matters, which are generally taught by a "same-sex nonparent" or other elder (Weisfeld, p. 114).

Phase Two: Ordinary Consciousness Transcended (Moore, 2001) is referred to as the transition phase by Van Gennep. In this phase, initiates are instructed in ceremonial and religious matters, cultural mores and practices, and personal conduct (Weisfeld, p. 115). Further, Weisfeld noted that boys receive more elaborate instruction during adolescence than girls (Weisfeld, p. 115). Using colorful language, Moore described the second phase of initiation as "nowhere, limbo, dissolution, Hell, sacred space ... the tomb, the belly of the whale, the womb of the tomb, and the tomb of the womb" (2001, p. 79). This is a time of dissolution of one's former comfortable existence and ways of living, with a sense of living betwixt and between statuses.

During the middle phase, initiates frequently encounter ordeals that they must endure, some of which are quite painful and frightening. The ordeals might entail the knocking out of a tooth, a scarring, the endurance of hunger, cold, heat, or some other kind of deprivation (Eliade, 1958, pp. 14–18). The function of ordeals in puberty rites of passage is that of submission, in which the unruly or rebellious initiate must subjugate himself to the elders as a precondition for admission into adult society (Weisfeld, p. 118). The wounding can also be viewed as a form of ritual humiliation (Moore, 2001, p. 86). Severe initiation ordeals may also promote male bonding and solidarity, especially in those cultures where group cohesion promotes survivability (Weisfeld, p. 118). Moreover, ordeals have a way of shocking the initiate into full awakening and out of complacency and clinging to the narcissism of childhood (Henderson, 1967, p. 56).

Many initiation rites require the subincision or circumcision of the male's penis. This practice has rich religious symbolism, but it also toughens the initiate by conditioning him to pain and deprivation. The initiate learns by way of pain and suffering that he can endure more than he thinks he can, and he learns that the world is a tough and unmerciful place when it requires one to take up the mantle of adult responsibility.

In Phase Three: Ordinary Consciousness Reconstituted, called the incorporation stage by Van Gennep, the initiate is returned and assimilated back into adult society as a renewed and transformed person. Although it is a return to ordinary time, the young man is not the same person as before. Often these changes are ritually and ceremonially dramatized by giving him a new name, wearing adult clothing for the first time, changing his appearance, and permitting him to engage in sexual activity (Weisfeld, p. 116).

An important concept in rites of passage is that of the *limen*, which in Latin means threshold, margin, or boundary (Moore, 2001, p. 82). It is the imaginary boundary line between the profane and everyday world of ordinary existence and that of the sacred world of charged and profoundly meaningful experience. Once a person has crossed the threshold, there is no going back to the previous childhood days. To cross the threshold is a dangerous journey into the unknown that takes the heroic traveler to places where he can learn much that is both good and destructive about himself (Campbell, 1968, pp. 77–79). Initiatory rites of passage are meant to be just such boundary-marking experiences, a significant life-changing experience in a young man's life and consciousness. After a young man passes through the limen, his life will never be the same.

Modern Western industrial culture has a dearth of initiatory rites of passage to aid in transitioning boys into mature manhood (Moore, 2001, p. 14; Tacey, 2001, p. 193; Greenwald, 1995, p. 266; Hollis, 1994, p. 16). Boys are forced to make themselves into men in some very inappropriate and destructive ways through membership in cults and gangs, indiscriminate sexuality, negativity, nihilism, depression, substance-abuse, risk-taking, and suicide (Tacey, 2001, pp. 112–119).

Military service is one of the last remaining routes to initiatory process and conforms to the three-fold pattern of rites of passage. Military service is a way for boys to become men and to be recognized and affirmed for their allegiance to a cause bigger than themselves that confers mature manhood upon them. According to Tacey,

> In a secular culture devoid of ceremonialism, war experience is one of the last vestiges of initiatory process. First, there is enforced separation from the childhood domestic scene. Second, there is a dissolution of the old self and an acquisition of a new identity. Boys were made to wear uniforms, had their hairstyles changed, behaved in regimented ways, and adopted new names: Corporal, Private, Sergeant, and so on. Youths were initiated by men into a society of men, with its own language, its distinctive ritual behaviors, its esoteric codes and rituals. In military service, male bonds were formed that lasted a lifetime and sometimes even transcended life itself. The risks and dangers of war also served a function: the old

self was to be threatened with death.... . If the young man
survives the ordeal, there is finally the hero's triumphant
return to the community. The young man has helped to save
the nation from the common foe, he wins the admiration
of society, and the nation feels politically and spiritually
regenerated by his efforts. (Tacey, 2001, pp. 120–121)

However, caution must be urged so that excessive militarism does not
become unnecessarily aggressive and violent. The code of the warrior mandates that the warrior's fierceness emerges from a principal concern for others
before himself. The warrior lives to serve by protecting others and by exercising self-control. The value of initiation in the code of the warrior is that
it teaches boys to become empowered and to submit to and serve the higher
authority; otherwise, he can become nakedly brutal and destructive (Moore &
Gillette, 1992b, pp. 150–155).

In the absence of any other initiatory route, some young men undertake
self-initiation experiences in wilderness settings apart from comfort and security. These settings provide opportunities for a young man to prove his mettle
removed from social distortions and where he must make it on his own. This
study focused on one such program called the School of Lost Borders.

For more than 25 years, the School of Lost Borders has been offering
wilderness experiences through which "every course is a rite of passage,
a border crossing from the past to the future, from the old to the new,
from the outward to the inward, from the self to the Self" (http://www.
schooloflostborders.com/lb/story/index.cfm). The courses structure their
programs for adolescents similar to traditional initiatory rites:

There is an element of perceived risk in every course. Time
alone in a natural place (solitude) and fasting (emptiness) and
exposure to the elements (vulnerability), and self-reliance
(self-trust), are the earmarks of Lost Borders. Certain old
ways of learning, such as story telling, councils of "elders,"
mirroring, four seasons teachings, and ways of empowerment, are also typical. (http://www.schooloflostborders.com/
lb/story/index.cfm)

Furthermore, each rite of passage experience takes careful note of
providing the requisite containment for the educational growth of the

whole person:

> The work of the teachers and guides involves the safe holding
> of an ancient container, a means of keeping the bridge steady
> as it were, as each student crosses a border unique to his / her
> own needs. The container is the course itself. (http://www.
> schooloflostborders.com/lb/story/index.cfm)

Designed for youth from the ages of 15 to 22, the 8–10 day course has a three-fold initiatory structure involving 3–4 days of group preparation called "severance," followed by 2–3 days of a solo experience called "threshold," and then 2–3 days of "integration and empowerment ("incorporation") in the elder's council (http://www.schooloflostborders.com/lb/trainings/detail.cfm).

Stephen Foster and Meredith Little, for many years the directors of the School of Lost Borders, have written extensively about wilderness initiations. *The Book of the Vision Quest: Personal Transformation in the Wilderness* (1992) is their book about the construction of a traditional rite of passage called the "vision quest," a native American initiatory rite. The initiatory process is deceptively simple—"a circle drawn in the dust, an empty form filled by the perceptions and values of the candidate"—but the rite is structured to access deep archetypal power and symbol (Foster, 1992, p. 22). The first part of the vision quest involves becoming mentally, emotionally, spiritually, and physically prepared for the wilderness experience and includes dealing with inner fears about the unknown, taking a medicine walk of a day's journey, preparing to fast by skipping meals, doing some guided imagination work focusing on making a clean break from the past, and preparing to journal their thoughts and experiences (Foster, 1992, pp. 32–37).

The heart of the vision quest is the threshold experience during which a person goes into the wilderness for the three to four day solo experience. The threshold experience is where sacred space and sacred time become one: "Past, present, and future become Now. And Now is defined as physical (the south), psychological (the west), mental (the north), imaginative (the east), mortal (earthward), and spiritual (skyward). All directions become one in Now" (Foster, 1992, p. 43). For the duration of the threshold experience no food is eaten. The fast has an ancient heritage as a method for attaining spiritual insight.

> The fasting process is one of readying the soil for a seed
> to be planted in it. The seeker empties the body so that the
> spirit may be cleansed and filled... . Your civilized veneer
> begins to crack... . You watch the way you occupy space,
> aware of the signs and marks you leave behind .... The earth
> becomes for you a single, whole, living entity, a Goddess.
> (Foster, 1992, pp. 46–47)

The purpose of the solo experience is to permit space for the initiate to
dream and finally to seek a vision—transcendent mystical knowledge—
about his life and purpose—"what your life has been and could be" (Foster,
1992, p. 55). During the threshold experience, the initiate may give himself
a new name that emerges from the process of the vision quest experience,
which is "potent medicine... . The specific object of self-mythology is to
transform or energize oneself with a name that signifies a story" (Foster,
1992, p. 51). One may build a fire, but it must be purposeful, and no sign of
it must be left behind (Foster, 1992, pp. 49–50).

At some point the initiate will find a particular place, called a "purpose
circle" that will be the place for the death-rebirth ceremony to take place
(Foster, 1992, p. 52). It must be constructed patiently and carefully and
be oriented properly to the six directions of the cosmos.

> When complete, your circle will outline the mythical terms
> of your death passage into birth. It will stand physically
> anchored to the six directional powers of the universe... .
> The circle will form a protective enclosure, a "ring pass-not,"
> a spherical interface of awareness between "inside" and
> "outside" that is mutually integrative, reciprocal, and healing.
> (Foster, 1992, p. 53)

On the last night of the threshold experience, the initiate is to enter the
purpose circle at dusk for the all-night vigil during which he cries out for
a vision (Foster, 1992, p. 53). Once the initiate steps out of the circle at
daybreak, the vision a person experiences will lead toward fulfillment in
his adult life (Foster, 1992, p. 56). Now it is time to "emerge" by removing
all traces of one's presence, scattering stones, and cleaning one's place of all
signs of human habitation.

The incorporation phase of the vision quest involves reuniting with people, telling one's story, and learning to live in two worlds. "One world is visionary, consecrated, and wholly natural, the threshold world of the Great Mother. The other world is the 'real' world of people, places, and things, the incorporation world of taking on the body." (Foster, 1992, p. 65) To nurture the vision quest experience, one can perform a simple daily ceremony of remembrance in a place apart or at times one may return to the wilderness for communion with nature. Although the vision quest is an experience in a particular place at a particular time, it is, in fact, ongoing and timeless, defying space and time, for it is a vision of the heart and animated from the deep sources of the Self. It is a transforming experience of passage from boyhood into adulthood.

In *The Four Shields: The Initiatory Seasons of Human Nature* (1998), Foster and Little expand on the various rites and ceremonies that can be used during the threshold experience. The rite that an initiate uses depends upon the unique needs and issues of the initiate as he prepares to undertake the vision quest experience. Working with an initiated elder, the initiate is asked to evaluate and articulate his feelings and intentions as they are prepared to enter the threshold. The "rites of fall" assist the initiate's transition to adulthood by stressing severance and individuation by "introduc(ing) powerful new earth-images of anima and animus to replace the archetypes of the parents, from whom there must be severance" (Foster, 1998, p. 140). The following are seven rites of fall:

RITES OF DAY: The Day Walk

Rise at dawn, leave your life behind you, and walk alone, without food, into the natural world. Choose an intuitive course that takes you to whatever elicits your interest. If you are currently dealing with a crisis or problem, take the problem with you and allow it to inform your steps as you wander. Do not think you have to cover as much ground as possible, or to needlessly expose yourself to danger. Walk with your senses open. Imagine yourself as an animal. Be wild. Try not to be heard or seen. Don't consult your watch. Find places to rest where you feel welcome. Practice being perfectly quiet, in a state of alert repose. If you need to, take a nap. Perhaps you will dream an important dream. Talk to yourself or to any other wild thing. Pray if you feel the urge. At sunset your walk is finished. (Foster, 1998, p. 142)

RITES OF NIGHT: The Night Walk

Go to a place where you can be absolutely silent and alone, surrounded by the mingled shadows of inward human nature. Invite the darkness in. Walk and sit all night with your feelings, your memories, the daily traffic on the streets of your psyche. Listen to the night, to the beating of your heart, to the rasping of your breath. Listen to your fear. Listen and wait. If you should fall asleep and dream, remember your dream. You have been separated from the light so that you can pass through a dark place. If you feel led, raise your voice to scream, moan, shout, or otherwise give vent to whatever feels trapped within. Practice ways of walking, standing, sitting that characterize your power to express and defend yourself. (Foster, 1998, p. 145)

RITES OF VISION: The Vision Fast

The time has come to confirm that you are no longer a child. You must be removed from the mothering arms of home, the reassurance of routine, and all that has been familiar to the emotional, reactive, comfort-seeking persona of summer. Innocence and trust must now be tried in the fires of initiatory experience. You will go alone, with an empty belly and a bare minimum of equipment, into the heart of wild nature, for four days and nights. There you will live with yourself in perfect solitude. You will surrender to the influences of the looks-within-place, the psychosphere, the soul of nature. In your outcast state you will find answers. You will drink at the springs of feeling and be filled with self-recognition. (Foster, 1998, p. 148)

RITES OF WALKING: The Walkabout

Go alone into the wilderness for seven days and nights, following a pre-set course that leads you into an adventure that confirms your death to childhood and rebirth as a mature man.... . With a minimum of food and shelter, you will have to exercise self-reliance, cooperation and nature, and a commitment to see yourself through hard times. You will follow a primitive road, walking at least 20 miles, camping each night at a new site a few miles down the road. Each day will represent a new ordeal in your initiation into maturity. (Foster, 1998, p. 155)

RITES OF INTERMENT: Alone in the Earth

Leave your life behind and enter a dark place in the earth (a hole, cave, or darkened lodge) and stay there for 24–48 hours alone without food, water, or artificial light. Take with you (the spirit or memory of) another person who has wronged you or you have wronged. Live with that person throughout the ordeal. Perhaps you will find a way to forgive or be forgiven. Pay attention to what you see, hear, and feel in the darkness. If you fall asleep and dream, remember the dream, for it will be relevant to current and future ways of symbolically characterizing yourself. If you wish, you may take a bundle of dried sage and a few matches to purify and bless your place of darkness or the "presences" that appear. You may also take a drum or rattle or some other means of accompanying your chanting and singing. (Foster, 1998, p. 157)

RITES OF SWEATING: Lodges and Saunas

At the door of the lodge you leave your life as a "child" behind. Stripped of your protective clothing, you enter the psychological world of naked feeling, as represented by this dark place of anonymity. Here you sit with the others and become aware of your ability to endure the closeness, discomfort, heat, and blindness. There will be times when the child rages at the door, screaming to be let out, to escape to comfort and safety. You will take the rebellious child into yourself and comfort him... . With the others, you will sing and pray for yourself and them, for healing, for the good of the community, for the earth. You will discover that part of yourself that is humble, that is nothing, that can grovel unashamedly. You will learn how to transcend what you mistakenly believed to be personal limitations. Finally, you will emerge from the darkness cleansed, illumined, new born. (Foster, 1998, p. 160)

RITES OF DREAMING

Go alone to a wild place with the specific intent to dream. Stay in that place, without food, for 24 hours. Sleep and dream. Be watchful for and record any dreams that may come, including daydreams, fantasies, reveries, out of body experiences, etc... . Elements of the dreams will help you to understand yourself and your mythical course. (Foster, 1998, p. 162)

There are eight rites of winter, six of which will be noted below, that function to assist the initiate's move into maturity rather than languishing in depression, victimization, rebellion, or narcissism.

RITES OF SELF-TRACKING

Spend a week fashioning an object representing your self out of some natural substance. Go alone with that object into a natural place where there are no paths or familiar landmarks and your boot tracks cannot be seen. Place that object on or in the earth and turn your back on it. Walk away from it without looking back for an hour. Then turn around, retrace your steps, and find the symbol.

RITES OF SURVIVAL

For ten days you must put away all your technological toys except for a knife and an emergency kit and learn how to live as your primitive ancestors did. With the aid of a teacher you will learn the basic rudiments of Stone Age survival, mastering principles, techniques, and secrets known for untold thousands of years but almost forgotten by modern culture. You will build shelters, make fire without matches, find water, fashion hunting weapons of stone, wood, and sinew, twist fiber into cordage, weave baskets, hunt, skin, preserve game animals, identify, gather, and prepare wild foods. Before you are done, you will taste the fruits of the illumination that comes from knowing the all-sufficiency of nature. (Foster, 1998, p. 177)

RITES OF OBSERVATION

Go alone into the wilderness for 48 hours with the intent to study a particular species and its relationship to the biosystem. Although you will have the opportunity to indulge your inner life and forget about the world you are

in, you will not be able to abandon your intention—which
is to examine the ways of the natural world. You will scru-
tinize a plant, tree, insect, reptile, fish, bird, or mammal
as thoroughly as you can, noting its growth stages, how it
propagates, defends, nourishes itself, how ling it has existed
in the evolutionary stage, how it is associated with other life
forms in its habitat, i.e., how it "belongs." Lastly, you will
observe the ways in which this species is related, in physical, psychological, mental, and spiritual ways, to yourself.
(Foster, 1998, p. 179)

SELF-DESIGNED RITES

Plan your own ceremony using only the stuff of the natural
world. In order to do so you must answer many questions.
What would be the purpose of the ceremony? For what reason would the ceremony be performed? What goal would it
accomplish? Would it be a ceremony marking a severance
from a former state? Would it be a ceremony that mirrors
the passage from a former state to a desired state? Would
it be a ceremony confirming the attainment of a desired
state? Who would benefit from the ceremony? How would
you mark the severance, threshold, and incorporation stages?
Who would witness the ceremony? ... Then go out on the
land and do what you planned to do. (Foster, 1998, p. 181)

RITES OF CONFIRMATION: The End of Addiction

For too long you have felt victimized by your own deeds,
addicted to patterns of shame, guilt, and self-disgust. No
longer will you enlighten your own darkness with the aid of
drug rushes that make you temporarily forget that you are,
in fact, killing yourself. Perhaps you already understand
that you cannot heal yourself without first accepting the
truth that you are addicted (to whatever it is), that you love
your life and want to live it, that you cannot salvage yourself without recourse to a kind of spiritual power. Alone or
with the help of others, you begin to prepare to leave the
addiction behind by watching your addictive behavior. You
work hard to understand why you are addicted. You resolve
to follow a course that leads to the end of addiction. You
envision life without this monkey on your back. Not until

you have taken firm steps toward your goal are you ready to participate in a passage rite in the wilderness that will test your resolve and confirm that you have symbolically attained a state of non-addiction. For four days and nights you will live alone, without food or adequate shelter, in the wilderness. Each morning you will rise to a day devoid of addictive behavior. You will drink plain water and flush the toxins from your body. Each night you will lie down a little emptier, a little cleaner. Gradually, your mind will clear. With clarity will come a new form of illumination unattainable with addiction. So you will signify that you have passed into a new life state. But your struggles will not be over … you must return with the illumination brought to you by your success and test it against the realities of your everyday life. You must find others who have freed themselves who know that freedom is won through constant self-control. (Foster, 1998, p. 190)

RITES OF CONFIRMATION

You are altering your life status. You are moving from one stage or phase to the next. You are changing worlds. And every time you change worlds, a part of you—the part you used to be—changes. And so you go into the wilderness alone, without food or adequate shelter for four days and nights, to confirm that the decision has been made, that the change of worlds has occurred, that you are ready to assume a new life status. For the confirmation to be meaningful, you will sacrifice a part of yourself (food, companionship, shelter). During the threshold time, you will perform a "death lodge" ceremony in which you die a symbolic death, and be reborn to your new life. (Foster, 1998, p. 192)

RITES OF RELOCATION

You know the time has come to move—from one life occupation to another, from one home to another. You are also aware that this relocation of body, psyche, mind and spirit will wreak a profound change in your life. You are, in fact, at a major transition, a crossroads, and you know the time has come to confirm that the new course has been taken, that the new life has begun. Therefore, you sever from your former home or

occupation and you go into the wilderness and fast alone for
three or four days and nights. (Foster, 1998, p. 194)

A group or council of elders convenes at the culmination of the threshold
event to listen to the initiate's story about his threshold experience and to
mirror to the initiate their impressions about how he has done in answering
the critical questions of the vision quest. The elders' mirror serves as a positive
validation of the initiate's quest and experience (Foster, 1998, pp. 131–132).

IMPLICATIONS FOR EDUCATING LATE-ADOLESCENT BOYS

With the disappearance of healthy and life-enhancing initiation rites from
schools and from the culture, it is imperative that serious work be done to
reinstitute and reconstruct validating, transformative rites of passage for
late-adolescent boys. The fact that most late-adolescent boys fit the description of Mama's boys, tricksters, or narcissistic personalities merely reinforces the need for transformative rites of passage that can usher boys into
mature manhood. The alternative is that boys' initiation hunger will drive
them to initiate themselves and others in immature, dangerous, and even
destructive ways.

Schools have a natural and built-in opportunity to provide a containing
environment as well as a mature adult mentor and guide where boys can
meet and receive initiatory training in the ways of mature manhood. If
space and a willing and properly trained (initiated) adult can be intentionally
established, the prerequisites for initiatory process can be met. Such a place
in the school setting would need space where boys can segregate from the
female population for a period of time in order to feel safe to talk about, act
out, and experience a healthy all-male environment and camaraderie.

The schools need to provide nurturing environments in which late-
adolescent boys can learn ways of being a man by receiving male-specific
instruction in a curriculum constructed with that focus in mind. This study
addressed some of the key components in future chapters, but the addition
of a character component is essential. Michael Gurian (1999) movingly
advocated for a new paradigm of manhood based on the four principles of
compassion, honor, responsibility, and enterprise (Gurian, 1999, pp. 231–250).
Additionally, he advocated teaching males about loyalty, duty, fairness,

virtue (values), decency, dignity, character, and discipline as part of honor training (Gurian, 1999, pp. 239–240). These concepts can become the cornerstone of the instruction given to males as part of their initiation training and preparation.

Most importantly, it is critical that a curriculum for late-adolescent boys incorporates a meaningful rite of passage as its culminating event. The rite of passage needs to follow the ancient pattern of initiation rites as outlined above. While there are many initiatory scenarios that could serve as a meaningful container for a rite of passage, this study advocates a wilderness-type experience as a proven approach. Absent any existing culturally sanctioned rites of passage for transitioning and validating late-adolescent boys into manhood, a traditional vision quest experience or a self-styled initiation experience with proper containment and adult guidance are imperative. Regardless of the initiatory route taken, the limen must be crossed, and the youth must become a man. Growth into maturity can be accomplished only when the youth's selfish individuality can find fulfillment in a greater transpersonal wholeness. Rites of passage can facilitate this life-changing and life-enhancing process.

CHAPTER SIX

UNIQUELY MASCULINE ISSUES: FINDING THE FATHER

I am that father whom your boyhood lacked
And suffered pain for lack of. I am he.
This is not princely, to be swept away
By wonder at your father's presence.
No other Odysseus will ever come,
For he and I are one, the same.
Then, throwing his arms around this marvel of a father
Telemakhos began to weep. Salt tears
Rose from the wells of longing in both men,
And cries burst from both...
So helplessly they cried, pouring out tears.

Homer's *The Odyssey*, Book XVI.
Translated by Robert Fitzgerald

Early psychoanalytic writers emphasized the negative role of a father in a son's development, preferring to emphasize the Oedipal conflict and picturing the father as a hostile, aggressive figure who was to be feared and submitted to

(Pollack, 1995, p. 42; Steinberg, p. 66). Subsequent research shows a more positive role for the father in a male child's development. First and foremost, a father's importance manifests in the father's ability to be a caring nonmother alternative, who draws the young boy into external reality. By doing so, the father helps the boy differentiate from his mother by encouraging him to separate from her as a part of normal development (Steinberg, pp. 66–67). In this way, the father becomes a safe and stable space in which the boy can experience independence and separateness (Steinberg, p. 67). Furthermore, the father facilitates the young boy's development of a positive gender role by serving as the principal object of focus in the external world and helps the young boy define his gender identity: "He emphasizes by his very presence that there is a way to be—masculine—that differs from the initial identification with the mother's way of being—feminine" (Steinberg, p. 68). Hence, the quality of the father-son relationship, to a great extent, will determine if a son will be secure or defensive in his gender role and identity (Steinberg, p. 69).

Recent research suggests that children have an innate drive to find and connect with their fathers. According to Pruett (2000), "Children and fathers hunger for each other early, often, and for a very long time" (p. 2). Pruett identified a number of positive father care influences on a child's development. Father "play" has long-lasting effects because a father tends to use his own body rather than a toy, and the play between a father and a child tends to be more nonconventional, emphasizing activation-exploration themes (pp. 27–28). Furthermore, father play tends to take on a more rough-and tumble quality and novelty-seeking behaviors, as well as exploring more vigorously and widely the world's environment (pp. 29–30). A father tends to carry his child in the football position with the child facing forward so the child can see the world *en face* (p. 29). Concerning problem-solving, a father tends to tolerate his child's frustration when he attempts something new, which plays a role in promoting the expectation of achievement in children (p. 31). When discipline is involved, a father tends to be more emotionally distant while emphasizing the societal effects of the consequences of misbehavior (p. 32). In the area of communication, father-style talk tends to be more complex, using bigger words and longer sentence structures (p. 33). In the following passage, Pruett quotes Myriam Miedzian on the impact of fathering on young boys.

> Boys raised with nurturant, caring, involved fathers develop a sense of their father's primary male identity on which they can model themselves from the youngest age. They do not need to prove that they are real men by being tough, violent, obsessed with dominance. Their model of masculinity includes nurturance, caring and empathy experienced from their fathers. Since they are secure in their masculinity, they do not have the need to look down on or disparage everything feminine in order to establish a masculine identity. (Pruett, p. 182)

A sufficiently nurturing, affectionate father is indispensable for helping a young boy develop competency in the instrumental / active dimension of the male gender role. This masculine nurturing is the foundation on which male individuality develops. This essential, father-mediated core of masculine identity remains as the boy learns to separate his identity and personality from his father in order to form his own unique personality.

THE ABSENT FATHER

The absent father is a man who is emotionally uninvolved and physically absent from his children. The result is a rather painful experience of father loss on the part of boys, often referred to as a wound. Father absence has become a major social, economic, and health issue in contemporary American society.

The rise in father absence is the result of two significant demographic trends: an increase in divorce and the rise in unwed childbirth (National Fatherhood Initiative website: https://fatherhood.safeserver.com/fatherfacts/intro.htm.). The divorce rate between 1965 and 1980 more than doubled since the 1960s and has leveled off to between 40–50 percent of all marriages ending in divorce or separation. Divorce alone affects approximately one million children annually (National Fatherhood Initiative website: https://fatherhood.safeserver.com/fatherfacts/intro.htm.). There has been an equally significant increase in the number of unwed childbirths, with a 600 percent increase in unwed childbirths between 1960 and 2000. This factor affects 1.3 million children annually. Cohabitation also increased significantly at the same time (National Fatherhood Initiative website: https://fatherhood.safeserver.com/fatherfacts/intro.htm.).

Negatively, father absence is a major social ill. Child abuse in single parent families is almost double that of two-parent families (America's Children: Key National Indicators of Well-Being. Federal Interagency Forum on Child and Family Statistics. Washington, D.C.: GPO, 1997). With all other variables being equal, boys who are raised outside of two-parent families are more than twice as likely to end up incarcerated as those in intact families (Harper and McLanahan, August 1998). Furthermore, adolescent use of illegal drugs in single parent and stepparent families is double that used by teens in two-parent families (Hoffman and Johnson, 1980). Children born out of wedlock and who remain in a single-parent family or whose mother later married have significantly poorer math and reading scores and diminished academic performance than children from intact households (Cooksey, 1997). In 1999, 6.3 percent of married-couple families with children, compared to 31.8 percent of single-parent families with children, were living below the poverty line (U.S. Census Bureau. Current Population Survey).

In more than 100 parent-child relational studies, father love was noted as being just as important as mother love as a predictor of children's and adolescent's social, emotional, and cognitive development. Researchers stressed that the presence of a loving and nurturing father was equally as important as that of a loving and nurturing mother for an offspring's well being. Furthermore, the withdrawal of love by the father or the mother was equally significant in negatively affecting emotional instability, self-esteem, depression, and aggressiveness. In some studies the absence of father love was a more significant factor in delinquency and conduct problems, substance abuse, and general mental health and well being than other variables (Rohmer and Veneziano, 2001).

According to the National Fatherhood Initiative, children with fathers who live with them in the family are more prone to have a close and permanent relationship than those children whose fathers do not live in the family. Children born to cohabiting parents are three-times more likely to experience father absence than children born into intact families, while those born to unmarried non-cohabitating parents are four-times more likely than those children in intact families to experience father absence. However, children who live with involved, loving fathers in the family experience healthy self-esteem, demonstrate empathy and socially-appropriate behavior, and have lower rates of high-risk behaviors such a drug use, truancy, and criminal activity (Top Ten Father Facts. National Fatherhood Initiative website: https://fatherhood.safeserver.com/fatherfacts/topten.htm.).

Beyond the statistics about father absence, David Blankenhorn (1995) warned that we are losing the cultural idea of the father. Echoing a number of researchers, Blankenhorn stated that fatherhood, more than motherhood, is as much a cultural invention as it is a biological one. As a cultural construction, it is postulated on cultural scripts that guide and prescribe certain ways of acting and thinking about fatherhood (p. 3). Our culture has failed to "to sustain or create compelling norms of fatherhood (that) amounts to a social and personal disaster" (p. 4). From a personal standpoint, the ultimate result of the devaluation of fatherhood is narcissism—"a kind of me-first egoism"—which results in "our society's steady fragmentation into atomized individuals, isolated from one another and estranged from the aspirations and realities of common membership in a family…" (p. 4).

From a psychological point of view, the father's absence makes problematic the son's relation with his father, requiring an explanation that is often mistaken for wanting to know why that person is not present. Therefore, sons will either idealize or devalue their fathers, "misidentifying with them, and struggling with shame and guilt themselves" (Osherson, p. 29). Frequently, sons blame themselves or project some secret weakness for the father's absence. Consequently, these misidentifications become difficult to untangle and rewrite with appropriate explanations (Osherson, pp. 28–30). For those sons who were raised in a family with an all-suffering father, the masculine fate is to be like dad and to suffer as he did.

> Father never escaped; he worked hard, and that becomes our task as well. To be a loving son means to work hard and suffer the manly pains that Dad did. Not to do so means to leave your father. It can be difficult to let go and partake of happiness as an adult when father is unhappy and suffering. (Osherson, 1986, p. 33)

Additionally, a son may idealize his father and grow up with the perception of him as saintly or heroic. He may not be able to feel he can ever live up to his father's stature unless he himself attains the same level of heroic idealization in his own family (Osherson, pp. 33–34). Furthermore, the father may be seen as secretly vulnerable. Traditional father roles in the family mandate that the father assumes the real-world instrumental financial and material provider role, while the mother assumes the expressive, affective tasks in the family. Over time, sons learn about their fathers through their mother's viewpoint, often a mistaken or skewed image of their fathers and masculinity. Moreover, sometimes sons become surrogate husbands to their mothers, thereby creating "male vulnerability—a sense that something was wrong with the father that could never be discussed" (Osherson, pp. 34–38).

The result is that young men grow up with a view of their fathers as either too strong or too weak. Men, consequently, grow up either fearful of hurting their fathers or being hurt by him. According to Osherson, "These two themes are acted out over and over again in the … lives of men: the search for and rejection of our fathers. We want redemption and want to destroy them." (p. 45). This kind of wounding to young men is devastating and difficult to overcome. It becomes internalized in them as an inner image of the wounded father (Osherson, p. 27). It also becomes projected as father hunger.

FATHER HUNGER

Father hunger is the deep, but often unconscious, longing young men, and even older men, have for affirmation from male authority figures. It is the need men have "for an older, wiser, or stronger man to guide him, believe in him, affirm him, concretely touch him, challenge him, and correct him" (Rohr, 2004, p. 87). It is complicated by males' culturally and developmentally conditioned inability to express their need for affirmation and validation from other men. Boys, especially, need "male mothering," a kind of intentional yet practical and affectionate instruction by the father. This kind of attention helps boys move beyond the secure nest of home and his mother to where he can encounter the outer world with self-confidence. When a father is absent and unable to support and guide the son, this absence leaves the son with "a life-long and gnawing sadness" (Rohr, p. 88).

Rohr asserted that boys are genetically hard-wired to need other males (2004). They find healthy expression in bonding relationships with a coach or with a mentor, in the esprit de corps of boys in an all-male school, and in the general manner in which boys, young and old, look in admiration to older men who are heroes in their eyes. Sheehy (1998) cited research from the *Journal of the American Medical Association* that suggested that boys need a "sense of connectedness" to their fathers. It is not the quantity of activities that matters but the quality of caring and connection they have with their father that forges the bonding (p. 166).

Boys who experience father hunger describe it as a kind of vacuum or void left in their hearts. According to James L. Schaller, M.D. (1999), many people have a father hunger void inside them that has a significant effect on their lives. Schaller listed the following descriptors of father hunger in a person:

- When I think about my father, I become emotional-insecure, sad, or angry.
- When I'm with my father, I don't act like myself; I'm either childish or grandiose.
- I consider my father wonderful, but others think I'm fooling myself.
- I feel numb toward my father.
- I have trouble with competitiveness.
- My motivation is poor because I feel beaten down.
- I have difficulty establishing relationships.
- I move too quickly into new relationships.
- I'm confused about my identity; it's not as if my father ever made me feel good about myself.
- I don't feel like a real man.
- I feel unattractive.
- I feel incompetent.
- It is difficult for me to relax.
- I have problems with my sexuality.
- Being assertive is hard for me.
- People seem to feel that I violate their boundaries.
- I'm afraid to get too close to others.
- I fear being abandoned.

- Authority makes me uneasy.
- My father's criticism hurt me too much. Now I have difficulty accepting criticism.
- God often feels a million miles away.
- I have little interest in spirituality.
- When my father does not provide the emotional support my mother needs, my mother unknowingly tries to get me to provide that support.
- My father confides in me too much.
- My father and I do not talk openly and honestly about our lives.
- I keep trying to please everybody-especially father-types or mentors.
- I run to things and people to nurse myself in a compulsive way.
- I am rarely satisfied.
- I live with a vague, diffused fearfulness.
- My mother's boyfriend annoys me.
- My stepfather and I do not get along very well.
- I am a parent who worries I am repeating my father's and grandfather's mistakes.
- Sometimes I feel like an orphan. (from The Search for Lost Fathering. James L. Schaller, M.D. Chapter 1-"Everybody Needs a Father." (www.personalconsult.com/books/lostfathering1.htm)

Schaller concluded that this unhealed wound associated with the father has left many people "with a void, an injury, a psychic thirst that only a father can quench (that) ... is nearly universal" (from The Search for Lost Fathering. James L. Schaller, M.D. Chapter 1-"Everybody Needs a Father." (www.personalconsult.com/books/lostfathering1.htm.).

RECONNECTING WITH THE FATHER

Canada (1999/2000) recommends the following suggestions for helping boys connect with their fathers through the school setting:

- Reach out to boys early and get them to talk about their feelings, which is easier when they are young.

- Make sure boys take risks in safe, developmentally appropriate ways such as sports, but also expose them to new experiences such as walks, sailing, and dancing.
- Give boys more positive messages of self-worth and reduce the number of negative messages from others.
- Ensure that boys have positive role models who take an interest in their moral, intellectual, and emotional development. Monitor what boys see and hear through the media.
- Find a place for spiritual and moral education.
- Expose boys to different cultures and points of view.
- Have a multilayered support system, perhaps involving parents, grandparents, aunts and uncles, coaches, teachers, and other caring adults. (Canada, 1999/2000, pp. 140+)

Fuller and Olsen (1998) provided a number of ideas for involving fathers in their sons' education, such as including fathers' names on invitations to school functions to make explicit that both parents are welcome and expected. Another idea is for schools to offer a few father-only or father-child events. A further recommendation is for schools to be sensitive to male styles of communicating in meetings because some fathers prefer to focus on business first and socializing as a later and secondary priority. Furthermore, schools need to be flexible in scheduling meetings to accommodate work schedules.

Schools need to have father-friendly environments that include posters and media portraying fathers in a positive light. One way to do this is to solicit the active involvement of fathers in sharing their experiences and skills in clubs, projects, games, coaching, judging science projects as well as other less traditional activities. Taking these types of proactive steps will help to involve fathers in their sons' school experiences and lives (Conderman, pp. 140+).

In order to reconnect with the father, the son will need to examine his life and the ways in which he has been affected by his father's presence as well as his absence. It will require a journey of remembering, and the remembering will engender grief (Harris, 1996, p. 130). Male grief for the absent father is complex with many facets and nuances of loss, failure, incompleteness, inadequacy, silence, and misunderstanding (Harris, p. 130; Hollis, p. 117). Honest grief is cleansing and healing, a better remedy, however painful, than succumbing to depression or narcissistic self-absorption. The grief process will teach a boy how to fill the inner emptiness creatively.

A number of healing strategies are available to confront and deal with the father wound and father hunger. Harris advocated an honest personal addressing of the timeless questions of life: "What is the purpose of my life? Why am I here? What am I doing? What does my heart say? How do I live?" (Harris, p. 143). Answering these questions forces a person to address his or her inner integrity and to listen to the myriad inner voices that demand loyalty and to make choices that bespeak of who one is and what one stands for.

Osherson (1986) recommended that boys do an in-depth exploration of their fathers' life and experiences as a way of coming to an understanding of the father's own personal suffering. By doing so, the son may be more empathic of the father's faults. These feelings of empathy may help him forgive his father. This recovery of the personal father's past has several benefits.

> In learning about their fathers, sons can come to see them as separate people, different from them. That can help the separation-individuation process, as the son realizes that he is responsible for his own identity as a man, that he is not chained to his father's attitudes and values. So the process of exploration may lead to an acceptance of father, even if not a deep connection with him. (Osherson, p. 211)

Hollis (1994) echoed Osherson, citing Jung's observation that the unlived life of the parent is the greatest burden that the child has to carry. Hollis advocated that the son study without judgment the father's wounds and how they were passed on to him:

> Each father's son must ask himself, "What were my father's wounds? What were his sacrifices, if any, for me and oth-ers? What were his hopes, his dreams? Did he live out his dreams? Did he have emotional permission to live his life? Did he live his life or the Saturnian tapes? What did he receive from his father and culture that hindered his journey? What would I have liked to know from him about his life, his history? What would I have liked to know from him

about being a man? Was he able to answer such questions, however tentatively, for himself? Did he ever ask them? What was my father's unlived life, and am I living it out, somehow, for him?" (Hollis, p. 119)

By asking these important questions of the father, even if he is no longer living, the son can have a more realistic picture of his father, and the father becomes a man more like his son. In this way, a reconnection with the personal father can begin.

Drew (2003) wrote an extensive guide for reconnecting with the absent father and for healing the father wound. Her method is a step-by-step self-help process that begins with releasing unresolved longing and anger toward the absent father, reframing the painful memories of the past, and empowering self-fathering. Two final steps involve accepting the father wound and the direction it has taken the son's life and building healthy, supportive relationships that promote self-healing and understanding (pp. 7–8). Drew's book is a manual of exercises that can be done alone or in groups to facilitate a reconnection with the absent father or healing of the father wound. The manual provides a number of appropriate exercises for working with boys and their coming to grips with father absence, including those fathers that are abusive, judgmental, or distant (pp. 17–21). The following exercise assists boys in becoming aware of the ways in which their fathers influenced their personalities and their problems:

WHAT KIND OF FATHERING DID YOU HAVE?

Read questions A through D below. In your journal, write out answers to any of the questions, which you feel apply to you and your dad. You may respond to one or more categories. Be specific, including as many details as you can recall. When describing feelings, use simple words like "hurt," "angry," "lonely," "sad," and "afraid"—to keep you in contact with your emotions rather than your thoughts. If two or more men acted as your father, start with the one toward whom you feel the greatest charge. If you feel you have significant issues with the others, re-do the exercise, focusing on each in turn.

A. Was your father absent?
   1. What were the conditions of his departure: death, suicide, divorce, military duty, extended travel, imprisonment, desertion?
   2. How old were you at the time?
   3. What feelings can you remember about his leaving?
   4. Did you ever think your father's absence was your fault?
   5. Did you talk about your dad being gone? How did your mother, siblings, grandparents, family friends, and others react to his absence?
   6. Did you exhibit an early independence? Describe what you did.
   7. Have you felt impeded in career development? In what way?
   8. Are you afraid that people you love will leave you?
   9. Can you identify any specific relationship problems that reflect your early experience with your father?

B. Was your father abusive?
   1. Recall some of the ways he was verbally, physically, or sexually damaging. How did you feel during and after these events?
   2. Do you have a sense that you've blocked out any memories or feelings from your childhood?
   3. If so, can you guess what kind of abuse you are repressing?
   4. How did you feel about the way others did or did not protect you?
   5. Did your father exhibit addictive behaviors?
   6. Describe any problems you may have had yourself with overweight, substance abuse, or other compulsive behaviors?
   7. Have you gotten into trouble with any authorities?

C. Was your father judgmental?
   1 In what ways was he severe with you? Give examples of the comments he made or rules he enforced?
   2. How did he humiliate or stifle you? Give examples of the comments he made or rules he enforced.
   3. How did you feel before, during, and after these events?

    4. How did his judgments about you affect you later as an adult?
    5. Describe any mask you put on or false self you developed in order to please your dad.
    6. In what kinds of self-criticism do you engage?

 D. Was your father distant?
    1. Describe in detail how he separated himself from you.
    2. Recall three specific times when he wasn't available to you. How did you feel inside?
    3. What did you get from your father's attention? Were your actions successful? Do you continue the same behavior now with loved ones and authority figures?
    4. If you had a step-father, how old were you when he came on the scene? Examine the nature and trace the history of the relationship you had with him. (Drew, pp. 23–25)

The following exercise uses visualization and creative imaging to help boys understand how they are relating to their fathers now:

LOCATE DAD WITHIN YOU

Sit comfortably and close your eyes. Breathe deeply, letting yourself get very quiet. After several minutes, feel where your father is *in your body.* Open yourself to the experience of locating where you physically hold your dad inside you.

A. Is he in the center or attached to the bottom of your heart?
B. Is he in the pit of your stomach, caught in your throat, or hiding at the back of your head?
C. What does he feel like?

Now imagine that the part of your body where you have discovered your dad can communicate.

A. Does this site have a message for you?
B. What does it say? Let the phrases come quickly. Don't intellectualize about them. If you draw a blank, give the emptiness a voice.

C. If you hardly knew your dad, where in your body do you sense his absence? Let whatever feeling is associated with that place speak. (Drew, pp. 32–33)

Writing a letter to one's father can be an effective way to access feelings about one's father and to give vent to tightly-held emotions as is illustrated in the following exercise:

LETTER TO YOUR FATHER

Tell your dad in a letter what's in your heart: all your anger, hurt, fear, needs, forgiveness, and love, in that order. This is your chance to write anything to him that remains unexpressed. Don't worry about spelling, punctuation, or your literary style. It doesn't matter if your letter is polished or not. Let whatever is inside come out. (Drew, p. 56)

One facet of reframing and appreciating the father is to honor him despite his flaws and imperfections and to try to see him in the larger context of his accomplishments.

HONOR YOUR FATHER

Ask yourself the following questions about your father:

A. Was he a responsible human being?
B. How did his friends and peers see him?
C. What kind of worker was he at his job and around the house?
D. Did he belong to a service-oriented church or fraternal club?
E. Did he do anything of larger value creatively or for the community?

Write down how you honor your father. Using your dad's first name, complete the following sentence: *"honor my father (state his name), for ... ."* (Drew, pp. 77–78)

There are a number of options concerning reconnecting with the father: break off the relationship completely, accept the relationship as it currently exists, or move toward a closer relationship. In order to move toward a closer relationship, it is important that the son initiate the contact with the absent father, requiring making oneself vulnerable. Accepting the father as he is now and changing the way one treats one's father are key components to reconnecting with him (pp. 133–134). The following strategies can be used to connect with the father:

STRATEGIES TO CONNECT WITH YOUR DAD

A. Give your dad a hug the next time you see him.
B. Take your father out to lunch on a regular basis.
C. Spend a few days away on a mini-vacation with just your dad.
D. Sit down with your father, possibly with a tape recorder, and get his version of the family history.
E. Create a videotape about your father's life as a present to him. (Drew, pp. 140–142)

It is even possible to reconnect emotionally and spiritually with the absent father who is deceased.

ENCOUNTER YOUR DECEASED DAD

A. Talk to your dad out loud or just internally.
B. Write to your father in journal form.
C. Collect physical objects that belonged to your dad.
D. Search out and meet your father's relatives and friends.
E. Make a pilgrimage to your father's burial site.
F. Ask your father to make contact with you in dreams. (Drew, pp. 146–148)

These exercises can be used or adapted to work effectively with late-adolescent boys in reconnecting with the absent father and healing the father wound. Although there is no easy, quick fix for these issues, nevertheless, there is hope that the father wound can be accepted and worked with in a positive manner that will help boys to reconnect to their absent fathers in a positive and self-affirming way.

IMPLICATIONS FOR EDUCATING LATE-ADOLESCENT BOYS

Rather than using the Oedipal story as the paradigmatic explanation for a man's relationship with his father, a more appropriate myth is that of *The Odyssey* and the relationship between Odysseus and his son, Telemachus (Harris, pp. 23, 81–82; Osherson, pp. 49–51). Fighting the Trojan War and struggling to return home, Odysseus has been absent from his son for twenty years. During that time, Telemachus has grown to the verge of young adulthood under his mother's tutelage and the negative role models of her ravaging male suitors. Odysseus is merely a legend in his son's mind and heart. Clearly, Telemachus is suffering a terrible father wound caused by Odysseus' long absence. As is vividly told in the poignant passage at the beginning of this chapter, both men long for each other, as do many fathers and sons today long for connection with each other. When they finally meet, Telemachus initially rejects the man before him as an imposter, an apparition from the gods, but Odysseus proclaims his real humanity to his son, and a tearful reunion follows. This point is important because it is the father's responsibility to permit the son to experience his full humanity while giving up unrealistic projections of the father image as well in order to help the son assume his adult responsibilities (Harris, p. 82; Osherson, p. 50). In short, Odysseus models mature, confident manhood to his son, thereby helping Telemachus to assume manhood himself. The same task is necessary even today as Osherson (1986) wrote, "How to be a strong and present man in new, unfamiliar situations" (Osherson, p. 50). Telemachus' yearning is the same yearning of modern sons' desire to connect or reconnect with their fathers in order to find a foundation upon which the son can rely.

A curriculum for late-adolescent boys needs to incorporate a consideration of the role of the father in the son's life and to foster a reconnection with the absent father. The strategies used in a curriculum for late adolescent boys will vary to include those already mentioned in this chapter and the more evocative ones through the use of movies that vividly confront father absence and the father wound, such as Mel Gibson's *The Man Without A Face* (1993). Boys have an unarticulated need for their fathers despite the absence of their fathers from their lives because of various circumstances. By recovering the absent father in their lives, boys can develop "a fuller, trustworthy sense of masculinity, a way of caring and nurturing, of being strong without being destructive" (Osherson, p. 229).

CHAPTER SEVEN

ARCHETYPES OF A MATURE
MASCULINE IDENTITY

There is a Great Code which, when followed, leads a person towards
personal wholeness, and that this Great Code is, in fact, your two million
year old DNA.

Robert Moore, Ph.D.

C. G. Jung was the first to use the term *archetype* in 1919 (*Collected Works 8*, paragraph 270). The term has Greek roots dating back to classical times meaning "prime imprinter." Although Jung worked extensively with mythological and psychiatric materials to elucidate his experience of archetypes, nevertheless, there is abundant corroborative proof from diverse human populations that Jung was correct in his statement that "the collective unconscious contains the whole spiritual heritage of mankind's evolution, born anew in the brain structure of every individual" (*Collected Works 8*, paragraph 342). Moreover, archetypes are universal patterns of behavior and feeling as well as universally recurring symbols and themes that are biologically based and conditioned by evolution (Stevens, p 52), something which Buss (1999) called "evolved psychological mechanisms." At its most basic formulation, an archetype, according to Jung, "is a pattern of behavior" (*Collected Works 18*, paragraph 1228). Archetypes also have a psychic structure that serves to organize experience, especially concerning to gender categories and "the dichotomizing of existence into opposites of masculine and feminine" (Steinberg, pp. 19–20). Additionally, archetypes are composed of cultural material that completes the structure.

> The unconscious supplies as it were the archetypal form, which in itself is empty and irrepresentable. Consciousness immediately fills it with related or similar representational material so that it can be perceived. For this reason archetypal ideas are locally, temporally, and individually conditioned. (*Collected Works 13*, paragraph 476)

Archetypes possess a basic duality of consciousness / unconsciousness, symbolical / instinctive, and psychic / nonpsychic. Therefore, according to Stevens, archetypes are "actualized both on the objective level of outer and on the subjective plain of inner conscious experience" (p. 71). In summary, archetypes are "systems of readiness for action, and at the same time images and emotions" (p. 71).

Moore & Gillette (1992a) posited that the archetypes are "hard-wired" into human genes, and so they "represent transpersonal human psychological characteristics" (Moore & Gillette, 1992a, p. 33) that exist in all persons. As such, archetypes serve as channels of psychological energy that manifest particular patterns of thought, feeling, and behavior.

MOORE & GILLETTE'S MODEL OF THE MATURE MASCULINE ARCHETYPES

Moore & Gillette (1990, 1992a, 1992b, 1993a, 1993b) theorized that the human Self is constructed on Jung's concepts of the "quaternio" and "double quaternio" as explained in his essay on "The Structure and Dynamics of the Self" found in *Aion* (1959). The structure of the Self is a pyramid shape with the four major masculine archetypes called King, Warrior, Magician, and Lover forming a quadrant of the pyramid (Moore & Gillette, 1992a, p. 38). Each archetype is represented as a triangle with the base of the triangle representing the bipolar Shadow split in the archetype itself, which must be integrated by the Ego in order to attain the fullest expression of the archetype as represented at the top of the triangle (Moore & Gillette, 1992a, p. 45). The upward movement of Ego consciousness has the purpose of reconciling the opposite Shadow poles of the archetype and integrating them into consciousness, thereby becoming whole and better able to access the archetype in the process (Moore & Gillette, 1992a, p. 45).

> Each of the poles of the split Shadows of the four major archetypes possesses insights and strengths that, when the Ego integrates them, contributes to a consolidated sense of Self. Each of the opposites, when united, reveals the "transcendent third" of the archetype in its fullness. By overcoming the splitness in the bipolar archetypal Shadows, a man comes to feel inwardly empowered. And, in a sense, while he is *building* internal masculine structure he is also *discovering* the pyramid of the masculine Self, which has always been within him, at his core. (Moore & Gillette, 1992a, p. 45)

The bipolar Shadow archetypal forms can be considered immature because they are not integrated and remain undeveloped until they emerge at certain developmental stages. Moore & Gillette (1990) theorized that the first archetype to emerge is the Divine Child, followed in turn by the Precocious Child, the Oedipal Child, and finally the Hero. The boyhood archetypes are the antecedents of the mature masculine archetypes. "Thus, the Divine Child, modulated and enriched by life's experiences, becomes the King; the Precocious Child becomes the Magician; the Oedipal Child becomes the Lover; and the Hero becomes the Warrior" (Moore & Gillette, 1990, p. 15). These four archetypes have a triangular structure and form a pyramid that illustrates the boy's developing identity.

Before examining the mature masculine archetypes, it is appropriate to examine the boyhood archetypes first because most boys manifest these immature patterns in adolescence to some extent before developing the mature masculine archetypes. The first, most basic boyhood archetype is the Divine Child. Its characteristics include magical empowering abilities, and its embodiment produces "an enormous sense of well-being, enthusiasm for life, and great peace and joy" (Moore & Gillette, 1990, p. 23). The bipolar Shadow manifestations are the High Chair Tyrant and the Weakling Prince. The High Chair Prince embodies characteristics of arrogance, negative childishness, irresponsibility, which is demanding and denigrating of others (Moore & Gillette, 1990, pp. 23–25). On the other side of the bipolar Shadow is the Weakling Prince, who has characteristics of helplessness, listlessness, and depressed passivity (Moore & Gillette, 1990, pp. 25–26).

The Precocious Child boyhood archetype manifests itself in males as a sense of adventure, wonder, and curiosity in the outer and inner worlds, and a tendency toward introversion and reflection with an impulse to share insights and talents with others, and a propensity for knowledge and intellect. The bipolar Shadow is the Know-It-All Trickster, with a proclivity for playing tricks and practical jokes on himself and others. He is manipulative and enjoys intimidating others with his comments by being verbally abusive and deceptive. Although this archetype causes males to be envious and to have an authority problem, they cannot take responsibility for themselves or their actions (Moore & Gillette, 1990, pp. 28–33). The other side of the bipolar Shadow of the Precocious Child is the Dummy. This archetype manifests as naivete, unresponsive, and dull, but "his duncelike behavior may mask a hidden grandiosity that feels itself too important (as well as too vulnerable) to come into the world" (Moore & Gillette, 1990, p. 33).

The third boyhood archetype is the Oedipal Child, which can be seen in a male as a sense of wonder and deep connectedness in his inner and outer worlds, warmth, affection, and spirituality (Moore & Gillette, 1990, pp. 33–34). One bipolar Shadow side of the Oedipal Child is the Mama's Boy who cannot disconnect from his mother. The embodiment of this archetype includes never being satisfied with a mortal woman (the Don Juan syndrome) and autoeroticism. "He does not want to do what it takes to have union with a mortal woman and to deal with all the complex feelings involved in an intimate relationship" (Moore & Gillette, 1990, pp. 35–36). The other Shadow pole of the Oedipal Child is the Dreamer, which isolates boys who retreat into the inner world of imagination, and which results in a person's accomplishing little and becoming withdrawn and depressed (Moore & Gillette, 1990, pp. 36–37).

The last and most advanced form of the boyhood archetypes is the Hero. This archetype usually manifests itself during adolescence. Its bipolar Shadow manifestations are the Grandstander Bully and the Coward. The Grandstander Bully in a male has characteristics of dominance and superiority that are masking a sense of insecurity. He is a loner who has a false sense of his own self-importance and ability and who feels invulnerable and unable to acknowledge his own limitations (Moore & Gillette, 1990, pp. 37–39). The Coward archetype manifests itself in males who cannot stand up for themselves and who give in to others despite feeling invaded and run-over. However, he will erupt unexpectedly in aggressive, abusive verbal and / or physical attacks on others when he becomes exasperated (Moore & Gillette, 1990, pp. 39–40).

When mobilized, the Hero archetype helps a boy make the transition from boyhood to begin facing into manhood by assisting him in making the break with the Mother and in asserting his independence and abilities.

> The Hero enables him to establish a beachhead against the overwhelming power of the unconscious (much of which is experienced as feminine, as Mother). The Hero enables the boy to begin to assert himself and define himself as distinct from all others, so that ultimately, as a distinct being, he can relate to them more fully and creatively. (Moore & Gillette, 1990, p. 40)

To be able to make this transition, the Hero in the boy must encounter his limitations and confront his own dark, unheroic side as well as encounter true humility. Two conditions characterize true humility: knowing one's limitations and getting the help one needs (Moore & Gillette, 1990, p. 41). When these conditions are met, boys will be prepared for initiation into manhood (Moore & Gillette, 1990, p. 42).

According to Moore & Gillette, the primary archetype of mature masculinity is the King. It is unique in that it embodies the archetypal energies of the Warrior, Magician, and Lover, in addition to its own essential patterns and energies (Moore & Gillette, 1992a, p. 60). Moore & Gillette viewed the King as similar to Erikson's Generative Man concept and Gilmore's manhood concept (Moore & Gillette, 1992a, p. 149). In its bipolar Shadow forms, the King is embodied as the Tyrant or as the Weakling. However, in its fullness the King manifests a four-fold pattern as The Center: Reconciler of Opposites, Transforming Vessel, Procreator, and Structurer.

As The Center, The King establishes and furthers civilization as the *axis mundi* (Eliade) symbolized by the throne from which he organizes chaos (Moore & Gillette, 1992a, p. 114). Much like the Chinese symbol of the Tao, the King, the reconciler of opposites, unites in himself as the center opposing forces of spiritual and physical, God and man, life and death, light and darkness, and good and evil (Moore & Gillette, 1992a, pp. 114–118). As Transforming Vessel, the King is the repository of enormous divine energy, so much so that it must needs be channeled and contained in order to keep from overwhelming everything around it (Moore & Gillette, 1992a, pp. 122–126). The third pattern of the King is as Procreator, a life-giver in a physical and a spiritual sense, one "that is always saying 'yes' to life, 'yes' to the new, 'yes' to creativity" (Moore & Gillette, 1992, p. 126). The King archetype blesses, admires, and holds others in high regard and willingly offers himself sacrificially for the good of the world (Moore & Gillette, 1992a, pp. 130–133). The fourth pattern of the King is as Structurer, that which brings order in the outer world as well as in the inner world of consciousness (Moore & Gillette, 1992a, pp. 133–142).

Using Erikson's Generative Man concept, Moore & Gillette described the following contemporary vision of masculinity embodying the King archetype:

> Protector, provider, procreator, a generative man is a Center for world building, an *axis mundi* around which others may rally. At his Center he is unassailable. He provides stability to his inner world, and to others who come to him looking for order in themselves. His own impulses are reconciled at his Center, and through his experience of this he helps others to do the same. As a Transformer he makes usable the creative life-force he carries within him. Others draw from him a sense of their own empowerment. He may be a Procreator in the specific sense of fathering children he cares for and teaches. Certainly he is a Procreator in the broad sense of initiating creative advance in the world he has been given to steward. And he is a Structurer, establishing calm in the midst of chaos, and facilitating order through determined action. He is committed to the preservation and the extension of a civilized, yet vigorously instinctual way of life. In these ways he incarnates the potential in the actual,

the sacred in the profane. He is an image of mature masculinity toward which we may all strive. (Moore & Gillette, 1992a, pp. 155–156)

This image of mature masculinity is encoded in human DNA as a potential ready to be embodied in men.

The Warrior, the second mature masculine archetype, has its bipolar Shadow poles embodied as the Masochist and the Sadist. As an archetypal pattern, the Warrior is "alive, vivid, crackling with energy," (Moore & Gillette, 1992b, p. 100) anticipating something about to happen and mobilizing to meet the challenge. Likewise, the archetype mobilizes an ecstatic heightening and sharpening of the senses, and it powers up one's ability to be assertive about one's life, needs, and goals (Moore & Gillette, 1992b, pp. 100–101). However, it enables boundary setting and protects one's psychological as well as physical space, while giving one the ability to trust and to share with others (Moore & Gillette, 1992b, pp. 102–104). As the archetype of controlled aggression, it enables a man to have courage to face fearsome obstacles, and it anesthetizes him to withstand tremendous suffering and pain in order to attain a goal for a higher cause (Moore & Gillette, 1992b, pp. 104–109). The Warrior archetype assists a man by helping him set goals, by providing him with self-discipline, and by energizing him to attain his goals. The Warrior archetype's capacities work in a man's mind and emotions, providing him with "greatly heightened vigilance, sharpened perceptions, and the capacity to discriminate between friend and foe" (Moore & Gillette, p. 110). The Warrior enables a man to be faithful to a "Transpersonal Other," which Moore & Gillette identify as God, or the King, but it can be anything to any other worthy cause larger and greater than oneself (Moore & Gillette, 1992b, pp. 114–115). Finally, the Warrior archetype maintains a purposeful detachment in order to protect one's self and boundaries from inappropriate encroachment, and in order to make way for renewal and growth, it can be a destroyer, "attack(ing) whatever is wounding and damaging, whatever causes despair, depression, injustice, oppression, whatever is cruel or discouraging or making demands that are abusive" (Moore & Gillette, 1992b, pp. 115–116).

Moore & Gillette concluded their discussion of the Warrior archetype with the following summary statement that highlights the relationship of the Warrior archetype to the other mature masculine archetypes:

> The Warrior serves the King. The King is the Warrior's Transpersonal Other, the focus of his loyalty, the source of his causes. The Magician gives the Warrior aid in reflecting on his commitments. The Magician enhances the clarity of the Warrior's thought processes and strategies, and provides the Warrior with inventive technologies. The Lover helps the Warrior to be humane and compassionate. In conjunction with these other archetypes the Warrior becomes an essential component of the Generative Man in his empowered wholeness (Moore & Gillette, 1992b, p. 117).

The Warrior brings controlled aggressiveness to the other archetypes and merges with them into a dynamic whole in order to complete the structure of the Self. Together, they balance and interact with each other to form an essential part of mature masculine identity.

The third archetype of the mature masculine is the Magician, and its bipolar Shadow manifestations are the Innocent One and the Detached Manipulator. The Magician is the most introverted and reflective of the masculine archetypes, urging a man into the exploration, manipulation, and communication of unseen and hidden knowledge (Moore & Gillette, 1993a, pp. 63–67). Often associated with shamans, medicine men, priests, and healers, they were the "guardian(s) of esoteric knowledge and the technician(s) of sacred power … of natural laws and psychological dynamics" (Moore & Gillette, 1993a, p. 70). The Magician archetype manifests as a knower and the technician of power. As Knower, the Magician archetype enables a man to locate and steward sacred space and time by being familiar with and adept at navigating the inner psychic worlds and by assisting others to experience them in positive and transformative ways such as initiation rites of passage and in therapeutic settings (Moore & Gillette, 1993a, pp. 105–148). The Magician archetype enables a man to balance and transcend opposites in the inner world and to contain the forces that overwhelm him (Moore & Gillette, 1993a, pp. 183–185). Therefore, the archetype permits a man to analyze and identify the core issues or problems that others cannot see, including knowing himself and his own inner dynamics. "He sees the shadow in himself and others, and faces the reality of death. At the same time he lives out of a deep inner joy, knowing that ultimately life triumphs over death" (Moore & Gillette, 1993a, p. 188). As Technician of Power, the Magician archetype is employed in the service of healing. Using psychospiritual leadership, men accessing the Magician archetype heal sick people via the initiatory scenario, initiate boys into manhood, interpret dreams, and communicate with spirits (Moore & Gillette, 1993a, pp. 191–192). In short, all of the Magician archetype's functions "can be seen to be evoking, containing, and accessing archetypal energies" (Moore & Gillette, 1993a, p. 193).

The fourth mature masculine archetype of Moore & Gillette's Great Code is the Lover, the archetypal energy of "vivid, spontaneous, and channeled Libido … feeling … relatedness and of hidden connections" (Moore & Gillette, 1993b, pp. 135–136). The Lover archetype's desire for pleasures is unlimited, unconditional, without boundaries, and manifested in a man as "the hunger for sex, for sensual experience, for procreation, and for a comprehensive sense of well-being," that awakens a man to his own feelings (Moore & Gillette, 1993b, pp. 137–138). However, this archetype demands instant gratification of pleasure that impels a man to sensual and sexual connection with the feminine (Moore & Gillette, 1993b, pp. 139–140). The Lover archetype makes a man aware of the embodiment of spirit in the world and the experience of God and provides him with a sense of meaning by means of "spiritualized *eros* and *agape*" (Moore & Gillette, 1993b, pp. 139, 143). Because this is the archetype of connection, the Lover not only becomes embodied in ecstatic cultural forms, such as art and music, but also it works to promote harmonious order within persons and within societal institutions (Moore & Gillette, 1993b, p. 144).

The Lover archetype is closely intertwined with the other three archetypes, and, in turn, needs the other three archetypes to become embodied in such a way as to be life enhancing.

> The other three mature masculine archetypes need the Lover in order to avoid falling into sterility, schizoid manifestations, or sadism. The Lover provides them, through his passionate valuing of the other, with their generativity and their reason for being. Because of his regard for the other, he keeps them from remaining immature and narcissistically self-involved. He gives the King the passion to make a world,

and provides him with the "creative" aspect of the creative ordering that is the hallmark of the ruler on the Primal Hill. The Warrior draws from the Lover motivation for aggressive pursuit of good, and for wielding his sword against the King's enemies, chaos, and death. And the Lover provides the Magician grounds for stewarding the sacred space the Lover reveals, and for aiding human beings in their quest for initiation into healed and more integrated ways of living. (Moore & Gillette, 1993b, pp. 108–109)

As the archetype of connectedness and feeling, the Lover presses the other archetypal energies toward relatedness and embodiment in a man as *eros* and *agape*, physical and self-sacrificial love.

OTHER MATURE MASCULINE ARCHETYPES

Another mature masculine archetypal energy is Phallos. In *Phallos: Sacred Image of the Masculine* (1987), Eugene Monick has written an insightful book in which he explicated the historical, psychological, and mythological aspects of Phallos, the erect penis, as a primal mark of maleness which has both an inner and an outer reality. Monick asserted that Phallos has god-like qualities that are not under his control; it is a sacred symbol of male identity and authority that "opens the door to masculine depth" (pp. 9–10). Phallos is a man's inner masculine god-image, which recapitulates resurrection repeatedly with its capacity to return to life after death.

Phallos is erection, not flaccid penis. Physical phallos has become a religious and psychological symbol because it decides on its own, independent of its owner's ego decision, when and with whom it wants to spring into action. It is thus an appropriate metaphor for the unconscious itself, and specifically the masculine mode of unconscious (Monick, p. 17).

Phallos also has religious qualities in its autonomous capacities inasmuch as a man, who, no matter how much he wishes to, cannot will phallos to obey. Like the transpersonal, phallos has a mind of its own (Monick, p. 22). Phallos is also an object of fascination, with an almost magical ability to propel one to a religious experience, which Moncick terms "phallic thrall" (p. 27).

Psychologically, Phallos is the life-task for a male, the process of becoming one's own man by separating from instinctual phallic strength to a social phallic purpose and then again to instinctual phallic responsibility (Monick, p. 6).

> The inner quality which prompts and feeds masculine development is phallos. A male knows this because of the importance to him of his masculine organ in its energized, invasive, penetrating mode. Hard phallos is a quality of youth and early manhood, the sign of heroic stance, sword raised high upon silver steed. As age descends upon a man, his hardness changes, becomes less apparent, less the signature of his body, less urgent to him concretely. Rarely do older men announce to the world their significance in ways so important to men of middle age: the building of new business, houses, marriages, alliances with women. Emergent wisdom interferes. Mellow phallos takes center stage, an aspect always present in masculinity but likely to have been dormant, overlooked, certainly undeveloped in younger, more callow males. (Monick, pp. 48–49)

Phallos is also an image of the *axis mundi*, the center around which everything revolves, possessing both masculine and feminine characteristics in a union of opposites. Phallos is the creative energy of a New Consciousness wherein there will be masculine and feminine parity and thus integrating Old Consciousness (matriarchal) and the Present Consciousness (patriarchal) (Monick, p. 77).

Mythologically, the archetypal pattern of Phallos is embodied in Hermes, the Greek messenger of the gods and conductor of the dead to Hades, after whom herms, boundary marking stone piles, were named. Possession and ownership are characteristic of Phallos (Monick, p. 78). Another Phallos figure is the Roman god, Mercurius, depicted as an androgynous, quixotic, deceptive, trickster. "The spirit in Mercurius is male instinct, spirit corked up in the male body that wants expression through phallus. Uncorked, Mercurius becomes the *one* animating principle of all created things" (Monick, p. 82). Mercurius has that ability to appear and disappear suddenly, leaving his unmistakable mark, enlivening and making a man potent, both sexually and intellectually (Monick, pp. 83–85). Another figure from Greek mythology is Dionysus, the god of the vine, associated with ecstasy and known as the suffering god, who is characterized as a bit crazy and unbalanced. He is intimately connected with femininity, causing intense feelings bordering on hysteria, and termed by Aeschylus "the womanly one" and "man-womanish" (Monick, p. 86). Dionysus is the combination of "chthonic masculine (phallos) and chthonic feminine (womb), together expressing irrationality and orgy, bound together" (Monick, p. 87). Therefore, Dionysus represents the integration and the confusion of masculine and feminine qualities in the archetypal image (Monick, p. 88). According to Monick,

> Chthonic phallos is the means by which a man moves through ego limitation to ecstatic merger with the archetypal world in sexuality. It is the numinous source of his being as a male. It is the silent god within, prompting his creative action, standing behind his erectile strength, facilitating the explosion of his fertilizing seed. Chthonic phallos is the hidden source of masculine power dark because of hiddenness, capable of catastrophic rage, but capable also of tender love and keen attention, based upon instinctual nature and need. (Monick, p. 95)

Together, these mythological figures evoke certain energies and patterns that comprise the archetype of Phallos. When properly accessed, Phallos can be a unifying archetypal pattern as part of a mature masculine identity.

ACCESSING THE ARCHETYPES

The archetypes should not be romanticized. They are impersonal and imperialistic and will control a man unless he develops an appropriate Ego-archetypal axis by differentiating himself from the archetype by becoming conscious of them. Moore & Gillette offered the following caution against too close an identification with the archetypes.

> They do not want to share the psyche and be balanced one against the other. Each wants complete hegemony. But we do not want to *be* an archetype. Maturity is getting to a place of strength where none of the archetypes can take us against our wills and possess us. We don't want to let go of any of them either. The archetypal energy we can hold

on to will be a *source* for everything we do. And because
the source is in the collective psyche, it will never run dry.
(1992a, p. 190)

A man will be possessed by an archetype unless he is aware of it and
has a healthy relationship with it. Otherwise, he will become vulnerable to the
destructive bipolar Shadow manifestations of the archetypes by manifesting
them in himself and in the world in unhealthy and potentially life-threatening
ways (Moore & Gillette, 1992a, pp. 191–192).

With this caveat having been said, it is nevertheless possible and helpful
to access the mature masculine archetypes in one's life as they provide
images of completeness and authenticity. A number of techniques can be
used to access the archetypes and to appropriate personally their patterns
and energies.

The first technique is the use of active imagination to provide an opening to the unconscious wherein the Ego can share its contents. Included
under active imagination is prayer and meditation from religious traditions
through which one seeks to get in touch with a Transpersonal Other or by
whatever name one calls God. Associated with active imagination techniques is visual imaging. Each of the archetypes has an associated, embodied
symbol. For the King, it is the scepter, for the Warrior it is the sword, for the
Magician, his wand, and for the Lover, the phallus (Moore & Gillette, 1993b,
p. 69). Imaging these archetypal forces in one's mind through meditation,
prayer, or any purposeful reverie assists in objectifying the archetypes' patterns and energies and permits the ability to establish a connection with
them (Moore & Gillette, 1992a, p. 213).

Another technique for appropriating archetypal energies is to internalize the positive images of the archetypes through art, music, literature, and
the movies. Collecting pictures, paintings, and other symbols of the archetypes and invoking the archetype while looking at these images helps to
manifest the archetypal patterns and energies within oneself. Again, the
point is for the Ego to access the archetypal energy by establishing a connection and a relation with it but not to become possessed by it. Useful
images of the King archetype include Egyptian pharaohs and Chinese
emperors on their thrones, pyramids, ziggurats, and mandalas. The Warrior
archetype can be visualized in pictures or drawings of a samurai warrior,

a medieval knight in his armor, or a General George Patton dressed in full uniform with medals. The Magician archetype finds expression in pictures or drawings of Confucius, Merlin, Black Elk, and Jung. The Lover archetype is expressed in pictures and drawings of Dionysus or any type of art that excites the senses. Music offers a vast variety of sounds that evoke various archetypal patterns and images, especially the Lover archetype with its appreciative consciousness (Moore & Gillette, 1993b, p. 193). Drumming and other highly rhythmic sounds evoke the Magician archetype (Moore & Gillette, 1993a, p. 185). Reading biographies about men who particularly embody one of the archetypal energies is also useful. Movies provide striking visual and auditory images of the action of the archetypal patterns as they are played out. Examples of literature and movies are too numerous to list.

A third technique for accessing archetypal energies is through bonding with and modeling other men who themselves are further along the road of masculine maturity. Bonding with other men reinforces male identity against regression and promotes social goals and protection (Moore & Gillette, 1992a, p. 233). According to Gilmore (1990) and Tacey (1997), manhood is socially constructed as much as it is brain and genetically endowed, and the company of other men helps a man not only to become a man but also to develop into full masculine maturity. Despite the imperfections that all humans possess, admiring and emulating men who embody positive aspects of masculine maturity aids in accessing and embodying these mature masculine patterns and energies in oneself.

A fourth technique of appropriating the archetypal energies is through purposeful action. The more one acts "as if" one embodies the archetypal pattern, the more self-fulfilling and empowered with the archetype one will become (Moore & Gillette, 1990, pp. 154–155). It is a matter of getting in character with the energy. By practicing calmness and reaching out to empower others, the King archetype becomes accessed. Taking up the discipline of martial arts or some athletic training regimen helps to empower the Warrior. Acting as if you have something wise and insightful to say to someone asking for help will activate the Magician. Dining and playing can access the Lover's energy and pattern.

IMPLICATIONS FOR EDUCATING LATE-ADOLESCENT BOYS

Modern industrial cultures suffer from a dearth of positive, life-enhancing masculine images and models. At their worst, manhood ideals are depicted as destructive, manipulative, and narcissistic—hardly anything worth emulation by young men. Consequently, exploring and accessing the positive archetypal patterns and energies of the deep masculine is the preferred and optimal route toward authentic, mature masculine embodiment. Rather than slavishly adhering to the current dysfunctional and destructive cultural scripts, accessing the mature masculine archetypes offers late-adolescent young men the freedom to develop genuine, innate predispositions in order to become the fullest possible manifestations of mature masculinity.

A gender studies curriculum for late-adolescent boys needs to incorporate a component on the mature masculine archetypes in order to assist young men in identifying these archetypal patterns when they are embodied in themselves and in others. The inclusion of the mature masculine archetypes is an absolutely necessary corrective measure to counter the defective cultural male images available to adolescent boys for emulation. When these mature masculine patterns are recognized, it is possible for young men to access and integrate these archetypal patterns and energies appropriately into their lives. By doing so, young men's lives can be enhanced and fulfilled.

Knowing and accessing the archetypes can be personally empowering to young men and can lead to enhanced communication, self-understanding, self-actualization, and a sense of fulfillment. The renowned mythologist, Joseph Campbell, characterized the journey of life as one of finding and following "your deepest harmony and bliss" (Thompson, p. 24). When inner archetypal life and outer living are integrated, and one is living an authentic life, harmony and bliss can be realized. As Jean Shinoda Bolen (1989) wrote,

> Bliss and joy come in moments of living our highest truth—moments when what we do is consistent with our archetypal depths. It's when we are most authentic and trusting, and feel that whatever we are doing, which can be quite

ordinary, is nonetheless sacred. This is when we sense that we are part of something divine that is in us and is everywhere. (Bolen, p. 287)

The danger is in the failure to live authentically and to succumb to living via the debilitating collective scripts of the contemporary culture. This concept was put another way when Jesus asked the following question, "What does it profit a man to gain the whole world, and forfeit his soul?" (Mark 8:36 KJV)

CHAPTER EIGHT

ENCOUNTERING THE FEMININE: SEXUALITY AND RELATIONSHIPS

Love is the answer, but while you're waiting for the answer,
sex raises some pretty interesting questions.

Woody Allen

The war between the sexes is the only one in which both sides
regularly sleep with the enemy.

Quentin Crisp (1908–1999)

In 1992, author and family therapist John Gray burst on the pop self-help scene with his best-selling book *Men Are from Mars, Women Are from Venus: A Practical Guide for Improving Communication and Getting What You Want in Your Relationships* (1992), and in the past thirteen years he has sold more than 30 million spin-off books about relationships between men and women. Gray's thesis stated that men and women have different communication styles that affect their relationships with the opposite sex. He asserts that male intimacy cycles and female self-esteem fluctuations are at the heart of these differences. He urged men and women to accept the other sex's unique ways of expressing love and provided numerous strategies for helping couples meet each other's emotional needs.

Gray's books are so popular that they seem to have tapped into an unmet need in the public zeitgeist concerning problematic relations between the genders (Buzzard, Karen S. Falling. 2002, pp. 89+). While hugely popular, Gray's books are not without critics. Peterson (2000) critiqued Gray's books as offering a gender ideology that polarizes the sexes and highlights the differences between the genders by "tell(ing) men and women what actions to perform in order to generate the polarized sexes / genders and (hetero)sexuality that are supposedly 'natural' and 'original' (Peterson, Valerie. 2000, pp. 1+). Gray's "two sexes, two cultures" concept divides men and women into separate "discourse communities and describes them as cross-cultural" (Peterson, p. 1).

The predisposition in Western culture to distinguish gender as a binary of opposites is what is at issue here in Gray's works because of his presentation of male-female differences as subject-object binary. Cowlishaw (2001) characterized the subject-object male-female binary in the following way:

> Not only does the binary provide each side of the dichotomy with an already-determined attitude toward the other, it also produces a sense of "coupledom" because the two positions, subject (the knower, the observer, the actor) and object (the known, the observed, the acted upon), are mutually dependent. Each position defines the other... . In the Mars and Venus books, the "nature" of male "needs, preferences, and patterns of behavior" are those of the subject position--though Gray presents them as characteristics of men. Likewise, Gray's presentation of the "nature" of females is a description of the "needs, preferences, and behavior patterns" of the object position. Of course, there is no denying that men have tended to take / have access to / have thrust upon them the subject position, and that women have similar compunctions upon them to take the object position. Gray never denies this--but his assertion that adherence to these positions is the "natural" path to happiness for men and women does imply an essentialist assumption. (Cowlishaw, pp. 169+)

Other stereotypes are conveyed in Gray's treatment of sexuality, such as portraying men as naturally active and possessing an expertise in sexual matters versus the female, who is depicted as an inexperienced, submissive partner (Potts, 1998). Furthermore, according to Potts' critique, Gray demonstrated preferential treatment for intercourse over other forms of sexual activity as well as a partiality for heterosexual intercourse as a means of self-completion (Potts, p. 154).

This short critique of John Gray's *Men Are from Mars, Women Are from Venus* illustrates the high energy and controversy surrounding the subject of sexuality and relations between the sexes. That such argumentation can take place over such a fundamental matter frequently perplexes men and frustrates women. Additionally, it does not help things that the various gender schools of thought entrench themselves in their positions and leave little room for dialogue and mutual understanding. However, to try to articulate and understand these points of view is important in order to provide a balanced and holistic perspective on how males encounter females and are, in turn, encountered in relationships and in sexuality.

What makes the task even harder is that the traditional models of male / female gender understanding and discourse have undergone tremendous change in the past fifteen years with androgyny emerging as a model of gender flexibility and adaptability that permits both masculine and feminine traits in a person (Strong et al., p. 138). Moreover, in recent years, the transgendered community has strongly advocated for the acceptance of "numerous genders and multiple social identities" (Strong, p. 148). According to Bolin (1997), the "complexity of gender offers serious challenges to scientific paradigms that conflate sex and gender" (Quoted in Strong, p. 148). Gender identity is a complex combination of biological and psychological factors. From the biological standpoint, masculinity and femininity are derived from the body's anatomical and genetic makeup. From the psychological standpoint, one is male or female based on gender assignation and gender identity (Strong, p. 149). Only occasionally do chromosomal or hormonal disorders make gender identity a problem (Strong, pp. 149–150). Nevertheless, it may be helpful to visualize gender as a continuum with numerous possible gender-variant combinations.

THE PSYCHOANALYTIC VIEW

Sigmund Freud asserted that infants were born with a sexual drive or instinct very similar to hunger (From Freud, "Three Essays on the Theory of Sexuality," 1925, pp. 240, 259 from Gay, Peter, Editor, 1989, *The Freud Reader*). The earliest stages of sexuality in infants are directed at the infant's own body, which Freud calls "auto-erotic," and "some pleasure which has already been experienced," such as sucking at the mother's breast (Freud, 1925, p. 263). Hence, sexual expression in infancy is connected to self-preservation functions such as procuring nourishment from the mother's breast. It is not until later that sexuality will become associated with human objects.

Freud maintained that children are polymorphously perverse because they can "be led into all possible kinds of sexual irregularities" (Freud, 1925, p. 268) through seduction or based on the pleasure principle. On the other hand, children progress through stages in which each stage has a focus on a particular erotogenic part of the body. The oral stage's erotogenic zone is the mouth. During the anal stage, the erotogenic zone is the anus. The genital phase of development has as its focus the genitals. The goal of sexual development is the "normal sexual life of an adult in which the pursuit of pleasure comes under the sway of the reproduction function and in which the component instincts, under the primacy of a single erotogenic zone, form a firm organization directed towards a sexual aim attached to some extraneous sexual object" (Freud, 1925, p. 272).

Because the final goal of sexual development is fraught with potential difficulties and fixations, a pleasurable act might become an end in itself, with the result that genital sexuality is only one possible outcome. Freud himself acknowledged the existence of varying degrees of bisexuality in males and females (Freud, 1925, p. 244) as well as sexual inversion in "men whose sexual object is a man and not a woman, and women whose sexual object is a woman and not a man" (Freud, 1925, pp. 240–241). Thus, there are many possible expressions of sexuality that can manifest in humans, much of which Freud noted was not neurotic (Freud, pp. 23–24).

Freud's Oedipus complex is the cornerstone of his theory of sexuality in which the child resolves his psychosexual relationship with his parents. The Oedipus complex is the process whereby a young child must overcome his desire to possess his mother sexually and to remove his father from the parent-child triadic relationship. The dissolution of the Oedipus complex occurs differently for boys than for girls.

> ... the boy's object-cathexis of his mother must be given up. Its place may be filled by one of two things: either an identification with his mother or an intensification of his identification with his father.... . In this way the dissolution of the Oedipus complex would consolidate the masculinity in a boy's character. In a precisely analogous way, the outcome of the Oedipus attitude in a little girl may be an intensification of her identification with her mother (or the setting up of such an identification for the first time)—a result which will fix the child's feminine character. (from *The Freud Reader. The Ego and the Id*, 1923, p. 640)

Freud called the Oedipus complex "the nuclear complex of the neuroses, and constitutes the essential part of their content" (1925, p. 290n).

> It represents the peak of infantile sexuality, which, through its after-effects, exercises a decisive influence on the sexuality of adults. Every new arrival on this planet is faced by the task of mastering the Oedipus complex; anyone who fails to do so falls a victim to neurosis. (Freud, 1925, p. 290n)

According to Freud, the pleasure principle is a central component of the sexual instinct. It is operative in the child's mental structures and processes from the beginning of life (Freud, Civilization and Its Discontents, 1929, p. 729). In his "An Autobiographical Study" (1925), Freud avowed, "Sexuality is divorced from its too close connection with the genitals and is regarded as a more comprehensive bodily function, having pleasure as its goals and only secondarily coming to serve the ends of reproduction" (1925, p. 23). The pleasure principle, separated from its linkage with the reproductive function, then, makes homosexuality an outgrowth of normal human bisexuality.

> Looked at from the psycho-analytic standpoint, even the most eccentric and repellent perversions are explicable as manifestations of component instincts of sexuality which

have freed themselves from the primacy of the genitals and
are now in pursuit of pleasure on their own account as they
were in the very early days of the libido's development. The
most important of these perversions, homosexuality, scarcely
deserves the name. It can be traced back to the constitutional bisexuality of all human beings and to the after-
effects of the phallic primacy. Psycho-analysis enables us to
point to some trace or other of a homosexual object-choice
in everyone. (Freud, 1925, pp. 24–25)

Despite these assertions, Freud finally concluded, "Anatomy is Destiny,"
(from *The Freud Reader*. The Dissolution of the Oedipus Complex, 1924,
p. 665); therefore, males and females tend to synchronize their anatomical makeup with their masculine or feminine sexuality. As a result, Freud
would be considered more of a biological determinist among the various
theories of sexuality because his views were consistent with the prevailing
view of the times that normal sexual relations were between a man and
a woman (Harding, 2001, p. 6).

Later psychoanalysts, such as Giddens (1992), referred to "plastic sexuality," indicating that definitions and practices of what is normal and what
is abnormal or perverse are changing. According to them,

The 'biological justification' for heterosexuality as 'normal,'
it might be argued, has fallen apart. What used to be called
perversions are merely ways in which sexuality can legiti-
mately be expressed and self-identity defined. Recognition
of diverse sexual proclivities corresponds to acceptance of
a plurality of possible life-styles ... 'normal sexuality' is simply one type of life-style among others. (Giddens, p. 179)

Giddens calls for a radical pluralism in which varieties of sexual expression are
possible and considered within the range of normal (Giddens, p. 179).

The Social Constructionist View

The social constructionist viewpoint starts by affirming that males are more
than their biological and anatomical makeup; they are primarily the construct of their interaction with a culture (Seidman, 2003, p. 45). Male and
female sexuality is the product of the conscious and unconscious cultural

gender scripts that define and mold sexuality and gender expression as well as the particular accommodations individuals make to those scripts (Kimmel and Messner, p. xv). Consequently, the sexuality experiences of men and women are not culturally or historically universal. Instead, they are profoundly variable and uniquely based on individual experience and other factors such as class, ethnicity, race, age, and sexual orientation (Kimmel and Messner, pp. xv-xvi). Lorber (1994) summarized the social construction of sexuality in the following way:

> Social constructionists argue that cultures and societies orga-
> nize sexual practices into approved, permitted, and tabooed
> patterns that are internalized by individuals and that the
> meanings of sexual behavior vary greatly over time and
> place. In this view, ideas about sexuality have a history,
> structure, and politics that affect any individual's develop-
> ing sexual desires and behavior. In the social constructionist
> view, ... sexualities are multiple, not unitary, and not physi-
> ologically or psychologically fixed for life; all are socially
> shaped. Approved practices are actively encouraged; permitted
> practices are tolerated; and tabooed patterns are stigmatized
> and often punis hed. Heterosexuality is as much a product of
> learning, social pressures, and cultural values as homosexu-
> ality. All sexual desires, practices, and identities not only are
> gendered but reflect a culture's views of nature, the purpose of
> life and procreation, good and evil, pleasure and pain; the
> discourses about them are permeated with power. (p. 56)

While the hegemonic sexual practice is genital and orgasmic sex, there is a great variety of sexual arousal and satisfaction that is based on differing sexual scripts for men and women, depending on whether they are hetero-sexual, homosexual, bisexual, transsexual, or transvestite (Lorber, p. 58).

Depending on labeling and categorization, in Western societies multiple sexual expressions exist that, according to Lorber, prove Freud's assigna-tion that human beings are polymorphously perverse.

> In Western societies we could say that, on the basis on *geni-*
> *talia,* there are *five* sexes: unambiguously male, unambigu-
> ously female, hermaphrodite, transsexual female-to-male,
> and transsexual male-to-female; on the basis of *object choice,*

> there are *three sexual orientations*: heterosexual, homosexual, and bisexual (all with transvestic, sadomasochistic, and fetishistic variations); on the basis of *appearance*, there are *five gender displays*: feminine, masculine, ambiguous, cross-dressed as a man, and cross-dressed as a woman (or perhaps only three); on the basis of *emotional bonds*, there are *six types of relationships*: intimate friendship, nonerotic love (between parents and children, siblings and other kin, and long-time friends), eroticized love, passion, lust, and sexual violence; on the basis of *relevant group affiliation*, there are *ten self-identifications*: straight woman, straight man, lesbian woman, gay man, bisexual woman, bisexual man, transvestite woman, transvestite man, transsexual woman, transsexual man (perhaps fourteen, if transvestites and transsexuals additionally identify as lesbian or gay)... . Sexual practices are even more varied. One can have sexual relations with men, women, both, one at a time or in groups, with oneself, or with no one (celibacy); one can erotically cross-dress or have sexual relations with cross-dressers; one can have sadomasochistic sex; one can have sex with animals, use fetish objects, pornography, sexual devices, and so on and on. (Lorber, p. 59)

Sexual identity and behavior have varied and undergone changes throughout history according to the economic and social norms of the societies in which they exist. Sexual practice also depends upon the politics of permissibility, depending on what is tolerated and what is punished at the time, especially as it relates adolescent males and females where "sexual politics establish the boundaries between conformity and deviance, and warn of the dire consequences of whatever practices are considered immoral or unsafe" (Lorber, p. 64). While current sexual practice in Western societies permits both men and women to engage in pleasurable sexual practices, including those that are experimental and short-term, the norm is that it should be "heterosexual, genital, orgasmic, and ideally, emotionally expressive" (Lorber, p. 68).

Sex norms differ for males and for females in Western society. Boys and girls grow up in homosocial worlds, but when they reach adolescence they are expected to form loving relations and sexual attachments with the opposite sex. What makes this problematic is that males are not permitted to display open affection for members of the same sex or a rejection of male friendships for other women. On the other hand, females moderate their emotional engagement with other women while they seek a long-term relation with a man. Moreover, women are expected to relate romantically to men first and sexually later, while males are supposed to be primarily sexual conquerors with numerous experiences and only secondarily have an emotional relation to one woman (Lorber, p. 69).

Further complicating the relations between males and females is what Rubin (2004) termed the approach-avoidance dance. From the time they were children and had to break away from their primary emotional connection to mother in order to bond with the father, men have been socialized to be autonomous from women. With that severance came the separation of emotion from thought with thought assigned to males and emotionality to females (Rubin, p. 386). In intimate relations between men and women, there is a "rational-man-hysterical-woman script" that gets played out (Rubin, p. 387). Rubin describes this script in the following way:

> All requests for such intimacy are difficult for a man, but they become especially complex and troublesome in relations with women. It's another of those paradoxes. For, to the degree that it's possible for him to be emotionally open with anyone, it is with a woman—a tribute to the power of the childhood experience with mother. Yet it's that same early experience and his need to repress it that causes his ambivalence and generates his resistance.
>
> He moves close, wanting to share some part of himself with her, trying to do so, perhaps even yearning to experience again the bliss of the infant's connection with a woman. She responds, woman style—wanting to touch him just a little more deeply, to know what he's thinking, feeling, fearing, wanting. And the fear closes in—the fear of finding himself again in the grip of a powerful woman, of allowing her admittance only to be betrayed and abandoned once again, of being overwhelmed by denied desires. So he withdraws. (p. 387)

Consequently, the modern heterosexual relationship has built into it a dilemma: the woman wants to talk about love while the man wants to make love (Lorber, p. 70).

Provoking even more questions and posing ever more problematic issues are the issues of those who are intersexed, who manifest ambiguous combinations of male and female anatomy, which are usually the result of prenatal chromosomal or hormonal imbalances. Hermaphrodites, males or females who have the anatomical sex characteristics of both sexes, comprise approximately 10% of all children born with ambiguous genitalia (Strong, p. 139). Another classification is the pseudohermaphrodites, those who are biologically male or female but with ambiguous-appearing genitalia at birth. Two chromosomal disorders are Turner Syndrome, a condition in which females are born missing an X chromosome, have nonfunctioning or absent ovaries and underdeveloped genitals, and present no breast development, and Klinefelter Syndrome, a condition in which males are born with one or more extra X chromosomes resulting in small testes and some additional weak female physical characteristics such as breast and hip development (Strong, pp. 140–141). Hormonal disorders cause males and females to develop physical qualities of the opposite sex. Androgen-Insensitivity Syndrome, also called testicular feminization, is a genetically inherited condition in which males are born with testes, but the body is unable to absorb testosterone; therefore, the body develops a female appearance while the testes remain inside the body, causing sterility (Strong, p. 144). Congenital Adrenal Hyperplasia is a condition in which a genetic female with ovaries and a vagina develops externally into a male because of a malfunctioning adrenal gland. Dihydrotestosterone (DHT) deficiency occurs in males when the body cannot convert the DHT hormone causing the male to have undescended testes until puberty and a clitoris-like penis, which at puberty the testes descend and a penis matures from the clitoris. Hypospadias is a malformation of the penis in males in which the opening in the penis is on the underside rather than the tip and the penis is small. Both abnormalities can be corrected surgically (Strong, pp. 144–145).

Another sexual identity issue is transsexuality, also known as gender dysphoria. People with this condition have normal genitalia but who identify with the other sex and feel trapped in the body of the wrong sex.

Consequently, they want to change their gender. Because the condition is a gender identity issue, it is very different from homosexuality. Usually, transsexuals seek surgery to align their genitals with their gender identity (Strong, p. 146).

The transgender phenomenon poses numerous challenges to traditional notions of sexuality. Increasingly, sexuality is being conceived as a continuum with many possible variations rather than simply as a dichotomy of male and female. Renfro, himself a transgenderist describes his identity and summarizes the position of the social constructionists when he writes,

> My identity, like everything else in my life, is a journey. It is a process and an adventure that in some way brings me back to myself, back into the grand circle of living.... My sense of who I am at any given time is somewhere on that wheel and the place that I occupy there can change depending on the season and life events as well as a number of other influences. Trying to envision masculine at one end of a line and feminine on the other, with the rest of us somewhere on that line, is a difficult concept for me to grasp. Male and female—they're so close to each other, they sit next to each other on that wheel. They are not at opposite ends as far as I can tell. In fact, they are so close that they're sometimes not distinguishable. (quoted in Strong, p. 149 from Feinberg, L., 1996, *Transgender Warriors: Making History from Joan of Arc to Rupaul*)

Lorber was more strident in her summary of the sex-gender issue when she said, "It is Western culture's preoccupation with genitalia as the markers of both sexuality and gender and the concept of these social statuses as fixed for life that produces the problem and the surgical solution for those who cannot tolerate the personal ambiguities Western cultures deny" (1994, p. 86).

THE ESSENTIALIST VIEW

The essentialist view of human sexuality and relations is represented in the fields of sociobiology and evolutionary psychology. The former emerged in the 1970s with E. O. Wilson, whose book, *Sociobiology: The New Synthesis* (1975), demonstrated how Darwinian selection was the basis on which animal and human species compete and cooperate. His book and the field of scientific inquiry it spawned are hugely controversial. A related field of inquiry is evolutionary psychology, a process that seeks to explain human behavior by using the insights gleaned from the fields of evolutionary biology, anthropology, cognitive science, and neuroscience. Evolutionary psychology proffers explanations for human behaviors based on universal problem-solving mechanisms that humans created in adapting to their evolutionary environments, and especially the passing of one's genes into future generations of offspring. Buss (2003) summarized this position by asserting that human beings are fashioned selfishly for "individual survival and genetic reproduction" (p. 152).

Dawkins (1989) was one of the first to argue that humans and other living beings are ruthlessly selfish genetic replicator machines that exist to transport their genes into the next generation. He points out that males and females are distinguished by the size and quantity of their sex cells with male gametes being smaller and more numerous than female gametes, which contribute large quantities of food supplies compared to the male sperm cells, which are only interested in infusing their genetic material into the egg as expeditiously as possible (Dawkins, p. 142). Over evolutionary time, the result is the development of two conflicting mating strategies: males pursue a short-term mating strategy of promiscuous mating with as many females as possible in order to transmit their genetic material through the sperm into as many females as possible (Dawkins, pp. 163–164), while females invest in long-term mating strategies by being more selective in their choice of mating partners and by selecting mates who will demonstrate a long-term commitment to the offspring (Dawkins, p. 164).

Human beings, then, are products of natural selection who possess valuable exploitable resources, through which "women are vehicles that can carry (a man's) genes into the next generation," and "men are sources of a vital substance that can turn eggs into embryos" (Ridley, p. 175). Accordingly, human beings have evolved a mating system characterized as "monogamy plagued by adultery" (Ridley, p. 176), "moderate polygamy," or "serial monogamy" (Miller, p. 195) with males generally acting as seducers and females as the seduced, and men being the aggressors and women the flirters (Ridley, p. 178). Miller (2000) echoed this conclusion when he said,

> Male humans generally invest more time, energy, and risk in sexual courtship, invest less in parenting, are more willing to copulate earlier in relationships with larger numbers of partners, and are less choosy about their sexual partners, at least in the short term. Female humans generally invest less in courtship and much more in parenting, are less willing to copulate early with large numbers of partners, and are more choosy. (p. 88)

All of these factors are predicated on the fact that there is a gender asymmetry in the size of the male's sperm and the female's eggs (Ridley, p. 179).

Despite the predisposition toward monogamy, women do resort to cuckoldry, which when coupled with concealed ovulation, makes infidelity highly asymmetrical. Women lose little when their husbands are unfaithful, but husbands may unknowingly raise another man's genetic offspring (Ridley, p. 237). Hence, men are deeply disturbed by a mate's infidelity, and jealousy is universal in human culture (Ridley, p. 235). In fact, according to Buss (2003), sexual jealousy is an evolved psychological mechanism to combat infidelity, producing either vigilance or violence (Buss, pp. 10–11). Accordingly, from the earliest hunter-gatherer societies the male rule has been to amass power and wealth in order to attract females who will birth his heirs. He wrote, "Wealth and power are means to women; women are means to genetic eternity" (Ridley, p. 244). On the other hand, the female hunter-gatherer rule has not changed either: "strive to acquire a provider husband who will invest food and care in your children; strive to find a lover who can give those children first-class genes" (Ridley, p. 244).

Evolutionary psychology is the latest scientific discipline to trumpet the theme that human behavior is the result of a series of biological adaptations through sexual selection (Miller, pp. 5–8). Miller asserts that sexual selection through mate choice is a powerful, creative, and direct form of evolutionary social selection and behavior (2000, pp. 13–38). Moreover, Miller contended that the human brain evolved by means of sexual selection through mate choice as a way of advertising fitness indicators, those physical and mental qualities that predict good genes to prospective mates (p. 111).

Evolutionary psychology holds the view that human propensities for music, humor, creative intelligence, and complex language are the results of sexually selected fitness indicators. "Sexual selection made our brains wasteful, if not wasted: it transformed a small, efficient ape-style brain into a huge, energy-hungry handicap spewing out luxury behaviors like conversation, music and art" (Miller, p. 134). According to Miller, sexual choice also influences the senses; therefore, the human brain evolved a propensity for pleasure and entertainment and for emphasizing "the role of sensation, perception, cognition, and emotion in sexual choice" (p. 158).

According to evolutionary psychology, fitness indicators guide sexual choice and are present across almost all cultures. Buss (2003) found that females universally prefer males with economic resources and high social status, those who are older than themselves, and those who display ambition and industriousness, emotional stability and dependability, intelligence, compatibility, physical size and strength, good health, love, and commitment (pp. 22–45). Females seek these qualities in men because the females have rich but fewer reproductive resources at hand and because the time and cost of gestating, caring for, and feeding offspring is borne by them almost exclusively (Buss, p. 19).

On the other hand, males evolved psychological mechanisms to detect a woman's reproductive value in order to maximize the future success of their genetic offspring in the next generation. Buss (2003), in a thirty-seven society cross-cultural study, identified two key male preferences in potential mates: youth and physical beauty (Buss, pp. 51–55). As a fitness indicator of reproductive value, males on average prefer their mates to be 2.5 years younger. Physical beauty is another universal fitness indicator for reproductive capacity with features such as "full lips, clear skin, smooth skin, clear eyes, lustrous hair, and good muscle tone, and features of behavior, such as a bouncy, youthful gait, facial expression, and a high energy level" (Buss, p. 53). Body shape is another evolved preference, with waist-to-hip ratio for women ranging from 0.67 to 0.80. The lower the ratio, the more attractive the female is to the male. Furthermore, bodily symmetry and sexual ornaments, such as the penis, the clitoris, breasts, and buttocks, are important fitness indicators, which Miller contended are the results of male and female choice (pp. 229–248). In conclusion, men universally desire beautiful, young, sexually faithful women who will remain with them until they die.

Regarding homosexuality, the essentialist school is hard-pressed to offer an adequate theory because of its predisposition toward a binary view of human sexuality, in which homosexuality would be eliminated through sexual selection (Buss, 2003, pp. 250–251; Miller, p. 217). This viewpoint recognized that only between two and four percent of the male population and an even smaller percentage of one to two percent of females have a primary orientation toward homosexuality and lesbianism (Buss, 2003, p. 251). Some researchers argue for the existence of a gay gene or "a series of genes that affect the sensitivity of certain tissues to testosterone" (Ridley, p. 265). One evolutionary theory for homosexuality is the kin altruism theory, which purports that homosexual genes can exist and pass on to the next generation by virtue of the fact that possessors of the gene invest heavily in their brothers' and sisters' genetic offspring. Another explanation offered is alliance formation theory by which homoerotic pleasure-seeking behavior evolved to enhance same-sex alliance formation. A third theory for homosexuality is the nice guy theory, in which homosexuality "is a relatively rare by-product of genes designed for another function—the production of 'feminine' traits such as empathy, sensitivity, tender-mindedness, and kindness" (Buss, 2003, p. 253). Unfortunately, these theories suffer from conceptual and empirical problems and leave this aspect of human sexuality a mystery (Buss, 2003, p. 251), while others say homosexuality is both nature and nurture (Ridley, p. 265).

Although male and female sexual strategies differ greatly and are cause for much conflict and tension, Buss noted the following formula for long-term cooperation between the sexes:

> Fulfilling each other's evolved desires is the key to harmony between a man and a woman. A woman's happiness increases when the man brings more economic resources to the union and shows kindness, affection, and commitment. A man's happiness increases when the woman is more physically attractive than he is, and when she shows kindness, affection, and commitment. Those who fulfill each other's desires have more fulfilling relationships. Our evolved desires, in short, provide the essential ingredients for solving the mystery of harmony between the sexes. (2003, p. 221)

However, male wealth and female beauty are not the only fitness indicators. Evolutionary psychology stresses a myriad of other criteria that humans have evolved to exhibit reproductive fitness, such as "through storytelling, poetry, art, music, sports, dance, humor, kindness, leadership (and) philosophical theorizing" (Miller, p. 429). Sociobiology, ethnology, and evolutionary psychology begin with the genes and progress through sexual mating strategy and end with social, cognitive, and sexual behaviors. Humans are alive now thanks to the unbroken chain of successful sexual relations because our genes had to pass into the next generation by means of sexual choice. Buss summed up this point of view very well when he said, "As individuals, mating permeates much of what we do. As a species, it defines who we are" (p. 286).

IMPLICATIONS FOR EDUCATING LATE ADOLESCENT BOYS

Given the divergent points of view raised in this chapter on sexuality, it is evident that no one point of view provides an exhaustive and comprehensive picture of masculine sexuality. Rather, each approach offers a valid and insightful perspective on human sexuality, and like a multi-faceted diamond, sexuality has many dimensions and aspects that shape masculine identity and sexual expression.

Rather than splintering into competing and intolerant ideologies, a synthetic view that can accommodate different perspectives is needed. Sexuality is a complex mix of genetic, psychological, and social components; therefore, attention needs to be given to the interaction of these components in the makeup of each person's sexual identity and expression. The findings of evolutionary biology and psychology point out that human beings are predisposed to certain behaviors and physical appearances because of genes, but this predisposition is not mere genetic determinism that means humans can act only in mindlessly predetermined ways. Genes predispose humans toward a certain physical makeup and behavior, but they do not lock human sexual expression and identity into closed systems of relating. Classical Freudian psychology asserts that there are complex interactive dynamics at work in individuals who are shaped by their unique personalities and histories in order to form their individual psychological makeup.

Therefore, genetic predispositions are molded by dynamic psychological forces to shape human sexual expression. Furthermore, social constructionist view highlights the complexity of cultural and societal influences and history that mold human behaviors and identities. Human sexual expression is not merely atomistic in nature; it is also the result of dynamic social forces at work shaping sexual identity and expression.

As we tease out the multitude of ways in which these three viewpoints interrelate and influence each other in humans, a rich and complex diversity of sexual identity and expression emerges. A single, monolithic view of sexual identity and expression no longer exists, if it ever did in the first place. Instead, there is plasticity to human sexual nature that is hardwired in the genes and shaped dynamically by complex psychological and social forces that are unique to each individual. Adolescent boys are in the throes of discovery of their sexual nature and identity by virtue of their development. It is vitally important that a curriculum addressing the sexuality of adolescent boys helps them to become aware of the rich and dynamic forces at work in themselves and in their world that shape their sexuality.

CHAPTER NINE

MATTERS OF HEALTH AND SPIRITUALITY

There is a silent health crisis in America ... it's (the) fact that, on average, American men live sicker and die younger than American women.

Dr. David Germillion
Men's Health Network

According to the Centers for Disease Control in Atlanta, men currently die on average six years before women compared to 1920 when men died on average only one year earlier than women ("Men's Health Facts" Website). It is no wonder when one looks at the big picture of men's health statistics: men die from the top 10 causes of death at higher rates than women, including four times more likely to die from suicide ("Men's Health Facts" Website). African American men are even more at risk than white men from dying earlier from homicide and they have a lower life expectancy in general ("Men's Health Facts" Website).

No wonder, men have the label of being the "weaker sex." Consider the following facts:

- 115 males are conceived for every 100 females.
- The male fetus is at greater risk of miscarriage and stillbirth.
- 25% more newborn males die than females.
- 3/5 of Sudden Infant Death Syndrome victims are boys.
- Men suffer hearing loss at two times the rate of women.
- Testosterone is linked to elevations of low-density lipoprotein, the bad cholesterol, and declines in high-density lipoprotein, the good cholesterol.
- Men have fewer infection-fighting T-cells and are thought to have weaker immune systems than women.
- By the age of 100, women outnumber men eight to one. (New York Times Magazine, March 16, 2003)

The disturbing facts highlight the health crisis in men. While there are distinct hormonal and physical factors that determine men's health, how they are socialized and conditioned through societal and cultural adaptation influences males to disregard their health.

MASCULINE GENDER ROLE STRESS SYNDROME

Eisler (1995) described the connection between male stress arousal and resulting health problems through his masculine gender role stress paradigm, which consists of five propositions. Sociocultural messages reward male attitudes and behaviors while punishing non-masculine (i.e. feminine) attitudes, resulting in instilling masculine gender role stereotypes in males. Therefore, little boys learn to attack aggressively rather than to cry when hurt because crying is perceived as feminine and not masculine. The result is that men use learned gender stereotypes to evaluate incoming threats and challenges and to guide their coping responses. "Masculine schema are lenses that shape men's appraisals of threat along the lines of traditional masculine gender ideology and also guide the selection of a response from a restricted repertoire of masculine coping behaviors" (Eisler, 1995, p. 213).

Hence, men typically display aggression when challenged rather than conciliatory responses. However, men display important differences in the degree of personal commitment to culturally accepted masculinity models, based on individual temperament, psychological makeup, and cultural experience. Consequently, gender role stress may result based on an individual's "excessive commitment to and reliance on certain culturally approved masculine schema that limit the range of coping strategies employable in any particular situation" (Eisler, 1995, p. 213). Therefore, some men experience stress when they lose in a competitive game while others cope with loss more easily, consoling themselves that they played well despite the loss. Finally, males experience masculine gender role stress when they perceive that they are not living up to culturally mandated masculine role expectations, "experiencing fear or by feeling that they did not appear successful or tough enough in situations requiring masculine appearances of strength and invincibility" (Eisler, 1995, p. 213).

A major approach to understanding the relation between health and masculinity is to examine the components of the masculine gender role that create stress and dysfunction for men. One measurement instrument used for this purpose is the Masculine Gender Role Stress Scale (MGRS) comprised of five indices assessing physical inadequacy, emotional inexpressiveness, subordination of women, intellectual inferiority, and performance failure (See also Thompson & Pleck, 1995, p. 152 and Eisler, 1995, p. 217). Two gender-role conflict instruments, GRCS-I and GRCS-II, developed by O'Neil, Helms, Gable, David, and Wrightsman (1986) (see also Thompson & Pleck, 1995, pp. 150–152) also assess men's thoughts and feelings about and the degree of conflict they experience in certain situations such as "(a) success, power, and competition, (b) restrictive emotionality, (c) restrictive affectionate behavior between men, and (d) conflicts between work and family relations" (Helgeson, 1995, p. 70). Research findings indicate fear of femininity as negative motivators for men's thoughts and behaviors (Helgeson, p. 70). A third set of scales, called the Masculine Ideology Scale (MRAS), which measures traditional male gender role attitudes, was developed by Pleck, Sonenstein, and Ku (1993) (Thompson & Pleck, 1995, pp. 145–146).

Generally, studies using these instruments indicate that traditional masculine gender roles result in higher stress and anxiety and lower psychological well being (Eisler et al., 1988; O'Neil et al., 1986). Furthermore, men highly identified with traditional male gender roles are more depressed (Good & Wood, 1995), have problems with interpersonal intimacy (Fischer & Good, 1997), are prone to cardiovascular reactivity (Watkins, Eisler, Carpenter, Schechtman & Fischer, 1991), and use fewer mental health services (Good, Dell & Mintz, 1989).

HOW MODERN CULTURE TEACHES MALES TO HANDLE PAIN

The notion of masculinity ideologies presumes that males are infused with societal expectations about masculinity by means of cultural messages, with health and illness as dynamic products of "cultural values and practices, social conditions, and human emotion and perception" (Sabo & Gordon, 1995, p. 3). One of the first messages boys learn is to be tough by denying any emotions of vulnerability and by adapting a stoic attitude; however, the result is a number of dysfunctional health consequences, such as the resort to substance abuse (Doyle, 1996) and suicide (US Bureau of the Census, 1997). Another cultural message is that males must be competitive and successful, frequently resulting in Type A behaviors including: "extreme aggressiveness, easily aroused hostility, sense of time urgency, and competitive achievement striving... . It is also characterized by an intense focus on central rather than peripheral information" (Hegelson, pp. 74–75). Consequently, men have a decreased awareness of health symptoms such as fatigue and precursory signs of a heart attack. (Hegelson, p. 75). Additionally, a number of related chronic health problems, such as anger and high blood pressure, are associated with masculine gender role stress (Eisler, 1995, pp. 207–225). Therefore, males must be aggressive, fearless, and invulnerable, prompting extreme and highly risky behaviors such as speeding in motorized vehicles. In fact, the principal cause of premature death in males under age 35 is motor vehicle accidents (US Bureau of the Census, 1997). Male invulnerability is expressed in the reluctance of males to seek heath care maintenance and prevention resources such as testicular cancer screening ("Men's Health," 1998). The cultural message that males must be independent contributes to male reluctance to seek medical services based on their emotional discomfort because such behavior implies dependence, vulnerability, and unmanliness (Komiya, Good and Sherrod, 1999). Sexual expression in males can be problematic because of cultural messages that males should not express emotional connectivity, resulting in multiple sexual partners with little communication and caring expressed, thereby increasing the risk of contracting sexually transmitted diseases (Brooks, 1995; Good & Sherrod, 1997).

There is a statistical fact that males die on average six years before females. A number of theories have been offered to account for this fact, including biological factors involving genes and hormones, as well as psychosocial factors that identify male ideology socialization in gender development. Masculine gender ideologies emphasize emotional inhibition through cultural messages such as "Big boys don't cry," requirements for independence and self-sufficiency through cultural messages like "Handle it yourself," and, most importantly, do not act feminine through cultural messages like "Don't be a sissy" (Stillion, p. 56). Coupled with the emphasis on competitive sports in American culture, boys are taught from grade school onward to suffer physical pain and deprivation in order to "play on the team" and "to be a man" (White, Young and McTeer, 1995, pp. 159–160). In order to attain these goals, males resort to a multitude of strategies for dealing with pain in order to avoid appearing weak and unmanly, namely by denying or hiding pain to the point of suffering disabling injuries (White, Young and McTeer, 1995, pp. 168–172). Together, these cultural messages become a self-fulfilling prophecy for young boys who develop into men. Consequently, they adopt an aggressive and often violent approach to living, which, in turn, compromises their health and contributes to premature death among them.

REVISIONING THE MALE BODY

In order to change the facts of life about destructive masculine lifestyles and mortality rates, it will be necessary to confront the cultural context and messages that teach males about masculinity, including challenging the widely accepted myths that shape the way males think and behave. The advertising world with the messages this segment of the culture constructs to appeal to men's insecurities as well as their unexamined assumptions about masculinity in order to sell their products must also be confronted.

Garbarino (1999) made the connection between superficial materialism and spiritual emptiness, when he wrote,

> The materialism of American culture does little to sustain children in times of crisis. Leather running shoes, jewelry, and designer clothes are not enough. The inherent weakness of superficial materialism may not be apparent when things are going well. But during challenging times the spiritual emptiness of shallow materialism is exposed for what it is, and crisis ensues. Violent boys who turn to robbery to feed their addiction to materialism load up their lives with fancy clothes, expensive shoes, cars, and jewelry. But it doesn't work. They are still in deep emotional trouble, and trauma intensifies this crisis. (p. 157)

A broader, healthier conception of masculinity needs to emerge to replace the traditional, narrow masculine gender ideology images and conceptions of aggressiveness, risk-taking, independence, stoicism, and emotional isolationism. These masculine gender ideology traits often result in greater dysfunctionality, poorer health, and shorter life expectancy in men. More complete, healthier masculine images are emerging, such as that of the "Green Man" (Blazina, 1997) as well as those articulated by Tacey in which masculine identity and imaging is caught up in *ecospirituality* (Tacey, 1997, 2004). By reconnecting with nature and natural processes as an "undivided whole," men can find a healing and wholeness in themselves and in their bodies (Tacey, 2004, p. 187).

In the future males need more support and education about the health issues they confront. Health education for males needs to be expanded and perhaps rearticulated in order to be more attractive to men seeking information and help. For instance, Eisler (2000) stated that the word "care" in "health care" has feminine connotations to men, so he recommends other associative phrases, such as "enhance optimal functioning" (Robertson & Fitzgerald, 1992) and "maximizing performance" (McGrath, 1998).

TOWARD A MASCULINE SPIRITUALITY

David Tacey (1997, 2004) is a Jungian academic who proposed a radical reformulation of masculinity as a means of addressing men's pain. Much of what is manifested as male disease and physical pain in our materialist Western culture is really a spiritual disconnection from feminine spirit, a profound lack of wholeness and disease:

> If men do not change, we will be wounded, handicapped, or maimed by the soul. Jung said that 'the Gods have become diseases,' not because they are diseases, but because in our materialist culture they have no way to express themselves other than as agents of pathology and as 'irritants' of change... . Gloria Steinem has said that men must overcome their fear of the feminine... . The feminine soul will, and often does, attack the feeling heart of a man... . Men sometimes have to suffer a nervous breakdown, unbearable stress, chronic fatigue, a broken marriage, the first heart attack, or a debilitating disease before they think about 'reconstructing' their lives. (Tacey, 1997, p. 195)

The reconstructing that Tacey calls for is a reunification of the feminine principle with the masculine that results in wholeness and creativity. Garbarino used the term "androgyny," and characterized it as adaptive and resilient, stating that "the more successfully people incorporate both traditionally masculine and traditionally feminine attributes, the more likely they are to master the situations they face" (Garbarino, p. 169). The return of the soul facilitates in men a new consciousness of their bodies, with a resulting awareness of their needs for healthy living and self-maintenance. The soul fosters an inner connectivity in order to produce insight, which can serve as a guide to inner and outer healing (Tacey, 1997, p. 90). The dysfunctionalities and diseases from which males suffer is a spiritual problem in which the absence of feminine spirit inhibits soul, which, in turn, prevents males from having a healthy and life-enhancing relation with their psyches, their bodies, or their world. Heroic patriarchal masculinity isolates and alienates males from themselves and others and deprives them of the very life-enhancing resources needed for health and wholeness. The consequence of the loss of the soul is summed up powerfully by Tacey who wrote, "When spirit is absent, there is no heart or soul in anything we do, because nothing connects our small human tasks and tribulations with a larger, redemptive vision" (1997, p. 127).

What is needed is a more inclusive universal spirituality that embraces wholeness. Such spirituality embraces "a new awareness of living in an enchanted spiritual universe" (Tacey, 2004, pp. 180–181) rather than being dominated by materialistic constructs that deconstruct, objectify, and devalue human life and nature. The old dualisms of subject / object, mind / body, mind / spirit, nature / God, and self / others that have been nurtured in materialistic Western culture will collapse and be redefined in a holistic cosmos where ultimate reality is mystically understood. "The world is full of God, Creation is Godful, because it is, and God makes it be (and) though God is eternal, perfect and transcendent above all, he is utterly and wonderfully *within* every part of his Creation" (bold and italics are the author's) (Zuck, John. "Biblical Panentheism: *The 'Everywhere-ness' of God—God in all things* Website).

When spirituality that envisions the divine indwelling in nature invites a sacred view of the cosmos, nature then becomes a place of healing, a place where humans can find renewal, restoration, and strength in body, mind, and spirit. Moreover, nature becomes a place of revelation where truths can be discovered and discerned in order to make life and our own individual lives meaningful and purposeful. To view nature as a source of life and as life nurturing is to recapture the ancient image of nature as Gaia, Mother Earth, "the feminine face of the divine" (Tacey, 2004, p. 182).

A spirituality that envisions the divine indwelling in everything also has a sacred view of humanity. God is not only out there, wholly unapproachable, but also he is within in our own human hearts. The concept of divine immanence has a deep connection to Christian mysticism (Fox, Matthew. "Some Thoughts on Thomas Berry's Contributions to the Western Spiritual Tradition" Website) and to the spiritual traditions of the other world's religions (Zuck, "Biblical Panentheism: *The 'Everywhere-ness' of God—God in all things* Website). All persons, in this view, participate in divinity and share in the original blessing. In his book *Original Blessing* (2000 Edition), Matthew Fox summarized original blessing in the following manner:

> *Goodness* is the natural state of the world. The world is *good!* Even when it seems evil, it's good. There's only goodness in God. And that same goodness is in us all. You can feel it in yourself. You know when you feel good

inside. Yes, you're God's child, too. You are *good!* Respect
yourself. Love the goodness in yourself. *Then put that goodness out into the world.* That's everybody's instructions.
Meister Eckhart goes to the heart of original blessing in
describing the *ancilla animae*, or spark of the soul, that is
in each of us. He writes that hidden in all of us is "something
like the original out break of all goodness, something like a
burning fire which burns incessantly. The fire is nothing
other than the Holy Spirit. (p. 5)

By recovering this kind of mindset about human nature and by educating young men with the notion of their original goodness, a new masculine spirituality could become the means of healing and liberation for
today's young men who are desperately in need of positive connections and
relations to themselves and to others, not isolation and negativity which is
characteristic of so much contemporary masculine ideology and pathology.
By reaffirming goodness in masculine spirituality, there is hope that males
can recover their health and wholeness as persons.

MEN AND COMMUNITAS

The anthropologist, Victor Turner, described "communitas" as the formation
of a communal bonding between equals during a state of liminality, a period
in ritual process experienced as betwixt and between (Turner, 1969, p. 95).
During a liminal period, according to Turner, people experience "the liberation of human capacities of cognition, affect, volition, creativity, etc., from
the normative constraints incumbent upon occupying a sequence of social
statuses" (Turner, 1982, p. 44). In other words, liminality has the capacity
to create personal and societal change and can become the crucible for
creativity and liberation that enhances transformation at the personal and
societal level. The betwixt and between time is a time when old structures
die and new, life-enhancing paradigms can emerge.

Communitas is the paradigm that must emerge out of a fractured patriarchal
order that has become dysfunctional and death dealing for males. The much-
needed emergent universal spirituality emphasizing androgyny and the sacred-
ness of all persons and things reinforces male connectedness, wholeness, and
community. "To allow all people to see that they are 'chosen people,' and to

show that the sky under which they live, labor, and love is a sacred canopy, ennobling their actions by a divine presence" (Tacey, 2004, p. 198). Males need to experience themselves in a transformational way, not as pre-determined traditional masculine ideology scripts but as whole, complete beings, connected in a sacred world and by nature intrinsically good. Communitas mediates that experience of belonging and joy that males experience when authentic self-acceptance and affirmation are found. When males can view themselves and each other in this way true health and healing can occur.

IMPLICATIONS FOR EDUCATING LATE ADOLESCENT BOYS

The statistics on male violence, health, and mortality tell a sad tale about males in Western culture and bear witness that the traditional masculine gender role ideologies are lethal to males. Clearly, the time has come for a revisioning of masculinity and a shift toward new paradigms that will embody guidance, support, and spirituality for males as healthy lifestyles and attitudes emerge from transformed images of what it means to be a man.

The task of a curriculum assisting late adolescent boys in making the transition into adulthood is to sensitize them about the masculine gender scripts that mold their lives. As emergent adult men, adolescent males need to understand the negative impact of these unexamined scripts on their lifestyles and choices, which result in greater dysfunctionality, poorer health, and shorter life expectancy. Moreover, males need a greater awareness of men's health issues and to be educated about healthy attitudes and lifestyles. However, at the heart of men's health is a healthy spirituality that brings balance and perspective to their lives. Such spirituality will be inclusive and open to the connections within by uniting masculine and feminine aspects of men's inner lives with the Great Mother / Heavenly Father aspects of the Godhead and by creating an enchanted spiritual universe where the natural order and human persons are viewed as sacred and good.

CHAPTER TEN

MATTERS OF MASCULINE DIVERSITY

Masculinity is not monolithic, not one static thing, but the confluence of multiple processes and relationships with variable results for differing-individuals, groups, institutions, and societies.

(Judith Gardiner, 2002)

We come to know what it means to be a man in our culture by setting our definitions in opposition to a set of "others"—racial minorities, sexual minorities, and, above all, women.

(Kimmel, 1994)

THE SOCIAL CONSTRUCTION OF MASCULINITY

A little over a decade ago, references about masculinity assumed that there was a single, monochrome definition that applied to all men regardless of race, ethnicity, or sexual orientation. Essentialism asserted that there were only two binary gender roles, masculine and feminine. This view mandated that all men should exhibit masculine behavior, and all women should perform feminine behavior.

On the other hand, the new social research that emerged in the 1990s clearly revealed that there was no one universal pattern of masculinity. Ethnological studies show that significant differences exist in the practice of masculinity between dominant forms and marginalized forms of masculinity, such as in homosexuality, in some cultures where homosexuality is a regular practice of masculinity, but in other cultures, it is not accepted as part of masculinity (Connell, 2000, p. 10). Recent ethnological studies emphasize the fact that multiple masculinities exist in different societies (Connell, 2000, pp. 8–9; Connell, 2003).

Responding to the challenges leveled by feminist writers about the construction of masculinity as it related to women, the profeminist men's movement articulated a second wave of new men's studies that viewed hegemonic patriarchy and masculinity as problematic while asserting masculinity as an essential component of gender studies (Brod and Kaufman, 1994). The new men's studies asserted that there were important differences among men and variances between masculinities. Since then, class and sexuality have received significant attention while the concern has been raised that men of color have not received appropriate attention (Awkward, 1998; Mirande, 1997). In order to achieve a comprehensive understanding of men, it is necessary to become sensitized to the diverse expressions of masculinities and their relations to hegemonic masculinity and women.

Connell (1995) articulated two pivotal concepts for understanding masculinities. The first is that masculinity is a patriarchal power structure exercised over women by subordinating women. Patriarchy subordinates women by controlling production relations by means of the gendered division of labor (Connell, 1995, pp. 74–75). The second is that masculinity uses the symbolism of difference as a way of differentiating masculinity by opposing femininity (Connell, 2000, p. 26). Hence, the symbolism of difference is employed to feminize non-hegemonic men, who are then labeled "other" (Paechter, p. 8). Men of color and other men who do not participate in hegemonic masculinity are consequently consigned to the category of other.

Connell distinguished four typologies of relations between masculinities. Hegemonic masculinity is the "configuration of gender practice that embodies the currently accepted answer to the problem of the legitimacy of patriarchy.

It guarantees (or is taken to guarantee) the dominant position of men and the subordination of women" that is achieved by means of a "correspondence between cultural ideal and institutional power" (Connell, 1995, p. 77). Hegemonic masculinity assumes many qualities that have been discussed elsewhere in this study, including those of aggressiveness, domination, competitiveness, stoicism, and control. Furthermore, a male must constantly validate his masculinity by proving himself over others, including women and other non-hegemonic men (Connell, 1995, pp. 83–84). Therefore, dominant masculinity is characterized by homophobia, whereby men fear other men as a defensive reaction to emasculation. Consequently, men project homophobic fear on "those deemed less than fully manly: women, gay men, nonnative-born men, men of color" (Kimmel, 1994, p. 135).

The second typology is Subordination, acknowledging the existence of "specific gender relations of dominance and subordination between groups of men" (Connell, 1995, p. 78). Noting the primary importance of sexuality, Connell stated, "The most important case in contemporary European / American society is the dominance of heterosexual men and the subordination of homosexual men" (Connell, 1995, p. 78). This subordination takes many forms, including political and cultural exclusion, legal and street violence, and economic discrimination, all of which relegate homosexual men to the bottom of the gender hierarchy (Connell, 1995, p. 78). Additionally, gayness can be easily equated with femininity, resulting in homophobic reactions. Homosexual men are not the only victims of subordination; some heterosexual men and boys who exhibit feminine attributes are also the object of hegemonic scorn and attack.

Connell's third typology is Complicity, in which he includes those "masculinities constructed in ways that realize the patriarchal dividend, without the tensions or risks of being the frontline troops of patriarchy" (Connell, 1995, p. 79). By patriarchal dividend Connell is referring to the economic and power benefits men generally accrue by virtue of the pattern of the subordination of women in general (Connell, 1995, p. 79). Hence, the patriarchal dividend mandates that men generally make more money than women, have higher and more powerful positions than women in corporations, and have more access to and hold positions of power in government and other centers of influence.

The final typology is Marginalized Masculinities, which differentiated from subordinated masculinities by virtue of the fact that marginalized masculinities exist outside of the "relations internal to the gender order" (Connell, 1995, p. 80). Marginalization occurs in the relations between masculinities of different classes or racial groups. Connell's work, as well as the work of Hearn (1996) and Mac an Ghaill (1996), posited an image of masculinity as a varied and varying complex of constructs and attitudes underlying men's social relations and not as an essential set of characteristics shared by all men. The diversity of masculinities results in conflicts among and between groups of men because the hegemonic group must account for its dominance, namely, that difference is inferior. According to Messner (1997), "Although it may be true that men, as a group, enjoy institutional privileges at the expense of women, as a group men share very unequally in the fruits of these privileges" (p. 7). Conformity to hegemony determines generally if a person belongs to a dominant or marginalized group because hegemonic masculinity cannot tolerate difference and perceives difference as a threat. Thus, hegemonic masculinity renders marginalized masculinities invisible and impotent by depriving them of status and power.

Connell's gender relations approach illuminates the different structures of gender and how they relate to each other by enhancing the understanding that there are many different ways of expressing gender. These varieties and variations of gendered practice are located in individual bodies that are shaped by society and culture. According to Connell, "Such body-reflexive practices are not internal to the individual. They involve social relations and symbolism; they may well involve large-scale social institutions. Through body-reflexive practices, more than individual lives are formed: a social world is formed" (2000, p. 26). At the macro level, gendered bodies act in relation to other gendered bodies in a process of shaping and creating gender. Therefore, locating and understanding the gender construction projects of other masculinities is vitally important. By doing so, insight into our own masculinity projects will emerge.

HOMOSEXUAL MASCULINITIES

One caveat must be asserted at the beginning of any discussion of a category of masculinity: there is no one monolithic category of homosexual masculinity.

Rather, there are numerous homosexual masculinities because homosexuality is not homogeneous (Connell, 1995, p. 160; Kurtz, 1999). There are subcultures and variations of homosexual masculinities based on the individual gender projects of these men's lives (Nardi, Peter, 2000, p. 7).

Despite the complexity of negotiations individuals must make in the multiple arenas of life that shape their identities, Connell proposes a model for analyzing homosexual masculinities. It consists of "(a) an engagement with hegemonic masculinity, (b) a closure of sexuality around relationships with men, (c) participation in the collective practices of a gay community" (Connell, 1995, p. 160). Together, these become defining moments in "the making of a homosexual masculinity as a historically realized configuration of practice" (Connell, 1995, p. 160).

To begin, it must be noted that the term homosexual originated in the late nineteenth century by German psychologist, Karoly Maria Benkert, who used it to denote life-long male-male sexual bonding (Greenberg, p. 409). The Western conception of homosexuality is a concept unique from other cultures that practiced male-male sexual relations as a temporary phase, such as that practiced by the New Guinea tribes as an initiation rite of passage (Greenberg, 1988, p. 32) or in age-based relationships, such as that practiced in ancient Greece (Greenberg, p. 147). In the Qing Dynasty in China, several male emperors had male harems as well as practiced male prostitution, but there was no distinct word for homosexuality because it was not viewed as an integral characteristic of a person's identity. According to Nick Yee, "Male-male sexual and romantic bonds were construed as relationships between two people as opposed to a psychological essence that defined either person. Moreover, these same-sex bonds were seen as a perfectly acceptable and natural way of life in Imperial China" (www.nickyee.com / ponder / social_construction.html).

In ancient Greece, there were no words for heterosexual and homosexual, for it was permissible for men to have passionate feelings for both men and women (Mondimore, 1996, p. 10). Same sex relations were routinely practiced with the primary distinction being between the one who took an active and insertive role and the one who assumed the passive and penetrated role. In Greek culture, only inferiors, such as women, slaves, and young boys who had not attained citizenship, known as the *eromenos* or *paidika,* assumed the passive and penetrated role. The Greeks held up the cultural ideal of a same-sex relation that was between an older man, probably in his 20s or 30s, known as the *erastes*, and a boy whose beard had not yet begun to grow. The relation was expected to be a temporary one, ending when the boy became an adult. The Greeks viewed the passive role as problematic, but to be attracted to other men was affirmed as a sign of masculinity (Greenberg, 1988, pp. 147–151).

Judaism, Christianity, and Islam had strong scriptural prohibitions against the practice of sexual sin. Judaism labeled sexual offenders as abominations who were to be cut off and killed (Leviticus 18:21, 20:13). Early Christian teaching, including passages from the New Testament and the early patristic writers, roundly condemned homosexuality and called for dire consequences for those who engaged in homosexual behavior (Greenberg, p. 233). Islamic *hadith* mandated the stoning to death of sodomites, although it seems that homosexuality and pederasty have been widely accepted in Arab society (Greenberg, pp. 177–178).

Intolerance toward homosexual practice reached its height during the latter 12th through 14th centuries as same sex practice was perceived as sodomy, a crime against nature (Greenberg, p. 276). Sodomites were defined by the acts they committed rather than as being the essence of a person (Greenberg, p. 278). Sodomy received severe penalties, such as being burned at the stake, but those who repented and changed their ways were granted reprieves.

The 18th and 19th centuries witnessed the decline of theological viewpoints and the emergence of secular and medical viewpoints, such as psychology, that articulated same sex acts as innately caused rather than voluntarily chosen. The tireless and unceasing efforts of Karl Heinrich Ulrichs (1825–1895) espoused a then revolutionary idea that sexual orientation was inborn and therefore natural (Mondimore, pp. 27–28). Consequently, the modern notion of homosexuality as an innate biological characteristic emerged (Greenberg, p. 404). However, homosexuality was widely considered as a defective or pathological expression of sexuality (Greenberg, p. 413). Widely referred to at the time as degeneracy theory, Krafft-Ebing used this theory to establish the scientific basis for the characterization of gay stereotypes for the next one hundred years (Mondimore, pp. 37–38).

The 20th century witnessed a radical redefinition of homosexuality as sexuality for the sake of pleasure became less stigmatized, and the sexual revolution of the 1960s inaugurated a diversity of open sexual expression (Greenberg, p. 457). The turning point for the gay liberation movement took place on June 27, 1969, with the Stonewall Inn riots in New York City, when homosexual men reacted violently to a police raid on a gay bar. This event has been affirmed as a rallying point for the gay movement because homosexual men began to organize nationally, calling for a reassessment of human sexuality and its place in society (Greenberg, p. 458). The result was gays began to form organized groups in major cities and on many college campuses. A new sense of identity was affirmed as individuals bonded together in unity. The AIDS epidemic makes problematic the future of homosexuality, as it has given rise to a new antihomosexual attitude while at the same time decimating large populations of homosexual persons. A deeper sense of unity in the gay population has arisen despite serving as a catalyst for gay bashing and discrimination (Greenberg, pp. 478–480). From this brief historical overview, it is evident that homosexuality has been variously defined and responded to throughout history based on the dominant hegemonic view at the time. Persons who engaged in these actions routinely found themselves subordinated, marginalized, and discriminated against despite the relative acceptance of homosexuality as a minor part of the sexual cultural landscape.

Moving from the historical to the individual, the social constructionist view of homosexual identity is that it evolves slowly in a person's awareness over time rather than an innate essence within a person. In his book, *Gay and Lesbian Identity: A Sociological Analysis* (1988), Richard Troiden used data generated from first-hand accounts of homosexuals themselves to posit a four-stage age-graded paradigm of homosexual identity development. According to Troiden, the first stage is the Sensitization Stage occurring between the ages of six and twelve where there is a sense of feeling different from one's peers. This feeling of difference is termed marginalization by sociologists. Troiden called children in this stage prehomosexual because they have no concept of homosexuality, and they assume that they will grow up to be heterosexual to assume dominant roles as parents. Along with a sense of difference, children during this stage become sensitized to labeling, such as *gay, queer,* and *faggot,* and to attitudes of contempt and disgust from peers. This antihomosexual bias lies dormant in a child's psyche for many years before emerging and inflicting damage in a person's adolescence or adulthood.

The second stage is Identity Confusion, which occurs during adolescence when there is a focus on a person's sexuality. At this point in development, a youth may experience conflict between his childhood identity and his emerging sense of self, thereby feeling excluded from others. Troiden identified four coping strategies employed to deal with the stress: denial, avoidance, repair, and acceptance. In denial a person maintains a denial of homosexual feelings and attractions; in avoidance, a person is cognizant of homosexual feelings but avoids confronting them; in repair, a person seeks to remediate his homosexuality by becoming heterosexual; and in acceptance, a person chooses to recognize, affirm, and validate his homosexual orientation. In addition to the other developmental tasks that take place in the critical adolescent phase, it must be stressed that all this conflict transpires and frequently causes disruptions in peer relations from teasing and harassment, both of which further marginalize and subordinate an adolescent in this stage of life development. Some consequences that result include, among other things, a restriction of emotions, a diminution of social contacts, formation of a false identity, a halting of intimacy skill development, and a predilection to perfectionism and caretaking of others rather than self.

The third identified developmental stage is termed Identity Assumption, which occurs between ages 19–21 and results in a refocusing of a person's social relations with other gay men. The primary challenge for young men at this point is to handle the social stigma of a new homosexual identity. Troiden identified the following four coping skills used to address this task: capitualization, minstralization, passing, and group alignment. Capitualization happens when a person succumbs to the negative sentiments expressed about homosexuality while acknowledging his homosexual identity. Minstralization is when a person portrays stereotypic and frequently exaggerated forms of homosexual behavior. Passing involves a person concealing his homosexuality publicly while privately acknowledging it to a limited group of associates, and group alignment is when a person immerses himself in a gay community to the exclusion of other heterosexual contexts. Frequently, a person's experience of "coming out" is fraught with negativity and isolation. AIDS is now a complicating factor in this process as well.

The fourth stage is the Commitment Stage, occurring between the ages of 21–24, during which the now young adult integrates his homosexuality into his lifestyle and sense of self and manifests it in his romantic and life choices. The issues of "coming out" are now resolved, and the young man becomes capable of self-identifying as a homosexual in his public identity, resulting in an increased degree of self-satisfaction and happiness (Troiden, 1988).

A fundamental experience of most homosexuals in their identity formation is that of stigmatization, the process of negative labeling with the purpose of characterizing a group of persons as unusual or morally degenerate. Stigmatization takes place at a number of different levels in homosexual experience. Despite positive gains for homosexuals, many states still consider private same-sex activity criminal. Additionally, certain occupations, such as the military, are denied to openly gay persons. Some homosexuals face a number of external risks, such as expulsion from their homes, beatings from classmates, job loss, and being passed over for promotions. Additionally, internalized stigmatization causes emotional hurt from expectation of rejection by friends and acquaintances and the loss of mainstream opportunities for sanctioned relations, such as marriage and parenthood, although this situation is currently changing. Overall, from a social perspective, homosexuality continues to be viewed as undesirable by many cultures, and many gay men experience negative consequences of shame and embarrassment for being self-identified as homosexual (Linneman, 2000, pp. 85–87). Stigmatization is the product of internalized homophobia, the fear of being perceived as unmanly, thereby propelling men to deny other men their manhood and causing men to engage constantly in the construction of their male identity out of fear of being misperceived as a homosexual. Fear and defensiveness about being labeled homosexual is *ipso facto,* a demonstration of a heterosexist and homophobic society (Linneman, p. 75).

There is much that homosexual men experience in common: a heritage of antipathy and homophobia toward their sexual orientation in general as well as a personal experience of marginalization and stigmatization toward their self-identifications as a homosexual person. However, it has been stressed from the outset that there is no one homogeneous experience of homosexuality; instead, there are subcultures and unique ways men construct and "do" their sexuality depending on a number of sociological variables: race, class, ethnicity, culture, religion, socio-economic status, and age. Each subgroup gender project must encounter and construct its masculinity in opposition to the hegemonic definition of masculinity, which Kimmel defined as "a man in power, a man with power, and a man of power ... [a man who is] strong, successful, capable, reliable, and in control" (1994, p. 125). Therefore, for example, Latino-American gays construct their sexuality against the backdrop of Roman Catholic Christianity with its strong prohibitions against homosexuality. Research statistics show that many gay men abandon their faith rather than deal with the complexities and ambiguities of affirming a gay identity and a strong Christian faith. "For most gay ... men, coming out in church has meant coming out of the church. The church has meant more than just a closet, the church has become for them a giant tomb smelling of death rather than life" (Rodriquez and Ouellette, 1999, p. 102). These men describe the distinctive demands and opportunities and the discordance and coherence that each aspect of being gay, male, Latino, and Christian presents in their construction of masculine identity (Rodriguez and Ouellette, p. 126). Recent social constructionist scholarship challenges the perpetuation of male and female stereotypes of "machismo / marianismo" sex-roles, in which women are characterized as submissive, maternal, and virginal while men are characterized as verbally and physically aggressive, frequently drunk, and sexually dominant (Cantu, 2000, pp. 227–228). Some scholars maintain that macho constructions of masculinity are expressions of inferiority vis-à-vis the dominant culture, yet others assert that this conception is deterministic and perpetuates a static view of Latino culture (Cantu, p. 228). Within this cultural context, sexual identity is defined not by biological sex but by the culturally prescribed roles of *activo / passivo* (dominant / submissive) assumed by the participants in which the "passive is defined and devalued as feminine, and the 'active' is defined as the dominant sexual script" (Cantu, pp. 228–229). However, these categories seem to be transforming because of U.S. migration and changing gender roles into a third category called *internacionales* (internationals) (Cantu, p. 229).

It is almost an oxymoron to refer to working class gay males because of the stereotypes surrounding working-class males. This group of males is largely defined by their socio-economic status and the Archie Bunker stereotype, prompting images of guys who work in close quarters with each other, talking about sports, women, and other physical activities and being largely devoid of emotional awareness. Moreover, this group stereotypically holds strong traditional views about male dominance-female submissiveness, and they are generally considered homophobic. Consequently, a working class homosexual does face difficulties balancing and managing his emotional and sexual needs against working class culture and acceptance of his homosexuality by members of the working-class. Furthermore, working class homosexuals are likely to find it problematic to meet their emotional and attachment needs in a cultural milieu that minimizes intimacy and emotional expression. Barrett (2000) summarized well the challenges facing working class gays when he wrote

> Negotiating a working-class masculinity, combined with such a masculinity's effects on social and sexual relations, could have positive and negative consequences for the working-class gay male. Although he may find his enactment of working-class masculinity a characteristic that is attractive to other gay males, class differences between himself and the more visible gay community might result in problems integrating with the more visible community. Second, to the extent he holds the cultural norms of working-class masculinity, he is likely to have trouble accepting his own homosexuality. Third, the components of the cultural norms around working-class masculinity (e.g., emotional detachment) work against maintaining supportive social and emotional relations with other gay men. Adding to these consequences is the fact that his nongay social relationships (including family and work) would be expected to be unaccepting of his homosexuality and thus potential sources of stress. Thus, the working-class gay male would be expected to be exposed not only to the broad, culture-wide stigma normally associated with homosexuality but also to the stigma of class. (pp. 177–178)

Therefore, working class gay writers allude to the sense of loneliness and isolation they experience from their cohort group as well as within their own personal relations (Barrett, p. 179).

The preponderance of the research data bears witness to the fact that homosexuality is a natural, normal sexuality for some, despite the challenges and obstacles homosexuals face as a subordinate minority in a hegemonically heterosexual, masculine society. According to Ward (2000), the social constructionist scholarship on masculinity stresses that "gay men and men of color neither share equally in the rewards of patriarchy nor experience and display masculinity in the same way as white, heterosexual men" (p. 152). This tie binds both diverse groups together.

MASCULINITIES OF COLOR

To conduct an analysis of men of color without stressing the role and influence of history in these men's lives is impossible. In essence, their history illustrates their role in relation to the dominant culture as the other and as socially marginalized by patriarchal institutions (Bucholtz, 1999; Dines, 1998). Nevertheless, men of color suffer a double bind because of their gender caused by their inability to attain dominant masculine roles (Bucholtz, 1999). Hooks, a leading African American social critic, characterized this Gordian knot of contradictory messages by saying, "Imperialist white-supremacist patriarchy is an integrated system of domination that will never fully empower black men" because "at the center of the way black male selfhood is constructed ... is the image of the brute—untamed, uncivilized, unthinking, and unfeeling" (2004, pp. xii-xiii).

From the outset, enslaved African men were indoctrinated to accept the notion of the patriarchal ideal of protecting and providing for their women and families (Hooks, p. 4; Bush, 1999, p. 49). Sadly, however, the legacy of slavery and white supremacist culture meant the destruction of African American men's dreams to meet these patriarchal ideals through the systematic elimination of any and all means of exercising personal control and leadership by resorting to methods of isolation, beatings, ridicule, and even killing (Bush, p. 49). As a means of survival, many African American males adopted a "go along to get along" pose as a means of avoiding white-supremacist reactions. According to Greer and Cobbs (1968), the effect is that many African American men have constructed a passive, nonassertive, and nonaggressive demeanor. "He has made a virtue of identification with the aggressor, and he has adopted an ingratiating and compliant manner" (Quoted in Hooks, p. 42). White-supremacist patriarchal culture utilizes a number of negative stereotypes of African American males in order to maintain control and to justify the mistreatment of African Americans according to hegemonic masculinist ideology standards.

During slavery, the African man was stereotypically labeled "sambo," a docile, childlike male who was unable to assert himself in the family and who, consequently, needed someone to rule over him (Marchioro, Kathleen. Website: www.siue.edu/SOCIOLOGY/journal/marchioro.htm). During Emancipation and Reconstruction, other negative stereotypic images were placed on African American men, such as the "Buck," a sexual metaphor for a black rapist as a symbol of "the personification of the black threat to white womanhood and, more importantly, to white male dominance" (Wallace, 1996, Quoted in Marchioro). Another image assigned to African American males was the "Brute," a violent, out-of-control beast, which racist white-supremacist ideology used as a mechanism of control and as a means to justify mob actions and lynchings (Marchioro, 2001). According to Hooks,

> Writing about this historical legacy in *Rituals of Blood*, Orlando Patterson states: "In all these stereotypes we find the idea of the slave as a dishonorable brute whose maniacal desires must be kept in check by the master's discipline, and whose word can be accepted only under torture.... Seeing the victim as the aggressor and as the 'white man's burden' is a classic instance of projection: at once a denial of one's own moral perversity and violence and a perfect excuse for them. The demonization of the Afro-American male in American society is still very much with us." Yet what makes contemporary demonization of the black male different from that of the past is that many black males, no longer challenge this dehumanizing stereotype, instead they claim it as a mark of distinction, as the edge they have over white males. (p. 48)

The "gangsta" persona that many young African American males assume perpetuates the negative racist / sexist stereotype that affirms "all black men are carriers of the violence we dread" (Hooks, p. 56). In fact, the statistics affirm that there is more African American male violence than ever before, and that most of this violence is "toward another black person whom they deem less powerful" (Hooks, p. 56). Dines (1998) argued that "both images serve to define Black men as outside the realm of (white) masculinity by constructing them as the "Other" (p. 291).

A critical but little-spoken of dynamic inherent in African American child-raising practice is that of "signifying," the parental practice of shaming a young boy's emotions by means of name calling, labeling, judgments, and sadistic teachings. Much of this shaming practice focuses around the sexual where boys are forbidden to express their pain because they must endure these rites of initiation in order to become men (Hooks, pp. 80–81). Parents feel this kind of training of young black males is essential to make boys tough, but this crushing of the male spirit in boyhood is better termed "soul murder" (Hooks, p. 87). African American boys face a double jeopardy striving to meet the demands of a patriarchal society that teaches them to be unfeeling and passive while at the same time forcing them to bear up under the crushing legacy of "a psychohistory that represents black males as castrated, ineffectual, irresponsible, and not real men" (Hooks, p. 88). Hooks continued by saying,

> It is as if black parents, cross-class, believe they can write the wrongs of history by imposing onto black boys a more brutal indoctrination into patriarchal thinking. Young black males ... learn early that manhood is synonymous with the domination and control over others, that simply by being male they are in a position of authority that gives them the right to assert their will over others, to use coercion and / or violence to gain and maintain power. Black boys who do not want to be dominant are subjected to forms of psychological terrorism as a mean of forcing them to embody patriarchal thinking. Shaming and rituals of disregard, of constant humiliation, are the tactics deployed to break the boy's spirit. (p. 88)

Hooks proceeded to identify a number of coping mechanisms that African American boys adopt to hide their shame, such as seeking to excel in sports. He wrote, "Acting out the patriarchal paradigm as competitive performers, black boys who excel at sports are able to shield themselves from the shaming and scorn directed at the boy who expresses his creativity in academic or artistic pursuits" (Hooks, pp. 94–95). Another coping strategy to keep the pain away and to control their rage is substance abuse and a culture of victimization.

> Excessive focus on the ways racism wounds male spirits is often evoked to deflect attention away from all other sources of emotional pain. That deflection is disempowering because it sends the message that there is nothing black males can do to create positive change since they are "powerless" to end white supremacy. (Hooks, p. 100)

The collective legacy of shaming at the hands of white-supremacist patriarchal culture wrecks individuals and their family lives and creates dysfunctionality, conflict, and abuse. Hooks concludes by identifying the plight of African-American males as a "crisis in the black male spirit ... perpetuated by widespread dehumanization, by the continued placement of black males outside the category of human, one that identifies them as animal, beast, other" (2004, p. 134).

Another dynamic affecting the masculine development of African American men is the absence of fathers and the resulting presence of matriarchy (Bush, p. 49). Patriarchal ideology teaches African American men that child raising and caregiving are women's work. (Hooks, p. 104). Consequently, African American fathers see their purpose as merely to impregnate women, thereby "prov(ing) their manhood in a patriarchal sense by making babies, not by taking care of them" (Hooks, p. 105). This wounded mindset has far-reaching consequences: lack of intimacy between fathers and children, lack of intimacy and conflict between husbands and wives, father abandonment of families, and family dysfunction (Hooks, pp. 107–117). Hooks stated,

> The core reasons for dysfunction in black families is blind allegiance to patriarchal thinking about sex roles and the coupling of that thinking with rigid fundamentalist religious beliefs. Dominator culture creates family dysfunction... . When racism is added to the mix dysfunctions are intensified. (Hooks, p. 117)

Unfortunately, patriarchal life scripts impose mandates on African American males to seek validation and fulfillment outside the home in the sphere of work, where money and material support take precedence over emotional bonding and loving and caring interaction with children (Hooks, p. 111).

Finally, it must be noted that African American males struggle under economic oppression by the dominant culture. Doris Wilkinson (1995) stated,

> The institution of slavery in the United States set apart the work and employment privileges of African American males and females from those of European heritage.... . In the process of equalizing the positions of African American men and women, enslavement embedded in the organization of work (created) a virtually permanent caste-like component up to the mid-twentieth century. By establishing and legally validating rigid separation between the races, the institution generated vastly disparate ranking in the class system. Thus, it was inevitable that the descendants of slaves would inherit this structural pattern. While political and economic inequalities mirror sex differences and gender roles, and while these link with class placement in the framing of US culture, racial ascription is far more pervasive in its impact, extent, intensity, historical meaning, and durability. (1995, p. 167)

The modern day work world continues to reinforce and embody white dominance in which African American males make consistently less than their white counterparts at the same job where access to job advancement is determined along color lines (Hooks, pp. 24–25). The current economic climate of downsizing and reduction in wages makes problematic the employment prospects of African American males for the future. Again, this pattern of treatment is typical for an oppressed, marginalized, and subordinated racial population to receive from a hegemonically white society.

By every socioeconomic and political indicator, African American males in America face a crisis, despite the notable success of certain African American individuals, such as professional athletes, entertainers, businessmen, and politicians. The majority of African American men lack self-confidence and self-esteem to make it (Hooks, p. 26). According to Hooks,

> A biased imperialist white-supremacist patriarchal mass media teaches young black males that the street will be their only home. And it lets mainstream black males know that they are just an arrest away from being on the street. This ... teaches

young black males that the patriarchal man is a predator, that
only the strong and the violent survive. (p. 27)

Too many African American males buy into the patriarchal culture of dominance, control, and materialism to the detriment of themselves and their
racial brothers. In his essay "It's Raining Men" (2004), Robert Reid-Pharr
captured the plight of African American males in contemporary America
when he wrote,

> The Black American Man, as the rhetoric of both the right
> and the left would have it, is the most *unfree* of American
> citizens. As huge numbers of black men in this country
> languish in prisons or under the stewardship of assorted
> probation and parole boards; as black men continue to be
> over-represented in the drug trade and among the legions
> of persons with chronic illnesses—H.I.V., cancer, heart
> disease, alcoholism, depression—as we give our lives over
> to violence or to a certain silent despair, we have become the
> very emblems of the ugliness, the bestiality, the barbarism
> by which the rest of America, particularly white America,
> can view itself as liberal and free. (p. 584)

African American males face a critical juncture at this moment in history.
Even as seemingly overwhelming social ills such as addiction, violence, and
death beset the black man, he must choose the path he will take. The old,
familiar path leads to death. As Hooks movingly put it,

> Until we begin collectively to protect the emotional life of black
> boys and men we sign their death warrants. Saving the lives
> of black boys and black men requires of us all the courage to
> challenge patriarchal manhood, the courage to put in its place
> alternative visions of healing black masculinity. (p. 159)

The courage and the wisdom to choose correctly are the challenges and
the promises of the African American male.

IMPLICATIONS FOR EDUCATING LATE ADOLESCENT BOYS

As the facts of subordinate and marginalized masculinities reveal, the
dominant masculine culture and ideology pose serious problems to males
because they seek to construct meaningful masculine identities amidst

a culture of bias and oppression of those deemed Other. While difficult and sometimes painful, analyses of masculinities must take place in order to promote an environment of understanding that can lead to constructive awareness and engagement. In the process, individual males can experience affirmation as the dynamics that shape their identities are identified and understood. Awareness promotes enhanced self-understanding. Furthermore, an enhanced awareness of the forces that drive and shape masculine identity can promote a constructive engagement with those dynamics, issuing forth in further discourse and challenges of those dynamics. Growth in maturity is the end product of such a process of analysis and inquiry.

At the collective level, analyses of the construction of subordinate and marginalized masculine gender groups by the dominant male group can be educational and enlightening and lead to constructive engagement with other groups and perhaps inner change in the dominant group. Awareness of the forces and dynamics that drive another's identity can lead to empathic understanding and engagement with those groups. This process can be liberating to everyone because each group strives to take the perspective of the other.

In a world where so many diverse groups closely interact with each other, empathic understanding and constructive engagement are imperatives for a curriculum seeking to help late-adolescent boys' transitions into manhood. Understanding others is a critical component to understanding oneself. Therefore, engaging in the process of analyzing the gender construction projects of subordinate and marginalized males assists young men in affirming as well as challenging the scripts that mold male identity.

CHAPTER ELEVEN

THE BOARDING SCHOOL AS AN INITIATORY EXPERIENCE

I believe that the work of creating short-term communities, support groups, ritual, and other cultural-specific events for men are essential for creating a culture which is gender equitable and committed to social change.

Onaje Benjamin, 1995

If you have not gathered wisdom in your youth, how will you find it when you are old?

Ecclesiastes 25:3

THE NEED FOR A CONTEMPORARY RITE OF PASSAGE

A vast amount of research and writing has been done on traditional rites of passage as a means of ushering young boys into manhood. The ancients intuitively recognized that manhood was best constructed through a pre-planned, ritualized series of ordeals and events that heightened a young man's consciousness and engaged him in a transforming experience that facilitated his transition into manhood. It was often a traumatic but necessary step in a crucible of change. At the conclusion of the rite of passage, the boy emerged as a man. The community welcomed him back and conferred upon him the mantle of manhood with full privileges and responsibilities that went with it.

The transition from boyhood to manhood is not one that occurs naturally, so rites of passage were devised to force the transformation. The intensity and duration of these rites varied according to local culture and needs, but their purpose was the same: transitioning boys into men. For millennia, the elder males in the society had the responsibility for conducting these rites and for stewarding boys through them. Cross-culturally, these rites of passage shared common elements: boys were removed from family and clan; the relation between mother and son changed from one of a child to that of a man; the history and customs of the society were transmitted through story, song, and dance; boys had to undergo frightening and often painful ordeals; and the new initiates' return was celebrated by the community.

The same need for initiatory rites of passage exists today. The problem is that in contemporary culture there are few or no initiatory rites of passage in existence. Furthermore, few elder men have any experience in ushering boys through rites of passage. Without healthy and validating rites of passage, boys will not make the transition into manhood; instead they remain stuck in a kind of eternal adolescence. Rubenstein described such a man in the following way:

> Do you know of any men who despite being adults still function on the model of boy psychology …? Imagine the frustration and internal stress of a man still continually seeking acknowledgment and power; wanting to be number one all the time, thinking he is the center of the universe, believing he will live forever, taking no responsibility for his actions and then on top of that looking for a woman who will mother him? It is a disastrous combination and one that often leads to either drugs or alcohol to numb out unhappy states of mind or the setting up of artificial environments at work or in relationships to create a false sense of success. ("Modern Day Rites of Passage as the Ultimate Form of Preventative Medicine." Website)

Dr. David Blumencrantz, Executive Director of The Center for the Advancement of Youth, Family, and Community Services is even more emphatic in advocating for contemporary rights of passage for youth. He wrote,

> Contemporary peoplemaking rites of passage are desperately needed. Especially rites of passage that focus on helping young people obtain meaning, identity and purpose, a deep connection with the natural world and building a sense of community between significant people in their lives. (www.bullfrogfilms.com/catalog/lost.html.)

Based on the facts and the presentation in chapters 1 and 5, today's young men need a carefully crafted, contained, transformative experience through which to accomplish their development into mature masculinity.

PLANNING A RITE OF PASSAGE

A number of rites of passage programs are offered commercially, most of which are wilderness experiences. Furthermore, most of the programs surveyed were coeducational as well as therapeutic in nature ("Rites of Passage." Website: www.pages.drexel.edu/~ages25/pgeneral.htm). Most notable is the School of Lost Borders, to which reference was made previously in chapter 5.

One of the critiques leveled by profeminist men and social constructionists is that the use of Native American rites of passage, rituals, and myth is anachronistic and racist (Kimmel and Kaufman, 1995, pp. 30–31). The mimicking of another's cultural enactments is viewed as troubling, as in the following passage:

> … leaders encourage what we might call "redface,"—the appropriation of Native American rituals and symbols—the drum, chants of "ho," warpaint, animal names, etc. And they imagine that these Native cultures expressed a deep spirituality, an abiding love and respect for nature, and a palpable sense of brotherhood. What they are really doing, we believe, is projecting onto these cultures their own longings and their own needs. Such a project relies upon racial, and racist, stereotypes. (Kimmel and Kaufman, p. 31)

While much of this criticism is overstated and misapplied, it is worth taking seriously when contemplating a social project such as constructing a rite of passage for late- adolescent boys. In fact, context does matter, and a contemporary rite of passage needs to address the question of what is an appropriate environment in which to conduct a rite of passage.

The answer being proposed in this study is that boarding schools are an ideal and appropriate context for rites of passage. Those who are engaged in work with boys in boarding schools have an extraordinary opportunity to assist young men in their growth and development from adolescence into adulthood. The three to five years a boy spends in boarding school are transformative. It is a time when the boy separates from parents and siblings, enters into an often strange and very demanding new existence, endures hardships, and learns to discipline his mind, body, and emotions in preparation for entry into the college years and adulthood.

The goal of the boarding school initiatory process for boys is threefold: (1) to provide for growth from boyhood into manhood, (2) to bond to the school community and its core values, and (3) to assist in establishing a new identity, with a new sense of self and responsibility. Boarding schools function much the same as the ancient initiation rituals. Consistent with all rites of passage, a boarding school rite of passage each year would inculcate the processes of separation, liminality, and re-emergence. In the separation phase, there is an acknowledgment that the boy has undergone a change in status and has become a member of the school community. This change in circumstances is highlighted by the enactment of a ritual of separation. In the liminality and intensification phase, the young man hears stories and receives training and instruction in his responsibilities as a member of the community. During the re-emergence phase, the boy's successful completion of the year's expectations is celebrated in a ritual of re-emergence that includes the bestowing of gifts and privileges. In each phase of the rite of passage, certain persons will be designated as the ritual elders who will assist the young men in the rite of passage. Additionally, careful consideration is given to the ritual space in which certain enactments take place.

This study will now outline a four-year rite of passage for a boarding school setting. For eleven years, I served as a faculty member at an all-boys boarding school in the mountains of central Virginia, known as the Blue Ridge School. The mission of the Blue Ridge School is to take academically struggling boys and guide them in developing skills and habits that will help them to become successful, mature young men in the world. In its almost 100 year history, the school has been dedicated to working with students from all walks of life on its rural 800 acre setting in the foothills of the Blue Ridge Mountains. Much of what follows is already in place at the school, although a great deal of the material presented herein is new. However, the content and the process that follows is completely my own conceptualization.

In the freshman year, the purpose of the rite of passage is to acknowledge formally that the student has made a significant, and perhaps a traumatic and painful, separation from home, by leaving his parents, siblings, and friends with all the attachments and meanings those relationships signify. This separation also includes the attachments the student may have to his former school and other significant institutions and organizations that have value to the student. For many students, this is a significant lifestyle change, requiring many physical, mental, and emotional adjustments. The separation ritual that is held the first weekend of the school year to mark the separation is a critical component of acknowledging this separation from home and the previous lifestyle. The ritual is held in the Gibson Memorial Chapel during which there are prayers by the Chaplain for new beginnings, for family, and for the Blue Ridge School. The tone is solemn, and the new student is called out by name and received into the Blue Ridge School family. Immediately after the chapel service, as a group, the new students go out into the woods on a campout for a day and a night. During this time, the new students and their adult advisors take part in a series of activities and games that facilitate the learning of each other's name as well as promoting bonding and class unity. Students are grouped to take responsibility for camping chores: fire and food preparation, meal cleanup, game and activities leadership, and team membership.

During the freshman year, students gather as a group each month to receive instruction from the school's resident historian about the history of the school and the founding personages who have positively influenced the school's growth and development. The instruction includes a discussion of the Blue

Ridge School's original mission to educate and serve the local mountain people as a way of highlighting the sense of social outreach and dedication to high ideals. The school's story is told many times during the year in different ways so that by the end of the year, the freshmen know the school's history. A key component in the telling of the story is incorporating the narration of the Herculean efforts on the part of Archdeacon Neve, who founded the original school. An additional part of the telling of the school story is the telling of students' own personal stories about how they came to learn about and decide to attend Blue Ridge School. In this way, the students' own personal stories are connected and become intertwined with the school's story. During the course of the school year, the freshmen learn the school's mission statement and the full names of the entire faculty and staff. Near the end of the year, the freshmen are subjected to an ordeal of memorization in which they must recite the names of the faculty, the mission statement, and write the key facts of the school's history. By doing and accomplishing these activities, the freshmen have a solid knowledge base about the school's people, values, and history in order to bond closely with the program and with each other.

Another component of the freshman rite of passage is the relation each boy develops with his adult advisor and his upperclassman Baron Brother. The adult and the older student assigned to each freshman serve in the capacity of a mentor to the boy and help him to navigate through the often-overwhelming novelty he encounters in his first year of boarding school. The relation the adult advisor and upperclassman form with the first-year boy is similar to that described as the ritual elder (see chapter 5) in the capacity of guide and instructor in the boy's emerging manhood and maturity and in telling the school's stories and ways in an insightful way that is helpful to the new student.

At the end of the school year, the freshmen engage in a ritual of re-emergence in the chapel, following a day and a night campout together. The purpose of the campout is to tell stories of the school year and to remember fondly the time together as well as to talk about the next school year. Good-byes are said in muted ways to those who are not returning. In the chapel ritual, the Chaplain, class advisors, and Headmaster congratulate the freshmen for a good year and then confer on them the school tie, a symbol of their successful completion of the first year at the Blue Ridge School.

The sophomore rite of passage has as its purpose the acknowledgment of the second year boys as "betwixt and between," meaning they have a status of neither a freshman nor an upperclassman. Additionally, these boys' new relations and increasing responsibilities to each other and to the school are acknowledged and affirmed. The second year rite of passage emphasizes the necessity and importance of personal growth and maturity in the acceptance of increased responsibilities and accountability.

The separation ritual for the sophomores takes place at the upper pond and cabin on the school's property, a scenic area highlighted by a small log cabin that was constructed entirely by hand under the supervision of a faculty member and a group of students a number of years ago. The cabin stands as a symbol of the students' constructive use of their time and talent for the betterment of the school—a point that is used in talking to sophomores about the opportunities they have for bettering themselves and their school. The overnight camping experience features the telling of student stories of what transpired over the summer as well as brainstorming about the upcoming year. The new students who enter as sophomores tell their stories of learning about the Blue Ridge School and why they decided to enroll. The sophomore adult advisors guide students to reflect on ways in which they have grown and matured in the past year as well as help the students to anticipate the challenges and opportunities of their second year.

During the school year, the instruction of sophomores focuses on the themes of service and honor. Connected with these themes is the telling of stories about some of the school's past personages who exemplify service and honor: the Rev. Dudley Boogher, a former longtime Headmaster who worked tirelessly to grow the school and to promote the mission of service to the mountain people, and Mrs. Bessie Turner, a faithful school secretary who devoted her life to the school and to the students and who was known as a dedicated, loving, and caring adult in the school community. Another central story in the Blue Ridge School culture is the medieval story of Parsifal, a squire to Sir Lancelot and a seeker after the Holy Grail. This story is read in sophomore English classes. It is highlighted for students as illustrative of the prized values of dedication to a quest, faithfulness, perseverance, integrity, and humility—values that are stressed as important components of good character. The Grail is stressed as a symbol of something worth dedicating oneself to and striving for, and the quest is emphasized as a metaphor for one's life as fraught with meaning and significance. An additional book, entitled *He: Understanding Masculine Psychology* by Robert Johnson, is read as well. This book introduces the sophomores to the concepts of male development as illustrated by the Parsifal and the Holy Grail myth. It is a first primer for second-year boys who will later encounter a more sophisticated men's studies curriculum in the junior and senior years. Other featured points of instruction include the Blue Ridge School Honor and Pride Code, which embody the core values of the school. Additionally, the school song, "Fight the Good Fight," which is sung at Opening Convocation, Commencement and other important occasions during the school year, is taught to the sophomores.

The testing phase of the sophomore rite of passage is comprised of memorization of the Pride Code, the school song, and the Parsifal myth. Additionally, the sophomores plan and undertake a group community service project on the school campus as part of their contribution to the community and as emblematic of their emerging sense of responsibility to the life of the community beyond themselves.

Again an adult advisor and an upperclassman Baron Brother are assigned as mentors to each sophomore to continue the guidance and instruction program begun in the freshman year. The guidance and instruction, however, are geared toward assuming more responsibility and maturity during the second year of boarding school. Together, the adult advisor and the Baron Brother engage the sophomore in the discussion of Johnson's *He* in an effort to help him understand the principles of male growth and development as he lives in the boarding school setting.

At the end of the sophomore year, the students participate in a re-emergence ritual that has as its central feature a coat and tie dinner in the dining room, which has been set formally for this occasion. The Headmaster and the sophomore class advisors attend this occasion. The students wear their school ties, which were conferred on them the prior year. During the evening, selected student leaders in the sophomore class give short addresses highlighting the accomplishments of their class during the school year. The adult advisors and the Headmaster respond with their own observations, affirming the students' continued growth and maturity as young men. At the end, each boy is called forward, and the adult advisors give each one a school lapel pin for his jacket as a symbol of the completion of the sophomore year.

The junior rite of passage has as its purpose the acknowledgment that the third-year students are upperclassmen with greatly increased expectations of them from the school community and higher levels of responsibility and accountability. During this year, some juniors are appointed Junior Proctors in the dormitories to assist the Prefects. Leadership is the central focus, especially leadership by example of supporting school and classmates in word and deed. The separation ritual for third-year boys takes place at the beginning of the school year with a two-day, one-night retreat on the campus where the group challenges the obstacles and apparatus of the ropes course and climbing wall. These activities are discussed as symbolic of the obstacles and challenges that the students will face in the next two years as upperclassmen, including anticipating college and responsibilities of life in general. Students are also challenged to analyze the strategies they adopted in dealing with and surmounting the obstacles. During the evening, the junior class advisors engage students in telling stories about their summer and in brainstorming what the next two years may bring. Students are encouraged to identify and articulate how they have matured in their thinking and behavior over the past year.

During the school year, the instruction of juniors focuses on responsibility and leadership, including the telling of the story about Mr. Hatcher C. Williams, a longtime Headmaster of the school, whose servant leadership was invaluable in making the school educationally strong. Mr. Williams viewed his work for the school as a Godly dedication and work of service. Additionally, during the junior year, students read in English class the Arthurian legend, which is discussed as a story about servant leadership and responsibility to a cause greater than one's self. Students also meet in groups to tell personal stories and to share their fears, dreams, and hopes in preparing for taking the SAT and the ACT, in assuming increased personal responsibilities, and in discussing the leadership elections that take place in the spring. Additionally, juniors work with their advisors about taking on the responsibilities as Baron Brothers to underclassman boys, thereby continuing the tradition that the juniors enjoyed when they were mentored by an upperclassman in their earlier years at school.

Another important story in the Blue Ridge School tradition is that of St. George and the Dragon. A large student mural of St. George and the Dragon is hanging in the school's dining room, and the image of the duo is imprinted on the school crest. The story emphasizes the values of dedication, faithfulness, and the archetypal warrior—qualities essential to the successful negotiation of the junior and senior years. Finally, juniors undertake the first part of the men's studies curriculum. The details of the curriculum will be discussed in the next chapter of this study.

The testing phase of the junior rite of passage involves having students engage in team building activities on the ropes course and climbing wall. Additionally, the juniors must memorize the school's code of conduct and be able to tell the story of St. George and the Dragon. Finally, the third-year students plan and undertake a complex, multi-day group community service project off campus.

The junior year re-emergence ritual consists of a steak dinner with the junior class advisors and the Headmaster present. The occasion is marked by the telling of the junior class story and accomplishments of the year by selected students. The junior class advisors respond by affirming the students' accomplishments, and the Headmaster responds by challenging the juniors to step up and assume the mantle of leadership of the school in their senior year. At the end of the speech, the Headmaster calls each student up by name and confers upon him the school crest, which he will wear on his jacket during his senior year. The Stepping Up Service immediately follows in the school chapel with the entire student body present. This service celebrates the retiring senior student leaders and confers student leadership positions upon the juniors. The ritual is quite dramatic as each senior leader steps down from his leadership position, goes out into the seated student audience, and invites his replacement junior student to step up into his new leadership position. Student leaders for the Honor Court, the Student-Faculty Discipline Committee, the Junior Proctors, the Sacristan and Verger of the Chapel, and the Prefects are all designated in this fashion. In this ritualized manner, the student leadership for the Blue Ridge School is transferred to the next class of students, and their abilities and responsibilities are affirmed and validated by the entire community.

The senior rite of passage has as its purpose the acknowledging and empowering of the senior class as leaders of the school, public commitments of accepting and affirming student assumption of responsibility for setting the tone of the school year and for their responsibilities as the student elders in the student body in order to mentor and lead by example the younger students. The senior separation ritual begins with a formal dinner at the Headmaster's house, for which the students dress up in their coats with school lapel pin and crest and school tie. Adults present include the senior class advisors and the faculty leadership advisors. Before dinner the students and faculty members divide into small groups for a discussion of the hopes for the new school year and the expectations of students' leadership roles. A key question is discussed: What do you wish your class's legacy to be in the school's memory? After dinner, selected small group members share a summary of their group's discussion with the entire assembly. At the end, the Headmaster affirms the senior class members and confers upon them their Senior Privileges for the school year, thereby giving them rights and privileges the rest of the students do not enjoy.

During the school year, the senior instruction is focused in the special Men's Studies class, the details of which will be discussed in the next chapter. Leadership, assuming manhood roles and responsibilities, and planning for an end-of-year vision quest are the central components of the instruction with seniors. Seniors meet in groups with their class advisors to tell stories and to share their future fears, hopes, and dreams for the upcoming year, for preparing to enter college, and for the visions of their paths in life. Additionally, seniors work with their class advisors to assume Baron Brother mentor responsibilities for underclassman boys. During the year, the story of the life of Mr. Jordan Churchill, a longtime, much-beloved Dean of Students and devoted man-of-faith is recounted by the school historian. Stories of Mr. Churchill resound with the same loving concern and sensitivity with which he reasoned individually with each boy who was in trouble and tell how Mr. Churchill labored tirelessly to help students be successful. Mr. Churchill is considered the quintessential Blue Ridge Man—a gentleman, a man of faith and devotion, dedicated to helping others, sensitive, and caring. Throughout the year, seniors are encouraged to look at their entire Blue Ridge School careers and to affirm their growth and maturity from boyhood and dependency into emerging manhood and independence.

The senior year testing phase focuses on the planning and participation in a Vision Quest on the school's property. The one-day, one-night solo experience takes place at the end of the school year on the school's vast, wooded, mountain property. The seniors also plan and execute a class service project and senior gift to the school as their legacy.

At the end of the school year, the senior re-emergence ritual begins with the Senior Class / Alumni picnic. The alumni return to Blue Ridge School for a weekend of socializing and activities, renewal and storytelling, during which the members of the senior class are invited to join and participate in the extended Blue Ridge School family. The seniors' transition from the Blue Ridge School community out into a larger life of college and beyond begins with this event. Commencement is the final event in the rite of passage for the seniors. At this time parents and family join the entire Blue Ridge School faculty and staff in celebrating the years and accomplishments of the graduating class of young men. The graduates are dressed in their school jackets complete with school lapel pin and school crest with their school tie—each a symbol of prior year achievements. The Commencement Service confers numerous awards and plaques upon members of the graduating class for outstanding achievements and accomplishments. At the end of the service, the diplomas are awarded and everyone stands and applauds the graduates for their success. The school song is sung in joyous, tearful voice to conclude to the service. Upon processing out of the chapel, the graduates run to the school lake, throw off their jackets and ties, and jump into the water. The action follows a tradition of defiance and liberation by other graduating classes, ignoring the prohibition against swimming in the lake. The action also becomes a kind of baptism of the new graduates into life beyond the Blue Ridge School. It is a beautiful and moving end to a four-year rite of passage as boys move from youth into emerging manhood.

IMPLICATIONS FOR EDUCATING LATE-ADOLESCENT BOYS

Although the preceding description is school-specific, it is not too difficult to extrapolate the principles involved in conceptualizing a rite of passage for any boarding school setting. A sensitive and thoughtful analysis of the unique culture, symbols, personages, and enactments that comprise a boarding school culture can become the elements in the construction of a rite of passage that can be meaningful in the lives of students. The process involves a social constructionist and analytical methodology combined with a knowledge and application of the extensive anthropological information available on initiatory rites of passage (see chapter 5 on initiation).

Initiatory rites of passage share common structural elements that include the element of separation, which occurs when a person is removed from his everyday world into a new environment; an element of liminality and intensification when the person is immersed in a new culture designed to enable inner transformation; and finally a return or re-emergence element, occurring when a person resumes a normal life as a qualitatively different person. By using the rite of passage structure and coupling it with context-specific elements found in the school culture, a meaningful, transformative process can be constructed. Furthermore, it is essential to devise sensitive and thoughtful rituals to accentuate the importance of these transitional phases for students as they move from one phase to another.

Careful consideration must be paid when considering the purpose and content of the rite of passage process and its accompanying rituals. These processes convey both overt and covert messages: hastily constructed or inadequately considered ritual processes can have unintended negative affects. Although the goal is to affirm boys and to assist them in the process of transition into maturity and manhood, there is a danger of slipping into a masculinist, misogynist ideology that unwittingly affirms a hegemonic masculinity at the expense of denigrating other expressions of masculinities or women. Although this is never the intended result, it is, nevertheless, an inherent danger to consider and avoid.

CHAPTER TWELVE

SUMMARY AND DISCUSSION

We need to take that Warrior energy, that which is very likely the most
noble thing in the male soul, and bring it into the service of an inclusive,
non-racist, non-sectarian, non-cultic vision about a world of justice and
peace.

Robert Moore, Ph.D., 2005

This above all: to thine own self be true
And it must follow, as the night the day,
Thou canst not then be false to any man.

Shakespeare, *Hamlet*, 1.3: 78.

A MASCULINE GENDER STUDIES CURRICULUM FOR LATE
ADOLESCENT BOYS: STRUCTURE AND KEY CONCEPTS

The following is an annotated outline of a two-year men's studies course
with the purpose of providing late-adolescent boys with a core of knowledge
that will assist them in making the transition from boyhood into manhood
(Mason, p. 61). The preceding chapters have sought to provide the necessary
background research and information to buttress the implementation of such
a course in a school setting (Mason, p. 110). This study has proposed

the boarding school setting as an ideal context in which such a course could be taught in conjunction with a rite of passage process (Mason, p. 110).

COURSE TITLE: MALE IDENTITY: WHAT DOES IT MEAN TO BE A MAN?

Purpose:

To provide a course and a context in which late adolescent boys can learn about and address masculine identity issues in order to promote growth and development into manhood and maturity.

Description:

This course will discuss the key conceptual issues and components that comprise contemporary masculine identity. In doing so, the class will encounter the academic disciplines of literature, history, anthropology, sociology, genetics, evolutionary and developmental psychology, and biology as each discipline makes its own unique contribution to the question of masculine identity. Additionally, the three interpretive perspectives on masculine identity—the psychoanalytic, the essentialist, and the social constructionist—will be discussed, analyzed, and debated. Concepts will be presented by means of readings, lectures, video presentations, and discussions. Throughout the course, students will be challenged to engage the material at an intellectual as well as a personal level in order to appreciate the personal impact these concepts have on their own masculine identity. Movies will be viewed as a way of illustrating the concepts as tphey are enacted in life contexts. Students will be challenged to plan and undertake a vision quest experience at the end of the course as a culminating activity.

Course Objectives:

1. To know the key conceptual materials presented in the course in order to identify and apply the concepts in one's own life.
2. To understand, articulate, and apply the key issues and ideas explaining the contemporary "crisis in masculinity."
3. To understand the role of patriarchy in men's and women's socialization.

4. To understand the changing gender role expectations of men throughout Western history.
5. To understand men's current status in American society from gender role and historical perspectives.
6. To understand, articulate, and apply the three interpretive perspectives on male identity—psychoanalytic, essentialist, and social constructionist.
7. To understand, articulate, and apply the effects of the Boy Code in life.
8. To understand, articulate, and apply the evolutionary biological explanation of sex differences.
9. To understand and articulate the unique brain structures found in males and the effects these structures have in male abilities.
10. To understand and articulate the role and effects of testosterone on male thinking and behavior.
11. To understand, articulate, and apply Erikson's, Jung's, and Levinson's models of human development as it relates to males.
12. To understand, articulate, and apply the dynamics of male wounding to oneself.
13. To understand, articulate, and apply the concept of "shaming as wounding."
14. To understand and articulate the effects of wounding in males.
15. To understand, articulate, and apply the techniques for confronting and acknowledging shaming and wounding in one's self.
16. To understand and articulate the need for male initiation.
17. To plan and execute a solo vision quest experience.
18. To understand and articulate the contribution the father makes in a male's psychosocial development.
19. To understand and articulate the problems associated with absent fathers.
20. To understand, articulate, and apply the concept of father hunger.
21. To understand, articulate, and apply strategies for reconnecting with the father.
22. To understand and articulate the meaning of archetype.
23. To understand, articulate, and apply Moore and Gillette's four boyhood and four mature masculine archetypes.

24. To understand, articulate, and apply Monick's concept of the Phallos archetype.
25. To understand, articulate, and apply techniques for accessing the archetypes.
26. To understand and articulate the psychoanalytic, the social constructionist, and the essentialist viewpoints on human sexuality.
27. To understand, articulate, and apply the concept of masculine gender role stress syndrome and gender scripting.
28. To understand, articulate, and apply how modern culture socializes males to handle pain.
29. To understand and articulate the components of a holistic, healthy spirituality.
30. To understand and articulate the concept of masculinities.
31. To understand, articulate, and apply the concept of hegemonic masculinity as it relates to women and other subordinate masculinities.
32. To understand and apply the concepts associated with the social construction of homosexual masculinities.
33. To understand and apply the concepts associated with the social construction of African American masculinities.
34. To understand and articulate the dynamics that comprise one's own expression of masculine identity.

Required Reading

1. Clatterbaugh, Kenneth. (1997). *Contemporary Perspectives on Masculinity.* Boulder: Westview Press. This well-written and detailed analysis of the current state of the men's movement identifies and analyzes eight distinct divisions based on their history, ideology and politics. This book is a very good sociopolitical overview of the factions in the modern men's movement.
2. Hooks, Bell. (2004). *We Real Cool: Black Men and Masculinity.* London: Routledge. An outstanding book analyzing African American masculinity from the social constructionist perspective. Hooks examines the impact "Imperialist white-supremacist racist patriarchy" has on African American men, candidly analyzing such topics as sexuality, work, parenting, and gangsta ideology. She concludes

with a hopeful advocacy of the healing work of love in the black community.

3. Johnson, Robert. (1990). *He: Understanding Masculine Psychology.* New York: Harper and Row. Johnson takes a Jungian approach to the analysis of the story of Parsifal and the quest for the Holy Grail myth as a story about masculine development. This book is easily accessible to younger male readers and is a good introductory text for a men's studies program.

4. Kilmartin, Christopher T. (2000). *The Masculine Self, Second Edition.* Boston: McGraw-Hill. The author is an acknowledged expert in the fields of men's issues, diversity, and violence prevention. This comprehensive textbook utilizes the latest in scholarly research and men's study theory to examine masculinity from a number of different perspectives. There is an extensive section on men's issues, covering topics such as work, relationships, health, violence, and the ever-changing definitions of contemporary society's definition of masculinity.

5. Kimmel, Michael. (1997). *Manhood in America: A Cultural History.* New York: Free Press. Kimmel is one of the giants in the field of men's studies and his cultural history of American manhood is among the very best treatments of the subject. His thesis is that manhood must be proved, and this proving of one's masculinity has been a shaping force in the culture and everyday lives of men. Kimmel presents an insightful analysis of how masculinity ideals have changed over time and concludes with the current crisis in manhood. This text would serve as an excellent first read in a men's studies course by setting the historical context for the discussion of definitions of masculinity.

6. Hollis, James. (1994). *Under Saturn's Shadow: The Wounding and Healing of Men.* Toronto: Inner City Books. A powerful and impassioned account of the current crisis in masculinity by a Jungian writer. Hollis contends that men struggle under a debilitating weight of Saturnian masculine expectations that men cannot meet. Using the myth of the overthrow of Cronos by his children, Hollis explains the causes of the current masculinity crisis in men and outlines a hopeful strategy for healing.

7. Moore, Robert and Gillette, Douglas. (1991). *King, Warrior, Magician, Lover: Recovering the Archetypes of the Mature Masculine.* San Francisco: Harper and Row. This instructive and insightful book by one of the leaders in the modern men's movement is about the influence of masculine archetypes in a man's psyche. Taking a Jungian approach, Moore and Gillette distinguish between the four immature, boyhood archetypes and their manifestations and the four mature archetypes of manhood. They outline strategies for accessing these mature masculine potentials in one's life.

Supplemental Materials

Videos

1. *A River Runs Through It.* This movie contrasts the lives of two brothers who share a love of fly-fishing but who have very different lifestyles and values. Both brothers face critical moments of decision—one in a healthy and life-enhancing way and the other in a self-destructive way.

2. *Colors.* This movie tells the story of two different men's transition into manhood—one a rookie police officer and the other, a young Latino male in an inner city gang. The movie pointedly shows the positive and negative sides of male initiation processes and their effects on one's masculine identity. This movie has a powerful gang-style initiation scene that is not for the squeamish.

3. *Dead Poet's Society.* Set in a boys' boarding school, the movie tells the story of young men who bond with their new English teacher. There is a powerful contrasting between the creative, positive mentor-teacher and a controlling, negative *senex* father with devastating effects on his son. There are numerous positive messages in this movie about masculinity and coming of age.

4. *Desmond Morris' The Human Sexes.* 6 video series. This TLC (The Learning Channel) series features anthropologist Desmond Morris as he explores the nature of sexual and gender expression and difference in culture. This series raises questions about essentialism and social constructionism as they relate to gender.

5. *Field of Dreams.* This is a powerful movie about a man's courageous decision to follow his dreams despite the personal costs to himself and his family and despite the criticism of others. This movie illustrates the concepts of father hunger, the absent father, and the Jungian concept of the spiritus rector as inner voice and guide.

6. *For Love of the Game.* This movie is about a professional baseball pitcher who has to face the double demands of working as a professional baseball player as well as nurturing a love relationship with a woman. The movie documents the inner thoughts and challenges a man faces in making critical decisions about life, love, and work.

7. *Gender: The Enduring Paradox.* This Smithsonian Institution video documents the socially-constructed and ever-changing world of gender throughout the life cycle. The video examines the paradoxical and contradictory cross-cultural expressions of gender in American society.

8. *Legends of the Fall.* This movie tells the story of a father and his three sons, the youngest of which dies in a wartime battle despite the oversight and protection of the middle brother. The middle brother's grief and failure is the basis for a powerful inner wound which drives his thinking and actions for the rest of the movie. This movie illustrates the themes of brotherhood, male identity, and most especially the significant effects of the masculine wound.

9. *Man Without A Face.* This movie tells a powerful story about a young boy who suffers from father hunger and from too much feminine presence and who wants to go off to a military boarding school. To do so, he must pass the entrance exam. He meets a badly disfigured male teacher who helps him to prepare. The movie poignantly illustrates the positive significance of the mentor relationship as well as a young man's developmental need to break away from mother and to bond with a positive male person.

10. *Mrs. Doubtfire.* This comedy is about a man who masquerades as a woman housekeeper in his ex-wife's home in order to see his children. In the process, important questions about masculine and feminine identity and ideology are raised.

11. *Saving Private Ryan.* This is a moving story about a band of soldiers and their platoon leader captain who have orders to find and remove

another soldier from wartime action. The movie illustrates the themes of male bonding, devotion to duty, self-sacrifice, and courage.

12. *Lost Borders.* This video by the School of Lost Borders documents teenagers who undergo a ten-day initiation ceremony including a three day-three night solo experience. The video provides helpful insight and information about a Vision Quest initiation-type experience and can be used as a preparation for the Vision Quest experience.

13. *The Fisher King.* This movie is a modern-day retelling of the "fisher king" legend. Befriended by an addicted media celebrity because he saved his life, a seemingly psychotic street person slowly emerges back into a healthy life. The themes of the wound, mentorship, and the quest as a journey to wholeness are dramatically illustrated.

14. *The Graduate.* A college graduate is "lost" and adrift in life after graduation. His encounter with the negative and positive aspects of the feminine is illustrated in this movie classic.

Additional Books

1. Blum, Deborah. (1998). *Sex on the Brain: The Biological Differences between Men and Women.* New York: Penguin. This is a well-researched and well-written book on the essential differences between men and women based on brain research and biology.

2. Bolen, Jean Shinoda. (1989). *Gods in Everyman: The Archetypes That Shape Men'sLives.* New York: Harper Collins. A Jungian analyst, the author presents the mythological gods of Olympus as archetypal images that influence the masculine psyche.

3. Foster, Steven with Meredith Little. (1992). *The Book of the Vision Quest: Personal Transformation in the Wilderness. Revised Edition.* New York: Simon and Schuster. This classic book tells about the Vision Quest experience by two experienced initiation guides. The book explains the components of a vision quest experience and helps persons plan and undergo one.

4. Gilmore, David G. (1990). *Manhood in the Making: Cultural Concepts of Masculinity.* New Haven: Yale University Press. This book is a groundbreaking treatment of the diverse cultural expressions of masculinity around the world. The author's

purpose is to show the universal, problematic and stressed nature of manhood.

5. Greenberg. David F. (1990). *The Construction of Homosexuality.* Chicago: The University of Chicago Press. This book is an extensively researched social history on the differing expressions and responses to homosexuality throughout history. It is a well-written and sensitive treatment of a subordinated masculinity.

6. Kimmel, Michael S. and Michael A. Messner, Eds. (2004). *Men's Lives, Sixth Edition.* Boston: Pearson. This book is a compilation of articles on men's issues written from a social constructionist perspective. Articles cover such topics as college masculinities, diverse masculinities, relationships, and work.

7. Lorber, Judith. (1994). *Paradoxes of Gender.* New Haven: Yale University Press. This book by a prominent feminist is a social constructionist view of gender. This book asserts that gender is a product of socialization and is an institutional construct like other components of culture. Her chapters on "Believing Is Seeing: Biology as Ideology" and "How Many Opposites?: Gendered Sexuality" are most enlightening.

8. Monick, Eugene. (1987). *Phallos: Sacred Image of the Masculine.* Toronto: InnerCity Books. Written from a Jungian perspective, this book is a scholarly explanation of "Phallos" as an archetype of masculinity. The author uses of extensive Jungian psychological, literary, and cultural resources.

9. Moore, Robert and Douglas Gillette. (1992a). *The King Within: Accessing the King in the Male Psyche.* New York: William Morrow. (1992b). *The Warrior Within: Accessing the Knight in the Male Psyche.* New York: Avon Books. (1993a). *The Lover Within: Accessing the Lover in the Male Psyche.* New York: Avon Books. (1993b). *The Magician Within: Accessing the Shaman in the Male Psyche.* New York: William Morrow. Moore and Gillette have provided a detailed explanation of the psychosocial dynamics as well as extensive mythological materials to illustrate the images of the four archetypes of the mature masculine—the King, the Warrior, the Lover, and the Magician.

10. Tacey, David J. (1997). *Remaking Men: Jung, Spirituality, and Social Change.* New York: Routledge. The author, a Jungian academic, offers a refreshing reassessment of masculine studies and the current debate over masculinity. This is one of the best men's studies books written from a Jungian perspective.

JUNIOR YEAR COURSE OUTLINE

Purpose:

To introduce juniors to the key concepts of men's studies and to provide a sociohistorical perspective on the changing nature of masculine identity.

1. Video: *Gender: The Enduring Paradox.*
    a. Essay question: What do you think are the essential characteristics of masculinity?
    b. Of femininity?
    c. What characteristics do masculinity and femininity have in common?
2. Sociohistorical Overview of Masculinity
    a. Mythological Foundations-see Mason, p. 1
    b. The Epic Male—see Mason, pp. 2–3; Doyle (1995), p. 28
    c. The Spiritual Male—see Mason, pp. 3–4; Doyle (1995), pp. 29–30
    d. The Chivalric Male—see Mason, p. 4; Doyle (1995), pp. 30–31
    e. The Renaissance Male—see Mason, pp. 4–5; Doyle (1995), pp. 31–32
    f. The Bourgeois Male—see Mason, p. 5; Doyle (1995), p. 32
    g. The Effects of the Enclosure Movement on Masculinity—see Mason, pp. 5–6; Kimbrell (1995), pp. 38–39
    h. Kimbrell's Four Archetypes of the "Masculine Mystique—see Mason, pp. 6–8; Kimbrell (1995), chapters 4–7, pp. 45–130
    i. The Self-Made Man—see Mason, pp. 8–9; Keen (1991), pp. 106–107
    j. The Psychological Man—see Mason, p. 9; Keen (1991), pp. 108–110
    k. The Post-Modern Man—see Mason, pp. 10–11; Keen (1991), pp. 110–111

l. Pleck's Masculine Sex Role Identity—see Mason, pp. 10–11; Pleck (1981)

m. Origins of the Men's Movement—see Mason, p. 12

n. Clatterbaugh's Eight Strands of the Men's Movement—see Mason, pp. 11–12; Clatterbaugh (1997), pp. 9–14

o. The Conservative Perspective—see Mason, pp. 12–14; Clatterbaugh (1997), pp. 17–40

p. The Profeminist Perspective—see Mason, pp. 14–15; Clatterbaugh (1997), pp. 41–67

q. The Men's Rights Perspective—see Mason, pp. 15–17; Clatterbaugh (1997), pp. 69–94

r. The Mythopoetic Perspective—see Mason, pp. 17–18; Clatterbaugh (1997), pp. 95–116

s. The Socialist Perspective—see Mason, pp. 18–19; Clatterbaugh (1997), pp. 117–136

t. The Gay Male Perspective—see Mason, pp. 19–22; Clatterbaugh (1997), pp. 137–156

u. The African American Men's Perspective—see Mason, pp. 22–24; Clatterbaugh (1997), pp. 157–176

v. The Evangelical Christian Men's Perspective—see Mason, pp. 24–26; Clatterbaugh (1997), pp. 177–193

3. Discussion questions

   a. With what masculinity ideals do you most identify? Why?

   b. With which men's movement perspective do you most agree and identify as the one that most closely fits your own self-understanding?

   c. With which men's movement perspective do you least agree and identify? Explain your reasons.

4. A Social Constructionist Historical Overview of American Manhood: *Manhood in America: A Cultural History.* (1997)

   a. The Birth of the Self-Made Man

   b. Born to Run: Self-Control and Fantasies of Escape

   c. Men at Work: Captains of Industry, White Collars, and the Faceless Crowd

   d. Playing for Keeps: Masculinity as Recreation and the Re-creation of Masculinity

e. A Room of His Own: Socializing the New Man
f. Muscles, Money, and the M-F Test: Measuring Masculinity Between the Wars
g. "Temporary About Myself": White-Collar Conformists and Suburban Playboys, 1945–1960
h. The Masculine Mystique
i. Wimps, Whiners, and Weekend Warriors: The Contemporary Crisis of Masculinity and Beyond
j. Toward Democratic Manhood
k. Essay: Explain how historical circumstances have influenced and molded the conceptualization and enactment of masculine identity in America from one time period to the next.

5. Video Series: Desmond Morris' *The Human Sexes*.
   a. "Different But Equal." Desmond Morris looks at the evolutionary reasons for men looking like men and women looking like women.
   b. "Language of the Sexes." The mating display signals of different cultures are explored and analyzed.
   c. "Patterns of Love." Morris raises thorny questions such as: Is it biologically natural for us to be faithful to one partner all our lives? Are we by nature monogamous or polygamous?
   d. "Passages of Love." This video explores the rituals that join and separate the sexes at every stage of life.
   e. "The Maternal Dilemma." Morris discusses the problems that living in cities have brought to the human species, how cultures have often favored the birth of boys over girls, and how different cultures cope with caring for a baby.
   f. "The Gender Wars." This video examines how western wedding rituals reflect the subordination of the woman to the man.

6. Essay questions
   a. Based on your viewing of the video series, *The Human Sexes*, identify the dynamics that influence the formation of gender identity. Discuss your view on the theory that one's gender identity can vary from one culture to the next.
   b. Based on your viewing of the video series, does Desmond Morris base his conclusions about sex differences based on innate

biological characteristics, or does he attribute the major influence on culture? Explain.

SENIOR YEAR COURSE OUTLINE

Purpose:

To expose students to the key concepts that comprise a men's studies course and to challenge them to engage personally the materials in such a way as to facilitate personal growth and awareness.

1. What is Men's Studies?
   a. Book: *The Masculine Self, Second Edition* (2000), pp. 3–19
   b. Exercise: Box 1.2: Thinking About Masculinity, p. 10
   c. Discussion questions
      i. Define "patriarchy" and explain how it equates to "power." Do you agree with the author's overall point of view?
      ii. Explain the interrelationship between "patriarchy," "power," "race and class." Where do you fit in this interrelationship?
2. The Current "Crisis" Among Men—See Mason, pp. 26–33
   a. Read: *The Masculine Self, Second Edition* (2000), pp. 234–262
   b. Activity: Box 12.2: The Question of Pornography—See *The Masculine Self, Second Edition* (2000), pp. 252–253
   c. Video: *The Graduate*
   d. Discussion questions
      i. What are some symptoms of "lostness" in today's generation of young men?
      ii. What other strategies and means do young men resort to as a way of coping with their problems?
      iii. Analyze the allure the feminine has for men who are experiencing lostness.
3. What Does It Mean To Be a Man Today?
   a. Book: *Under Saturn's Shadow* (1994)
   b. The Cronos-Saturn Myth—See Mason, p. 28; Hollis (1994), pp. 10–11
   c. The Saturnian Legacy—See Mason, pp. 28–29; Hollis (1994), p. 11, 12–27

    d. The Mother Complex-See Hollis (1994), pp. 28–61

    e. Male Wounding and Initiation Need—See Mason, pp. 26–29; 87–88

    f. Father Hunger—See Mason, pp. 118–120

    g. Video: *Mrs. Doubtfire*

    h. Discussion Essays

        i. Explain the effects of the "Saturnian legacy" in male's lives.

        ii. Identify the effects of the "mother complex" in your life.

        iii. Identify how the "Eight Male Secrets" operate in the life of the main character in *Mrs. Doubtfire*.

4. Male Biology

    a. Current Scientific Research—See Mason, pp. 52–55; Blum (1997); Buss (2003); Geary (1998)

    b. Current Neurobiological Research—See Mason, pp. 55–56; Gurian (1996; 1999; 2001; 2003)

    c. Male Brain Structure—See Mason, pp. 56–58; Gurian (1996; 1999; 2001; 2003)

    d. The Role of Testosterone—See Mason, pp. 58–59; Clare (2000); Gurian (1996)

    e. Read *The Masculine Self, Second Edition* (2000), pp. 51–55

    f. Discussion Essays

        i. Identify and explain the major unique brain structures in the male brain.

        ii. Explain the role and effects of testosterone in males.

5. Models of Masculine Development

    a. Developmental Models as Positive Life Maps—See Mason, pp. 77–78

    b. The Psychoanalytic View—See Mason, p. 34; 65–69

    c. Read: *The Masculine Self, Second Edition* (2000), pp. 64–80

    d. The Jungian View—See Mason, pp. 69–73

    e. Read: *The Masculine Self, Second Edition* (2000), pp. 80–83

    f. Levinson's View—See Mason, pp. 73–76

    g. Discussion Essays

        i. Explain each model's view of masculine development.

ii. Using each model's constructs, analyze the stage of development you are currently in and explain the dynamics and issues that effect your development and growth.

6. Discovering and Identifying the Masculine Wound
   a. The Fisher King Wound: Video: *The Fisher King*
   b. Shaming as Wounding—See Mason, pp. 81–87
   c. Shaming in the Literature—See Mason, pp. 87–90
   d. Facing Shaming and Wounding Productively—See Mason, pp. 83–85; Everingham (1995), pp. 94–119
   e. Video: *Legends of the Fall*
   f. Discussion Essays
      i. Examine your life and relationships and identify areas in which you feel "wounded" in some way.
      ii. Reflect on ways in which shaming and wounding have affected you.
      iii. Identify and try strategies to positively deal with your personal shaming and wounding issues.

7. Identifying and Connecting to Masculine Potentials
   a. What are archetypes?—See Mason, pp. 131–132; Moore and Gillette (1990), pp. 9–11
   b. Moore and Gillette's Boyhood Archetypes—See Mason, pp. 132–135; Moore and Gillette (1990), pp. 13–42
   c. Moore and Gillette's Mature Masculine Archetypes—See Mason, pp. 135–140; Moore and Gillette (1990), pp. 43–141; Moore and Gillette (1992a; 1992b; 1993a; 1993b)
   d. Phallos as Archetype—See Mason, pp. 140–142; *Phallos: Sacred Image of the Masculine* (1987)
   e. Other Masculine Archetypes—See *Gods in Everyman: Archetypes that Shape Men's Lives* (1989)—See Mason, pp. 262–263
   f. Accessing the Archetypes—See Mason, pp. 142–145; Moore and Gillette (1990), pp. 143–156; Moore and Gillette (1992a; 1992b; 1993a; 1993b)
   g. Discussion Essays
      i. Explain how archetypes influence thinking and behavior.

    ii. Identify which archetypes influence you most in your personality makeup.

    iii. Experiment with some of the techniques for accessing the archetypes and report on your experience.

8. Coming to Terms with Our Fathers

    a. The Positive Effects of the Father-Son Relationship—See Mason, pp. 113–115; Pruett (2000), pp. 17–100

    b. The Absent Father—See Mason, pp. 115–118; Osherson (1986)

    c. Effects of Father Hunger—See Mason, pp. 118–120

    d. Reconnecting with the Father—See Mason, pp. 120–127

    e. Read: *The Masculine Self, Second Edition* (2000), pp. 273–277

    f. Exercises for Reconnecting with the Father—See Mason, pp. 120–127

    g. Videos: *Man Without A Face* and *Field of Dreams*

9. Varieties of Sexual Identity

    a. Are there only two sexual identities?—See Mason, pp. 147–149

    b. The Psychoanalytic View—See Mason, pp. 150–152

    c. The Social Constructionist View—See Mason, pp. 152–157; Lorber (1994), pp. 55–96

    d. The Essentialist View—See Mason, pp. 157–162; Buss (1999); Miller (2000); Ridley (2003)

    e. Read: *The Masculine Self, Second Edition* (2000), pp. 212–220; 231–233

    f. Discussion Essays

        i. Explain the differences between the three viewpoints on sexual identity and their causes.

        ii. Discuss the "gender continuum" and the view that there are a number of varieties of gender expression.

        iii. What questions and / or concerns does the idea that there are multiple sexual identities rather than the traditional two raise for you?

10. Diverse Masculinities

    a. The Social Construction of Masculinities—See Mason, pp. 175–178

    b. Read: *The Masculine Self, Second Edition* (2000), pp. 263–273

c. Homosexual Masculinities—See Mason, pp. 178–186; Greenberg (1986)

d. Read: *The Masculine Self, Second Edition* (2000), pp. 222–230

e. Activity: Box 11.4: Are You Homophobic?—See *The Masculine Self, Second Edition* (2000), p. 229

f. African American Masculinities—See Mason, pp. 186–191

g. Read: *The Masculine Self, Second Edition* (2000), pp. 104–135

h. Activity: Invite an African American student and a homosexual student to talk with the group about their experiences living as a minority among a dominant sexual identity group.

i. Book: *We Real Cool: Black Men and Masculinity* (2004)

j. Discussion questions

   i. Explain the key concepts of the social constructionist view of masculinities.

   ii. React to the idea of "masculinities" rather than "Masculinity." Explain in detail.

   iii. How has the information on homosexual masculinities modified or changed your view of homosexual males? Explain.

   iv. How has the information on African American masculinities modified or changed your view of African American males? Explain.

   v. Write an analysis of your masculinity using the social constructionist methodology.

11. Men and Work

a. Read: *The Masculine Self, Second Edition* (2000), pp. 190–211

b. Video: *For Love of the Game*

c. Discussion Essays

   i. Identify the scripts that you see most often operating among men in the work world.

   ii. Do you think that the essence of a man should be defined by his work or by other qualities? Explain.

12. Masculine Health and Spirituality

a. The facts about male health statistics—See Mason, pp. 30–31; 165–166

b. Read: *The Masculine Self, Second Edition* (2000), pp. 165–166

    c. Masculine Gender Role Stress Syndrome—See Mason, pp. 166–168; Thompson and Pleck (1995)

    d. Read: *The Masculine Self, Second Edition* (2000), pp. 155–172

    e. How Modern Culture Teaches Males To Handle Pain—See Mason, pp. 168–169; Sabo and Gordon (1995)

    f. Revisioning the Male Body—See Mason, pp. 169–170

    g. Toward a Masculine Spirituality—See Mason, pp. 170–174; Tacey (1997; 2004)

    h. Video: *A River Runs Through It*

    i. Discussion Essays

      i. Analyze the Masculine Gender Stress Syndrome and identify where it has effects on you and other males.

      ii. Do you think American culture encourages healthy lifestyles in men? Explain.

      iii. Explain your personal spirituality and how it affects your lifestyle and decision-making.

13. Masculine Initiation

    a. What is initiation?—See Mason, pp. 93–94

    b. The Need for Initiation—See Mason, pp. 94–96

    c. The Prerequisites of Initiation—See Mason, pp. 96–97

    d. The Process of Initiation—See Mason, pp. 97–110

14. Planning and Executing a Vision Quest

    a. Book: *The Book of the VisionQuest: Personal Transformation in the Wilderness. Revised Edition.* (1992)

    b. Activity: Planning and Executing a Vision Quest experience as a means of seeking a future path in life.

    c. Video: *Lost Borders*

In addition to the curriculum for late-adolescent boys, it is important to undertake a screening and training process for adult advisors and teachers in this curriculum. It has been noted that adults function as a "ritual elder" in the capacities of instructor, mentor, and guide (Mason, p. 97). Careful attention needs to be used in selecting adults who understand the developmental and other issues late-adolescent boys confront, who are sensitive and supportive of boys' unique expressiveness and needs, and who have themselves made a wholesome transition into mature adulthood. Moore and Gillette (1990; 1992a; 1992b; 1993a; 1993b), Gurian (1996; 1999a; 1999b), Kipnis (1999), and others have written compellingly about the indispensability of mature men functioning as mentors and advisors in helping late-adolescent boys make a healthy transition through adolescence.

IMPLICATIONS FOR FUTURE RESEARCH

The foregoing study represents a beginning effort to identify and define the critical components of a curriculum that can facilitate the transition of late-adolescent boys into manhood. Some topics are quite well researched and much written material exists about them, but there are some topics that are not. More work needs to be done in gender identity curriculum development for adolescent boys. The Haverford School's Men's Studies Project is an outstanding example of a boarding school's dedication to research on late adolescent males and may be the only prep school program of its kind in the United States. Another example at the college level is the Men's Studies Project at the College of St. Benedict / St. John's University. There is a great need to expand this kind of research on late-adolescent boys to help them make a mature transition into adulthood.

Another issue for future research is the need for more ethnological studies and analysis focusing on late adolescent masculinities. Peer pressure and diversity play major roles in late adolescent identity formation; therefore, more work needs to be done on the multiple dynamics that mold masculine identity in specific contexts. The curriculum in this study proposes that late-adolescent boys identify and understand the dynamics that shape their masculine identity. The social constructionist methodology is a useful analytical tool in analyzing individual gender projects. Students could benefit from writing their own ethnological analyses as a means of becoming cognizant of the discourses and scripts that shape their lives. Collectively, these ethnographies could contribute to the fund of knowledge needed to address adequately the needs and issues of late-adolescent males.

Finally, this study has attempted to address the dynamics and issues that affect late-adolescent males by considering all the perspectives that comprise the literature on masculine identity. Frequently, the perspectives make polemical attacks on other perspectives rather than engage in a constructive dialogue that elicits a deeper and broader understanding. More scholarship needs to take a holistic approach to men's studies as a means of explicating the dynamics that affect men's lives. Echoing what was said at the beginning of this study, a "bio-psycho-social model of the construction of gender" (Pollack and Levant, 1995, p. 386) is needed. Perhaps even that paradigm is too limited and needs to take into account other diverse perspectives. It is a much-needed engagement that should take place when the lives of late-adolescent males in transition to manhood are at stake.

CONCLUSION

This study has attempted to present an overview and a curriculum composed of the bio-psycho-social dynamics that make up masculine identity and influence boys' transition from late-adolescence to manhood. In order to accomplish this objective, the psychoanalytic, the essentialist, and the social constructionist perspectives have been surveyed and presented in an attempt to provide a balanced account. Each perspective has been included in the gender studies curriculum proposed herein. The men's studies curriculum offered here draws on the research findings of a number of academic disciplines, including literature, history, anthropology, biology, neurology, developmental and evolutionary psychology, sociology, ethnology, and theology. Every effort has been made to provide a comprehensive yet brief overview of the key concepts involved in each chapter. Nevertheless, much more needs to be done to address other issues that affect the lives of late-adolescent boys that are beyond the scope of this present work.

A men's studies curriculum is more than just a communication of facts and concepts in a systematic manner. It is also an embodied presentation by a teacher-mentor-guide in the manner of the ritual elder in initiatory rites of passage. The teacher of a curriculum such as is proposed in this study needs to be psychologically healthy and aware, sensitive, knowledgeable about the needs and issues of late-adolescent males, and possess a capacity for establishing an empathic relation with this cohort. More men who possess these qualities are needed to work with late-adolescent males in order to make a positive difference in their lives.

According to social critics and the experts in the field of adolescence, adolescent males are experiencing a crisis in this present time. The Chinese character for crisis is written in such a way that its connotation is both a "time of danger" and a "time of opportunity." The male transition from boyhood into manhood has been universally acknowledged throughout millennia and across cultures as fraught with danger and opportunity. It is so easy to become stuck in boyhood ways and thinking and never emerge into manhood's ways and thinking. In this current age, when there are so many competing as well as negative messages about what it means to be a man, it is imperative that the challenge be met to address the needs of young men. This curriculum is offered as a way to grapple with the needs and issues of males making this dangerous yet opportunistic passage into manhood. With so much at stake in the lives of adolescent males, this important work must be done.

APPENDIX A

GURIAN–BRAIN GENDER DIFFERENCES

PART OF BRAIN	FUNCTION	SIMILARITIES AND DIFFERENCES	IMPACT
Amygdala	Part of limbic system involved in emotional processing	Larger in males	Helps make males more aggressive
Arcuate fasciculus	Curving bundle of nerve fibers in the central nervous system	Likely develops earlier in girls as evidenced by their earlier speech capabilities	Females speak in sentences earlier than males do
Basal ganglia	Control movement sequences when necessary, e.g., walking	Likely to engage more quickly in male brain—when required	Males generally quicker to respond to attention demands in physical environment
Brain stem	Connects brain to spinal cord; handles primitive drives	Male brain at rest here to greater extent	Faster, immediate and physical crisis response moves data to brain stem more quickly
Broca's area	Motor area for speech; processes grammatical structures and word production	More highly active in females	Improved verbal communication skills in females
Cerebellum	Contains neurons that connect to other parts of the brain and spinal cord and facilitate smooth, precise movement; balance; and speech	Stronger connecting pathways in female brain between brain parts	Females have superior language and fine-motor skills; males less intuitive, as fewer parts of brain involved in tasking

PART OF BRAIN	FUNCTION	SIMILARITIES AND DIFFERENCES	IMPACT
Cerebral cortex	Contains neurons that promote higher intellectual functions and memory, and interprets sensory impulses	Thicker in males on the right side of brain; thicker in females on the left side	Males tend to be right-brain dominant; females tend to be left-brain dominant
Cerebrum	Upper or main part of the brain, largest part of human brain, controls conscious and voluntary processes; the thinking center	Females use more volume and particular areas to do same tasks	Greater capacity to multitask in females; female cerebrum always active
Corpus callosum	Connects two hemispheres of the brain	Larger in females	Helps females coordinate two sides of brain better
Dopamine	An intermediate biochemical product in the synthesis of norepinephrine, epinephrine, and melanin; neurotransmitter	In healthy brains, few differences known between male and female patterns	Problems in dopamine and other select neurotransmitters a likely cause of brain disorders more prevalent in males, such as schizophrenia and autism
Estrogen	Several female sex hormones that cause estrus; shapes female brain	Much more present in females than males	In females lowers aggression, competition, self-assertion, self-reliance
Frontal lobe	Facilitates speech, thought, and emotion; produces neurons for skilled movement	Likely more active in females	Improved verbal communication skills in females
Hippocampus	Ridge along the lower section of each lateral ventricle of the brain; memory storage	Significant difference in size; larger in females; number and speed of neuron transmissions higher in females	Increased memory storage in females
Hypothalamus	Controls automatic body processes (heart beat, breathing, temperature); also controls sexuality differences	Female and male cell structures and patterns significantly different; denser in males; less dense in females	Males greater and more constant sex drive

PART OF BRAIN	FUNCTION	SIMILARITIES AND DIFFERENCES	IMPACT
Left hemisphere	Processes language in most people; reading, writing, math, verbal thoughts and memory, temporal, sequential language, linguistic consciousness, conscious self-image, defense mechanisms, projection, self-deception, denial	Usually better developed in the female brain; creates superiority at language tasks	Females superior at listening, communicating, all language-based learning
Limbic system	Amygdala, septal nucleus, hypothalamus, pleasure principle, hippocampus, memory, emotions	Female brain at rest here to greater extent	Moves sensory data up the neocortex more rapidly
Medulla Oblongata	Widening continuation of the spinal cord, forming the lowest part of the brain and containing nerve centers that control breathing and circulation	Likely increase in male brain-stem functioning implies stronger relationship to connections between medulla oblongata and resting male brain	Possible increase in SIDS death in males could be explained by this relationship; increased male aggression
Melatonin	Hormone produced by the pineal body; lightens skin pigmentation, inhibits estrus; secretion inhibited by sunlight	Likely higher concentration, at times, in females	May be partial explanation of females' increased sensitivity to bright light
Neocortex	Thin, gray outer layer of the brain's cortex; associated with human thought and higher intelligence	Difference in basic size of brain affects amount of brain material (male brains have greater mass)	Basic kinds of intelligence likely influenced by these differences
Neurotransmitters	Biochemical substances that transmit or inhibit nerve impulses at a synapse; deliver messages from one neuron to the next; vitally important in brain functioning	Some neuro-transmitters more prevalent in males, some in females	Clearly affect differences in how male and female brains process data

PART OF BRAIN	FUNCTION	SIMILARITIES AND DIFFERENCES	IMPACT
Occipital lobe	Detects and interprets visual images	Differences evident in divergent responses to light sensitivity	Females see better in lower light; males see better in brighter light
Oxytocin	Hormone of the posterior pituitary gland; increases contractions of the smooth muscle of the uterus and facilitates secretion of milk	Much more functionally present in females than males	Likely involved in mother-child bonding capacity being increased at birth
Parietal lobe	Perceives and interprets bodily sensations such as tough, pressure, pain, and temperature	In females, more data move through than in males; male brain better at "zoning out"	Females have more tactile sensitivity
Peptids	Brain chemicals; group of compounds formed from two or more amino acids; cortisol and endorphins	Same compounds exist in male and female, but significantly different levels among peptides	Low cortisol levels lead to feelings of euphoria; high cortisol levels can lead to despair
Pituitary gland	Secretes hormones influencing growth, metabolism, and activity of other glands	Likely more strongly or directly relates fight-or-flight data from hypothalamus to endocrine gland system in males	Males' fight or flight more rapidly engaged
Progesterone	Steroid hormone of the corpus luteum, active in preparing the uterus for fertilized ovum	Much more functional and present in females	Primarily to promote conditions for healthy pregnancy
Right hemisphere	Interprets emotional contents; tone of voice; facial expressions; gestures; melodic speech; social, musical, visual, spatial, and environmental awareness; unconscious self-image, body image, emotional and visual memory	Boys use right side of brain to work on abstract problems; girls use both sides	Males superior at spatial relationships

PART OF BRAIN	FUNCTION	SIMILARITIES AND DIFFERENCES	IMPACT
Sensory system	Includes two parts: receptors, which receive sensory input, and transformers, which take separate pieces of information and process into integrated knowledge	Clear differences throughout entire sensory reactive system	Different sensory strengths and weaknesses consistent in common male and female patterns
Serotonin	Both neurotransmitter and hormone; regulates body temperature, sensory perception, and onset of sleep	Gender difference in these physiological states likely explained partially through differences in amount and distribution of this monoamine	Basic differences in male and female sensory perception styles likely affected by serotonin levels
Synapse	Minute space between one nerve cell and another through which nerve impulses are transmitted	Likely high level of similarity in male and female brains	Subtle differences (affected by hormones?) could be partial explanation of different responsiveness in genders
Temporal lobe	Part of memory storage; recognizes some tones and volume	Stronger neuron connections in females would explain superiority in language tasks	Female connections and neuron pathways produce superiority at communicative tasks
Testosterone	Male steroid sex hormone	Much more present and functional in males	Increases aggression, competition, self-assertion, and self-reliance
Thalamus	Regulates emotional life and physical safety; processes incoming sensory information; tells us what's going on outside body	Processes data faster in females, especially at certain times in menstrual cycle	Greater stress and activity in female thalamus at varying times during menstruation

PART OF BRAIN	FUNCTION	SIMILARITIES AND DIFFERENCES	IMPACT
Vasopressin	Hormone secreted by posterior lobe of pituitary gland; increases blood pressure by constricting arterioles	Involved in water retention, blood pressure, and memory	Differences in males and females in all these areas suggest some differences in this peptide's involvement in males and females
Werencke's area	Links language and thought; word comprehension	Likely more highly active in females	Improved verbal communication skills in females

Source: From Gurian, 2001, pp. 20–26. Used with permission.

APPENDIX B

HALPERN—MALE AND FEMALE BRAIN DIFFERENCES

COGNITIVE TESTS AND TASKS THAT USUALLY SHOW SEX DIFFERENCES

Type of test / task	Example
Tasks and tests on which women obtain higher average scores	

Tasks that require rapid access to and use of phonological, semantic, and other information in long-term memory	Verbal fluency-phonological retrieval
	Synonym generation-meaning retrieval
	  Associative memory
	  Memory battery-multiple tests
	Spelling and anagrams
	Mathematical calculations
	Memory for spatial location
	Memory for odors

Knowledge Areas	Literature Foreign languages
Production and comprehension of complex prose	Reading comprehension Writing
Fine motor tasks	Mirror tracing-novel, complex figures Pegboard tasks Matching and coding tasks
Perceptual speed	Multiple speeded tasks "Finding As" – an embedded-letters test
Decoding nonverbal communication	
Perceptual thresholds (large, varied literature with multiple modalities	Touch – lower thresholds Taste – lower thresholds Hearing – males have greater hearing loss with age Odor – lower thresholds
Higher grades in school (all or most subjects)	
Speech articulation	Tongue twisters

Type of test / task	Example
Tasks and tests on which men obtain higher average scores	
Tasks that require transformations in visual working memory	Mental rotation Piaget Water Level Test
Tasks that involve moving objects Motor tasks that involve aiming	Dynamic spatiotemporal tasks Accuracy in throwing balls or darts
Knowledge areas General knowledge	Wechsler Adult Intelligence Scale Geography knowledge Math and science knowledge
Tests of fluid reasoning (especially in math and science domains)	Proportional reasoning tasks Scholastic Assessment Test – Mathematics Graduate Record Examination – Quantitative Mechanical Reasoning Verbal analogies Scientific reasoning

Males are also overrepresented at the low-ability end of many distributions, including the following examples: mental retardation (some types), majority of attention deficit disorders, delayed speech, dyslexia (even allowing for possible referral bias; stuttering, and learning disabilities and emotional disturbances. In addition, males are generally more variable.
*Source:*From Halpern, 1997, p. 1102. Used with permission.

APPENDIX C

LESSON PLANS AND ADDITIONAL MATERIALS

WHAT DOES IT MEAN TO BE A MAN?: A MEN'S STUDIES COURSE

Course Outline

I. What is Men's Studies?
Book: *The Masculine Self,* pp. 3–18
Video: The Enduring Paradox
Exercise: Read 1.1 and 1.2 and answer the following questions: What is masculinity? How do you define masculinity?
Exercise: Name some traditionally masculine roles and some traditionally feminine roles.

II. Sociohistorical Overview of Masculinity

III. The Current "Crisis" Among Men
Book: *The Masculine Self*
Video: **The Graduate**
Video: **Colors**
Essay: Analyze the two movies viewed and identify the core problems from which the main characters suffer from.

IV. What Does It Mean To Be A Man Today?
Book: *Under Saturn's Shadow*
Video: **Mrs. Doubtfire**
Essay: In your opinion, does the main character get treated fairly by the "system" with regard to his children? What does it say about masculinity when a man can get away with acting like a woman?

V. Male Biology
Book: *The Masculine Self*
Video: Desmond Morris' *The Human Sexes* **"Different but Equal"**

VI. Models of Masculine Development
Book: *The Masculine Self*

VII. Discovering and Identifying the Masculine Wound
        Video: **The Fisher King**
        Video: **Legends of the Fall**
        Exercises: Everingham
VIII. Identifying and Connecting to Masculine Potentials
        Book: *King, Warrior, Magician, Lover*
  IX. Coming To Terms With Our Fathers
        Book: *The Masculine Self*
        Video: **Man Without A Face**
        Video: **Field of Dreams**
        Video: **Dead Poet's Society**
        Essay: Write an essay in which you identify the main character
        with which you most relate to as he deals with his "father." Tell
        why you identify with this character.
        Exercises: Drew, Where Were You When I Needed You, Dad?
   X. Varieties of Sexual Identity
        Book: *The Masculine Self*
        Handouts: A New Approach to Handling Sexual Ambiguities,
        Male Sexual Scripts, Female Sexual Scripts, Contemporary Sexual
        Scripts
  XI. Diverse Masculinities
        Book: *The Masculine Self*
        Book: *We Be Cool*
        Essay: Write an analysis of your personal masculinity.
 XII. Masculine Health and Spirituality
        Book: *The Masculine Self*
        Book: Gurian, The Ten Integrities
        Video: **A River Runs Through It**
        Essay: Where are you with your spirituality? Identify and explain
        the key components of your beliefs and how they support your self
        understanding as a man.
XIII. Men and Work
        Book: *The Masculine Self*
        Video: **For Love of the Game**
XIV. Masculine Initiation

XV. Planning and Executing a Vision Quest
Video: Desmond Morris' *The Human Sexes* **"Passages of Life"**
Video: **Lost Borders**

I. Topic: What is men's studies?

Definition: The term "men's studies" is applied to courses and books that discuss men as a distinct gender or social, cultural or sexual group.

- Course will focus on the key components that make men unique
- Multidisciplinary approach: biology, sociology, psychology, anthropology, evolutionary and developmental psychology, mythology, theology, history

Present key concepts found in *The Masculine Self*, pp. 4–5

1. Pleck's Male Sex Role Identity paradigm (*The Myth of Masculinity*)
2. Note Kilmartin's rationale for a men's studies focus (pages 4–5)

Exercise: Name some traditionally masculine roles and some traditionally feminine roles. Identify those roles that are now shared by both genders. Discuss.

Exercise: Read 1.1 and 1.2 and answer the following questions: What is masculinity? How do you define masculinity? Discuss.

Video: **Gender: The Enduring Paradox**

Study Questions:

1. What is the critical difference between the terms "woman / man" and "female / male" as descriptors?
2. List some stereotypes ascribed to girls / boys.
3. How do you account for the assertion made in the video that "throughout the world, men hold the power?"
4. What modern "rites of passage" are there in boys' lives?

5. Do you agree with the notion that "the core of femininity is to get children into the next generation?"
6. How do you react to the men who stay at home and do the "fathering" while the mother works outside the home?
7. Identify the factors that shape children into males / females.
8. List the attributes ascribed to a man / a woman?
9. How do you react to the idea that in American Indian culture there is a gender designation as "berdache?"
10. React to the notion of "gender diversity" and to the statement that "in Western society, there is no room for gender diversity."
11. React to the idea of "Black male energy" and the assertion that American society does not know how to handle this person.
12. What stereotypes are ascribed to Asian women / Asian men?
13. List some of the factors that influence gender.
14. "What men and women are is diverse." React to this statement.

II. A Socio-Historical Overview of Masculinity

Objectives:

*   To understand the role of patriarchy in men's and women's socialization.
*   To understand the changing gender role expectations of men throughout Western history.
*   To understand men's current status in American society from gender role and historical perspectives.

1. Definition of patriarchy. (Mason, p. 1)
2. Historical Overview of Masculinity Ideals
    *   Mythological Roots (Mason, p. 1)
    *   Epic Male (Mason, p. 2–3)
    *   Spiritual Male (Mason, pp. 3–4)
    *   Chivalric Male (Mason, pp. 4)
    *   Renaissance Male (Mason, p. 4–5)
    *   Bourgeois Male (Mason, pp. 5)
    *   The 16th Century Enclosure Movement and Its Implications (Mason, pp. 5–6)

- Kimbrell's Four "Masculine Mystique" Archetypes (Mason, pp. 6–8)
- Self Made Man (Mason, p. 8–9)
- Psychological Male (Mason, pp. 9)
- Postmodern Man (Mason, p. 10–11)
- Pleck's Masculine Sex Role Identity and Sex Role Strain Paradigm (Mason, pp. 10–11)
- Modern Men's Movement (Mason, pp. 12)
- Clatterbaugh's Eight Strands of the Modern Men's Movement (Mason, pp. 11–12)
- Conservative Perspective (Mason, pp. 12–14)
- Profeminist Perspective (Mason, pp. 14–15)
- Men's Rights Movement (Mason, pp. 15–17)
- Mythopoetic Men's Movement (Mason, pp. 17–18)
- Socialist Perspective (Mason, pp. 18–19)
- Gay Male Perspective (Mason, pp. 19–22)
- African American Men's Perspective (Mason, pp. 22–24)
- Evangelical Christian Men's Movement (Mason, pp. 24–26)

Essay: Based on the foregoing presentation, which manhood ideal do you most strongly identity with? With which manhood ideal do you least identify? Which of the modern men's movement perspectives do you most agree with? Least agree with? Why?

III. THE CURRENT "CRISIS" AMONG MEN

Objectives:

- To understand, articulate, and apply the key issues and ideas explaining the contemporary "crisis in masculinity."
- To understand, articulate, and apply the effects of the Boy Code in life.
- To understand, articulate, and apply the factors that contribute to the problems men have with gender role strain.

1. Read: Mason, pp. 26–33.
2. Video: **The Graduate**
3. Video: **Colors**

4. Joseph Pleck's, *The Myth of Masculinity* (1981) Masculine Sex Role Identity paradigm (Mason, pp. 10–12)

The Graduate viewing notes:

In the beginning of the film, note the "lostness" of the film's central character, Ben, and its symptoms: malaise, lack of direction, lack of motivation, emotional isolation. When Ben is questioned about his feelings and thoughts he cannot identify or articulate them, a condition known as "alexithymia." (Mason, pp. 86) Ben spends his days doing nothing—lounging in his room looking at his aquarium or lounging in his parents' pool—and his nights acting out in an affair with the wife of his parents' best friends.

The Graduate Discussion Questions:

1. What are some symptoms of lostness in today's generation of young men?
2. What other strategies and means do young men resort to as a way of coping with their problems?
3. Analyze the allure the feminine has for men who are experiencing "lostness."

Colors viewing notes:

In this movie, it is important to note the role (and absence) of male mentors in the healthy development and maturity of young men. In the absence of modern male rites of passage, "pseudo-rituals" of patriarchal masculinity emerge that are destructive. (Mason, p. 29) Note the devastating impact these rituals have on young Latino men and others who lack positive male mentors in their lives. Another important feature in this movie is the pervasiveness of violence which account for the alarming statistics about male mortality. (Mason, pp. 30) At the movie's end, there is a powerful yet brutal gang-style initiation enactment.

Colors Discussion Questions:

1. Describe the lostness of the gang members portrayed in the movie. Do you think they are aware of their lostness?

2. Identify some of the effects of inadequate healthy male figures in the gang members' lives.
3. What values do you think are taught to the young Latino boy in his gang initiation experience?

IV. WHAT DOES IT MEAN TO BE A MAN TODAY

Objectives:

- To understand, articulate, and apply Hollis' 8 male secrets to one's own life and circumstances.
- To understand, articulate, and apply the 3 Saturnian Legacies to oneself and to men in general.

1. James Hollis, *Under Saturn's Shadow* with 15 homework assignments based on the reading along with outline of the book.
   a. The Cronos-Saturn Myth (Mason, pp. 28; Hollis, pp. 10–11)
   b. The Saturnian Legacy (Mason, pp. 28–29; Hollis, p. 11, 12–27)
   c. The Mother Complex (Hollis, 28–61)
   d. Male Wounding and Initiation Need (Mason, pp. 87–88, 92–94)
   e. Father Hunger (Mason, 118–120)
2. Video: **Mrs. Doubtfire**
3. Discussion Questions for Personal Growth
   a. Explain the effects of the "Saturnian Legacy" your own and in men's lives in general.
   b. Identify the effects of the "mother complex" in your life.
   c. Identify how the "Eight Male Secrets" operate in the life of the main character in *Mrs. Doubtfire*

Mrs. Doubtfire viewing notes:

Note the legal system's handling of the divorce between the parents and the presumption of custody with the mother. This pretext is the premise upon which the gender charade is based for giving the father more visitation access to his children. Note also the gender comparisons between the men in the movie: the straight new boyfriend, the gay brother and his partner, and the cross-dressing father. The diversity of masculinity expressed in this movie raises complex and interesting questions about who is most authentic and healthy in his gender identity. Furthermore, the movie raises questions about the ambiguity of gender identity and traditional conceptions of what it means to be male and female.

Under Saturn's Shadow **Study Questions, p. Introduction-p. 11**

1. According to Hollis, what is the first requisite that men must do for healing? (pp. 8–9)
2. Explain the myth of Cronus-Saturn. (p. 10)

Under Saturn's Shadow **Study Questions, pp. 12–20**

1. What is the first Saturnian message? (p. 14)
2. What is the second Saturnian message? (pp. 14–15)
3. What is the third Saturnian message? (p. 15)
4. What is the purpose of a "rite of passage?" (pp. 16–17)
5. What are the 6 stages in rites of passage? (pp. 17–19)

Under Saturn's Shadow **Study Questions, pp. 20–27**

1. What is the first male secret? (p. 21)
   Do you agree or disagree with the author's assertion? Why or why not?
2. Define "power complex." (p. 23)
3. What is the second male secret? (p. 24)
4. Of what specifically are men afraid? (pp. 24–25)

Under Saturn's Shadow **Study Questions, pp. 28–35**

1. Name and explain the three levels on which life is enacted? (p. 29)
2. Define the "mother complex." (p. 29)
3. What is the third male secret? (p. 30)
4. According to Jung, the greatest burden for a child is the unlived life of the parent. Explain this idea. (p. 34).

5. What is the dark side of the mother complex? (p. 34)
6. Explain how the mother complex can operate in a man's marriage. (p. 35)

Under Saturn's Shadow Study Questions, pp. 35–43

1. Name the effects of fear in men's lives. (pp. 35–36)
2. React to the following quotation from the book: "When men feel the wound that cannot heal, they either bury themselves in a woman's arms and ask her for healing, which she cannot provide, or they hide themselves in macho pride and enforced loneliness." (p. 40)
3. Explain the role of the hero archetype. (p. 40)
4. Define the three levels men experience the feminine. (pp. 41–42)

Under Saturn's Shadow Study Questions, pp. 43–52

1. What is one of the greatest developmental tasks a man must achieve? (p. 47)
2. What are the consequences of being unaware of one's own anima? (pp. 49–51)
3. What possible outcomes result if a man does not become conscious of his mother complex? (p. 51)

Under Saturn's Shadow Study Questions, pp. 52–61

1. React to the following quotation from the book: "No man can be himself until he has confronted the mother experience.... Only through the courage to confront this potential abyss can he become independent and free of anger. If he till blames mother or women, he has not yet grown up; he still seeks protection, or avoids the domination, of mother." (p. 54)
2. Explain "birth separation" and its consequences. (p. 55)
3. What two kinds of wounds is a child most likely to suffer from his mother? (p. 56)

4. Name and explain the four possible ways anger might be processed. (pp. 57–58)
5. Explain the "virgin-whore" complex. (p. 60)

Under Saturn's Shadow Study Questions, pp. 62–71

1. Explain the "double-edged sword of wounding." (p. 64)
2. Name the fifth male secret. (p. 65)
3. According to Joseph Campbell, what is the significance of initiation and wounding? (pp. 65–66)
4. What is the meaning of ritual mutilation? (p. 66)

Under Saturn's Shadow Study Questions, pp. 72–82

1. Explain how athletics is a way of a youth's seeking initiation. (p. 72)
2. Name and explain the fourth male secret. (p. 73)
3. Explain what is meant when it is said: "What modern man most suffers from is the wounding without transformation." (pp. 75–76)
4. What is the masculine "double-bind?" (p. 77)
5. Explain what is meant by the quotation from the book: "Men's lives are violent because their souls have been violated." (pp. 79–82)

Under Saturn's Shadow Study Questions, pp. 83–91

1. Describe the dual nature of the Great Mother archetype. (p. 83)
2. Describe the dual nature of the father archetype. (p. 83)
3. Describe the mythology of the Great Mother. (p. 84)
4. Describe the mythology of the Sky Father. (p. 84)
5. Name the seventh male secret. (p. 85)
6. Explain the negative father complex (p. 87)
7. Name the three things sons need from their fathers. (pp. 89–90)

Under Saturn's Shadow Study Questions, pp. 91–99

1. According to Eugene Monick, how are men also wounded? (pp. 94–95)

2. In what ways does the son compensate for the father-son wound? (p. 99)
3. Name the eighth male secret. (p. 99)

Under Saturn's Shadow Study Questions, pp. 100–109

1. What role expectations is a man suppose to live up to? (p. 100)
2. How does a man begin the process of healing? (p. 101)
3. What are men afraid of? (p. 102)
4. How does a man begin to heal his fear? (p. 102)
5. In what four ways do men develop a distorted relationship to the feminine? (pp. 102–104)

Under Saturn's Shadow Study Questions, pp. 109–115

1. Explain why men live a false self. (p. 109)
2. Explain how and why men project their mother complex onto their significant other women. (p. 111)
3. Explain why Hollis advocates psychotherapy for men's healing. (pp. 114–115)
4. How does a man begin to heal his fear? (p. 102)

Under Saturn's Shadow Study Questions, pp. 115–123

1. Name the seven steps to healing. (p. 116)
2. Explain the process of "re-membering the loss of the fathers." (pp. 116–119)
3. What critical questions does a man need to ask in "remembering the loss of the fathers." (p. 119)
4. What are the central secrets of men? (p. 122)
5. What is the value of therapy for men? (p. 122)
6. Describe mentoring and its value. (p. 123)

Under Saturn's Shadow Study Questions, pp. 123–134

1. Explain what Hollis means when he says that men must "risk loving men." (pp. 123–125)

2. Name and explain the archetypal need a boy has from his father. (p. 127)
3. Discuss: "Being a man means knowing what you want and then mobilizing the inner resources to achieve it." (p. 128)
4. Explain what Hollis means when he says that a man must "recover the soul's journey." (pp. 130–133)
5. What does Hollis mean when he urges men to "join the revolution"? (p. 134)

V. MALE BIOLOGY

Objectives:

- To understand, articulate, and apply the evolutionary biological explanation of sex differences.
- To understand and articulate the unique brain structures found in males and the effects these structures have on male abilities.
- To understand and articulate the role and effects of testosterone on male thinking and behavior.

1. Current Scientific Research (Mason, pp. 52–55)
2. Current Neurobiological Research (Mason, pp. 55–56)
3. Main Brain Structure (Mason, pp. 56–58, 229–234)
4. The Role of Testosterone (Mason, pp. 58–59)
5. Read: Kilmartin, *The Masculine Self, Second Edition,* pp. 51–63 with exercise 3.1 entitled "Sociobiological Proposals" (p. 56)
6. Video: *Desmond Morris' The Human Sexes,* **"Different but Equal"**
7. General Discussion Questions:
   i. Identify and explain the major structures in the male brain and their effects in males
   ii. Explain the role and effects of testosterone in males

Desmond Morris' *The Human Sexes,* **"Different but Equal"** viewing notes:
WARNING: THIS VIDEO CONTAINS GRAPHIC NUDITY. Desmond Morris discusses the biological and genetic differences between males and females based on evolutionary and sociocultural influences.
"Different but Equal" Video Study Questions:

1. According to Morris, what makes males biologically unique? What makes females biologically unique?
2. React to Morris' statement that "our sexuality is flexible."
3. What physical features distinguish a male face?
4. What features distinguish male brains from female brains?

VI. MODELS OF MASCULINE DEVELOPMENT

Objectives:

* To understand, articulate, and apply Erikson's, Jung's, and Levinson's models of human development as it relates to males.

1. Read Mason, pp. 63–78
2. Read *The Masculine Self*, pp. 64–83
3. Developmental Models as Positive Life Maps (Mason, 77–78)
4. The Psychoanalytic View (Mason, pp. 65–69)
5. The Jungian View (Mason, pp. 69–73)
6. Levinson's View (Mason, pp. 73–76)
7. Discussion Questions:
    i. Explain each model's view of masculine development.
    ii. Using each model's constructs, analyze the stage of development you are currently in and explain the dynamics and issues that effect your development and growth.

Erik Erikson's Epigenetic Developmental Model

	A Psychosocial Crises	B Radius of Significant Relations	C Related Elements of Social Order	D Psychosocial Modalities	E Psychosexual Stages
I	Trust vs. Mistrust	Maternal Person	Cosmic Order	To get / To give in return	Oral-Respiratory Sensory-Kinesthetic (Incorporative Modes)
II	Autonomy vs. Shame, Doubt	Parental Persons	"Law and Order"	To hold (on) / To let (go)	Anal-Urethral, Muscular (Retentive-Eliminative)
III	Initiative vs. Guilt	Basic Family	Ideal Prototypes	To make (=going after) To "make like" (=playing)	Infantile-Genital, Locomotor (Intrusive, Inclusive)
IV	Industry vs. Inferiority	"Neighborhood," School	Technological Elements	To make things (=completing) To make things together	"Latency"
V	Identity and Repudiation vs. Identity Diffusion	Peer Groups and Outgroups; Models of Leadership	Ideological Perspectives	To be oneself (or not to be) To share being oneself	Puberty
VI	Intimacy and Solidarity vs. Isolation	Partners in Friendship Sex, Competition, Cooperation	Patterns of Cooperation and Competition	To lose and find oneself in another	Genitality
VII	Generativity vs. Self-absorption	Divided Labor and Shared Household	Currents of Education and Tradition	To make be / To take care of	
VIII	Integrity vs. Despair	"Mankind" "My Kind"	Wisdom	To be, through having been / To face not being	

Source: From Erikson, 1980, p. 178. Used with permission.

Carl Jung's Developmental Model

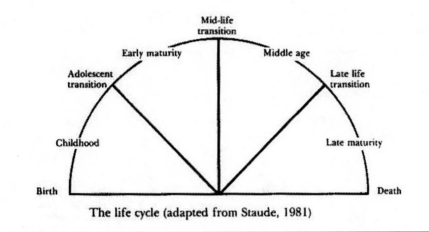

The life cycle (adapted from Staude, 1981)

Source: Diagram found in Stevens, 2003, p. 62. Used with permission.

Jung's Goal of Masculine Development

Union of the Opposites = Balance and **Freedom** in one's psychological make-up.

masculine–feminine
puer (adventurous, youthful attitude)–senex (conservative old man)
good–evil (shadow)
immanence (absorption in the moment)–transcendence (seeing the big picture)
self–world
body–spirit

Jung talked about "stages of development" in terms of consciousness.

First half of life=develop ego structure and appropriate persona and make one's place in the world. Jung="initiation into outward reality."

Second half of life = Jung = "initiation into the inner reality." Individuation, to become as much of an individual personality as one can be.

A series of integrations were necessary to accomplish this task:
ego-persona / shadow
ego-persona-shadow / anima / animus
anima / animus / Self

The stages of development of an ego-Self axis:

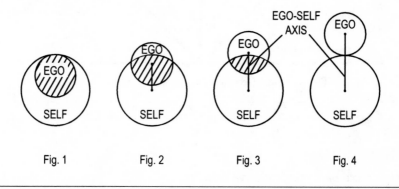

| Fig. 1 | Fig. 2 | Fig. 3 | Fig. 4 |

Source: Edinger, 1992, p. 5. Used with permission.

Five Stages of Masculine Development
1. Bonding / separating from the Mother
2. Hero Stage--identification with the Father
3. Anima Stage--returning to the feminine
4. Odysseus Stage--finding / living out a sense of mission
5. Dealing with God issue--life's meaning

Development as a sequence or spiral or circles which nest within each other.

Daniel J. Levinson's Life Structure Developmental Model

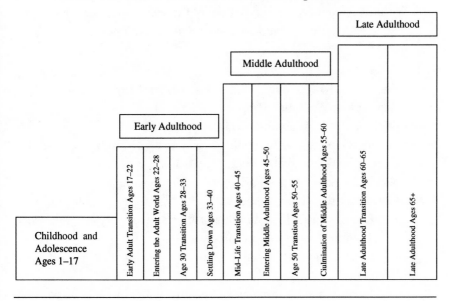

Source: From Levinson, 1987, p. 57.

VII. DISCOVERING AND IDENTIFYING THE MASCULINE WOUND

Objectives:

- To understand, articulate, and apply the dynamics of male wounding to oneself.
- To understand, articulate, and apply the concept of "shaming as wounding."

- To understand and articulate the effects of wounding in males.
- To understand, articulate, and apply the techniques for confronting and acknowledging shaming and wounding in oneself.

1. Read Mason, pp. 79–92
2. The Fisher King Wound: Video: **The Fisher King**
3. Shaming as Wounding (Mason, pp. 81–87)
4. Shaming in the Literature (Mason, pp. 87–90)
5. Facing Shaming and Wounding Productively (Mason, pp. 83–85)
6. Exercises (Everingham, 1995, pp. 94–119)
7. Video: **Legends of the Fall**
8. General Discussion Questions:
   i.   Examine your life and relationships and identify areas in which you feel "wounded" in some way.
   ii. Reflect on ways in which shaming and wounding have affected you.
   iii. Identify and try strategies to positively deal with your personal shaming and wounding issues.

The Fisher King Video Viewing Notes:

For background information on the myth of the Fisher King, read Johnson's *He: Understanding Masculine Psychology* (1990). The movie powerfully illustrates the effects of wounding and the need to undergo some kind of inner journey (quest) for healing. The positive mentor is a key concept in facilitating healing—one who guides and assists another to face the destructive effects of shaming and wounding in one's life.

Legends of the Fall Video Viewing Notes:

This movie illustrates the masculine wound and its effects on a man's life. Note also the effects of a powerful anima figure (Susannah, played by Julia Ormond) on the two older brothers. Note how the drive to be successful and the failure to protect one's kin are driving motives in these men's definition of manhood.

VIII. IDENTIFYING AND CONNECTING TO MASCULINE POTENTIALS

Objectives:

- To understand and articulate the meaning of archetype.
- To understand, articulate, and apply Moore and Gillette's four boyhood and four mature masculine archetypes.
- To understand, articulate, and apply Monick's concept of the Phallos archetype.
- To understand, articulate, and apply techniques for accessing the archetypes.

1. Read Mason, pp. 131–146
2. Read Moore and Gillette, *King, Warrior, Magician, Lover: Recovering the Archetypes of the Mature Masculine* (1991) with 13 homework assignments
3. What are archetypes? (Mason, pp. 131–132; Moore and Gillette, pp. 9–11)
4. Moore and Gillette's the Boyhood Archetypes (Mason, pp. 132–135; Moore and Gillette, pp. 13–42)
5. Moore and Gillette's Mature Masculine Archetypes (Mason, pp. 135–140; Moore and Gillette, pp. 43–141)
6. Phallos as Archetype (Mason, pp. 140–142; Monick, 1987, *Phallos: Sacred Image of the Masculine*)
7. Other Masculine Archetypes (Bolen, 1989, *Gods in Everyman: Archetypes that Shape Men's Lives*) Handout: "God Archetype Chart" (Mason, pp. 262–263)
8. General Discussion Questions:
   i. Explain how archetypes influence thinking and behavior.
   ii. Identify which archetypes influence you most in your personality makeup.
   iii. Experiment with some of the techniques for accessing the archetypes and report on your experience.

King, Warrior, Magician, Lover Study Questions, pp. 3–11

1. What are the pseudo-rituals in our culture? Name some. (pp. 5–6)
2. What are the two key factors in genuine initiations? (pp. 6–7)

256   CROSSING INTO MANHOOD: A MEN'S STUDIES CURRICULUM

3. Define collective unconscious. (p. 9)
4. Define archetypes. (pp. 9, 44)

King, Warrior, Magician, Lover Study Questions, pp. 12–27

1. Explain the structure of the archetypes. (pp. 14–15)
2. Define the Divine Child archetype. (pp. 15–23)
3. Define the High Chair Tyrant archetype. (pp. 23–25)
4. Define the Weakling prince archetype. (pp. 25–26)
5. How do you manifest these archetypes in your life?

King, Warrior, Magician, Lover Study Questions, pp. 37–45

1. What qualities make up the Hero archetype? (pp. 37–42)
2. Define the Grandstander Bully archetype. (pp. 37–39)
3. Define the Coward archetype? (pp. 39–40)
4. What is the significance of the death of the Hero archetype? (p. 41)
5. What are the four major forms of the mature masculine archetypes? (pp. 43–44)
6. Explain the ego as the metaphorical chairman of the board. (pp. 44–45)

King, Warrior, Magician, Lover Study Questions, pp. 49–63

1. Explain the preeminence of the King archetype. (p. 49)
2. Name the two functions of the King archetype. (p. 52)
3. Explain the King archetype ordering function. (pp. 54–58)
4. Explain the King archetype fertility and blessing functions. (pp. 58–63)

King, Warrior, Magician Lover Study Questions, pp. 63–73

1. Define the Tyrant archetype. (pp. 63–65)
2. Identify and explain where you see the shadow King manifesting at your school.
3. How do you correctly access the King archetype in your psyche? (p. 73)
4. Identify several adults in your life who manifest strong King energies. Explain how they exhibit this archetype.

King, Warrior, Magician, Lover Study Questions, pp. 75–88

1. What qualities make up the Warrior archetype? (pp. 79–88)
2. Identify several adults in your life who manifest strong Warrior energies. Explain how they exhibit this archetype.

King, Warrior, Magician, Lover Study Questions, pp. 88–95

1. Define the Sadist archetype. (pp. 89–93)
2. Define the Masochist archetype. (p. 94)
3. How do you correctly access the Warrior archetype in your psyche? (pp. 94–95)

King, Warrior, Magician, Lover Study Questions, pp. 97–106

1. Identify various professions that manifest the Magician archetype. (p. 98)
2. Identify the two Magician energies. (p. 98)
3. Explain the special knowledge possessed by the shaman. (p. 99)

King, Warrior, Magician, Lover Study Questions, pp. 106–118

1. What qualities make up the magician archetype? (pp. 106–110)
2. Define the Manipulator archetype. (pp. 110–115)
3. Define the Denying Innocent-One archetype. (pp. 115–116)
4. Explain how to access the Magician archetype in your psyche. (pp. 116–118)
5. Identify several adults in your life who manifest strong Magician energies. Explain how these adults exhibit this archetype.

King, Warrior, Magician, Lover Study Questions, pp. 119–131

1. Explain the symbolism of the erect penis. (pp. 119–120)
2. What qualities make up the Lover archetype? (pp. 120–126)
3. Identify two ways of life which most clearly manifest the Lover energy. Explain why. (pp. 129–131)

4. Identify several adults in your life who most strongly manifest the Lover energies.
Explain how they exhibit this archetype.

King, Warrior, Magician, Lover Study Questions, pp. 131–141

1. Define the Addicted Lover archetype. (pp. 131–138)
2. Define the Impotent Lover archetype. (pp. 139–140)
3. Explain how to access the Lover archetype in your psyche. (pp. 140–141)

King, Warrior, Magician, Lover Study Questions, pp. 143–156

1. Explain how self-appraisal is an effective strategy in accessing the mature masculine archetypes. (p. 145)
2. Describe the process of active imagination. (pp. 145–151)
3. Describe the technique of invocation. (pp. 151–153)
4. Describe the technique of admiration. (pp. 153–154)
5. Describe the technique of "acting as if." (pp. 154–155)

Boy Psychology

Divine Child	Precocious Child	Oedipal Child	The Hero
*Becomes the "King" archetype	*Becomes the "Magician" archetype	*Becomes the "Lover" archetype	*Becomes the "Warrior" archetype
*New life, peace, order	*Eagerness to learn, good student, multi-talented	*Passionate, sense of wonder,	*The archetype of adolescence
*Source of life with magical, empowering qualities	*Curious, adventurous	appreciation for connectedness	*Helps boy break with the mother and
*Self	*Introverted, reflective, see hidden connection in things	*Connected to the Great Mother	face the difficult tasks of growing up
			*Helps boy establish his independence and to experience his limits

(Continued)

T<small>ABLE</small> (Continued)

Divine Child	Precocious Child	Oedipal Child	The Hero
Active Shadow Manifestation			
"High Chair Tyrant" *Center of the universe *Unlimited demands *Grandiosity *Arrogance, childishness, irresponsibility, inflation, invulnerable, all-important *Perfectionist	"Know-It-All Trickster" *Plays tricks in life *Practical joker *Manipulator *Enjoys intimidating others *Mouthy *Makes many enemies *Good at deflating egos, "court jester" *Boys with authority problems	"The Mama's Boy" *Tied to Mama's apron strings *Fantasizes about marrying his mother *Get caught up in chasing the beautiful, yearning for union with Mother one woman to another *Autoerotic *Possessed by the feminine	"Grandstander Bully" *Intends to impress others, proclaim his superiority and dominance of others *Rageful displays *Loner: not a team player *Inflated sense of his own importance and his own abilities *Invulnerability *Locked in combat with the feminine, striving to conquer it and assert his masculinity *Doesn't know and unable to acknowledge his limitations *Denial of death
EXAMPLES: Stalin, Caligula, Hitler	Satan	Don Juan	Tom Cruise in *Top Gun*
Passive Shadow Manifestation			
"Weakling Prince" *little personality, no enthusiasm for life, little initiative *needs to be coddled, whining, complaining until dealt with *sarcastic, manipulative	"The Dummy" *lack personality, vigor, creativity *unresponsive, dull *lacks sense of humor *physically inept *naïve *may grasp more than he shows	"The Dreamer" *isolated and cut off from all human relationships *relationship is with intangible things and with the world of the imagination *accomplishes little, withdrawn and depressed	"The Coward" *extreme reluctance to stand up for himself in physical confrontation *bullied emotionally and intellectually *acquiesces to pressure from others

*Different archetypes activate at different developmental stages
Source: From Moore and Gillette, *King, Warrior, Magician, Lover* (1990).

Man Psychology

The King	The Magician	The Lover	The Warrior
*Archetype of order, blessing, and fertility	*Archetype of discernment and special knowledge (containing and channeling power), awareness, insight	*Archetype of vividness, aliveness, and passion	*Archetype of aggressiveness, motivation, alertness, mindfulness
*Activates last	*Thoughtfulness and reflection (detachment)	*Sensitivity, sensation, function	*Strategist, tactician
*Father energy	*Activates in a crisis	*Play and display	*Awareness of life's shortness and fragility
*Order=peace, calm, order	*Scientist	*Body without shame	*Decisive action, engagement in life
*Fertility=children, wife		*Deeply sensual	*Skill, power, accuracy, inner and outer control
*Blessing=mirroring and affirming		*Feelings of compassion and empathy	*Mastery of technology to achieve goals
*Stability and centeredness, balance		*Wants touching, to be touched, physically and emotionally	*Positive attitude, courage, fearless, takes responsibility for actions, self-discipline
*Vitality, life-force, joy		*No boundaries, but connectedness with world inside and outside	*Commitment to a higher ideal
*Guiding and nurturing others		*Aesthetic consciousness	*Loyalty
*Rewards and encourages Creativity in us and others		*Source of spirituality and mysticism	*Willingness to endure suffering, depravation of personal wants to achieve higher goals
*President		*Life is often unconventional, "messy"	*Soldier
		*Opposed to rigid "law"; confronts the conventional	
		*Artist and psychic	

Active Shadow Manifestation

"The Tyrant"	"The Manipulator"	"The Addicted Lover"	"The Sadist"

(Continued)

TABLE (Continued)

The King	The Magician	The Lover	The Warrior
*Hates, fears, envies new life *Destructive *Insecure *Exploits, abuses others *Ruthless, merciless in pursuing his self interest *Sensitive to criticism, makes him feel weak and deflated	*Withholding and secretive *Cynical detachment from human values	*Lostness, victim of his own sensitivities *Eternally restless, always looking for something *No boundaries *Don Juan Syndrome	*Passion for destruction and cruelty *Compulsive, self-driven, workaholic patterns

Passive Shadow Manifestation

"The Weakling"	"Denying Innocent One"	"The Impotent Lover"	"The Masochist"
*Lacks centeredness, calmness, and security within himself; leads to paranoia	*Wants power but doesn't want responsibility *Hides truth for sake of achieving and maintaining power of his own	*Experiences life in an unfeeling way *Lack of enthusiasm *Boredom, listlessness *Chronic depression *Lack of connection with others; cut off from themselves *Sexually inactive	*Pushover, whimpy *Takes far too much abuse for far too long and then explodes in a sadistic outburst of verbal and even physical violence

*Archetypes are energy fields in the psyche
Source: From Moore and Gillette, *King, Warrior, Magician, Lover* (1990)

God Archetype Chart

God	Archetypal Roles,	Jungian Psychological Type / Sense of Time	Psychological Difficulties	Strengths
Zeus, God of the Sky and Lightning Realm of Will and Power	King, Sky Father Executive, alliance maker, Philanderer	Usually extraverted Definitely thinking Both intuition and sensation Present and future	Ruthless, Emotional immaturity, Inflation	Ability to use power, Decisiveness, Generativity
Poseidon, God of Sea, Earth-Shaker, Realm of Emotion and Instinct	King, Earth Father, Instinctive, emotional man, Implacable enemy	Either extraverted or introverted, Definitely feeling, Past and Present	Destructive emotionality, Emotional instability, Low Self-Esteem	Loyalty, Access to feelings
Hades, God of the Underworld, Realm of Souls and the Unconscious	King, Recluse	Definitely introverted, definitely sensation, Timeless	Social invisibility, Depression, distortion of reality, Low Self-Esteem	Rich inner world of images, Detachment
Apollo, God of Sun	Successful goal-setter, Sibling	Usually extraverted, Usually thinking, Usually intuition, Future	Emotional Distance, Arrogance, Venom	Ability to set goals and reach them, Appreciation of clarity and form
Hermes, Messenger God	Communicator, guide, Trickster	Usually extraverted, Definitely intuitive, Usually thinking, Aware of past, present, future	Impulsiveness, Sociopathy Eternal Adolescent	Capacity to understand meaning, Communicator of ideas, Friendliness
Ares, God of War	Warrior, dancer, lover, Embodied man	Definitely extraverted, Definitely feeling, Definitely sensation, Immediate present	Emotional reactivity Scapegoat and abuser, Low self-esteem	Integration of emotions and body, Emotional expressiveness

(Continued)

Table   (Continued)

God	Archetypal Roles,	Jungian Psychological Type / Sense of Time	Psychological Difficulties	Strengths
Hephaestus, God of the Forge	Craftsman, Creative man	Definitely introverted, Definitely feeling, Definitely sensation, Present	Social inappropriateness, Buffoon, Low Self-Esteem	Creativity, Capacity to see and make beauty, Skill with hands
Dionysus, God of Ecstasy and Wine	Mystic, Wanderer, Ecstatic Lover	Either extraverted or introverted, Definitely sensation, Immediate present / timelessness	Distortions in self-perception, Substance abuse, Poor self-esteem	Appreciation of Sensory Experience, Love of Nature, Passionate Intensity

From Bolen, *Gods in Everyman: Archetypes That Shape Men's Lives, 1989.* Used with permission.

IX. COMING TO TERMS WITH OUR FATHERS

Objectives:

- To understand and articulate the contribution the father makes in a male's psychosocial development.
- To understand and articulate the problems associated with absent fathers.
- To understand, articulate, and apply the concept of father hunger.
- To understand, articulate, and apply strategies for reconnecting with the father.

1. Read Mason, pp. 113–129
2. Video: **Field of Dreams**
3. The Positive Effects of the Father-Son Relationship (Mason, pp. 113–115)
4. The Absent Father (Mason, 115–118)
5. Video: **Man without a Face**

6. The Effects of Father Hunger (Mason, pp. 118–120)
7. Reconnecting with the Father (Mason, pp. 120–127)
8. Exercises for Reconnecting with the Father (Mason, pp. 120–127)

Field of Dreams Viewing Notes:

This movie delves into the psychological burden of unlived dreams and the conflicts of fathers and sons. Ray is in the midst of his mid-life crisis when he hears a voice say "If you build it, he will come." The voice begins an improbable journey of discovery in which he rediscovers and encounters his father, reconciling long-ago conflicts and painful memories between them. Note that the voice requires a willingness to risk on Ray's part in order to gain the benefit of new insight necessary for the next part of his journey of discovery.

Man without a Face Viewing Notes:

This movie explores the dynamics of the absent father in a young boy's life and his father hunger. The result is a powerful mentor relationship with a seriously disfigured teacher-father figure. Note the positive effects of a healthy male-male mentor relationship.

Key Questions to Ask Yourself about Your Father

* Each father's son must ask himself:

1. What were my father's wounds?
2. What were his sacrifices, if any, for me and others?
3. What were his hopes, his dreams?
4. Did he live out his dreams?
5. Did he have emotional permission to live out his life?
6. What did he receive from his father and his culture that hindered his journey?
7. What would I have liked to know from him about his life, his history?
8. What would I have liked to know from him about being a man?
9. Was he able to answer such questions for himself?
10. Did he ever ask them?
11. What was my father's unlived life, and am I living it out, somehow, for him?

Statements For and About Men

"Being a man means knowing what you want and then mobilizing the inner resources to achieve it."

"I am my journey"

X. VARIETIES OF SEXUAL IDENTITY

Objectives:

To understand and articulate the psychoanalytic, the social constructionist, and the essentialist viewpoints on human sexuality.

1. Read Mason, pp. 175–192
2. Read *The Masculine Self*, pp. 212–220, 231–233
   i. React to Kilmartin's distinction between males' views of the *Madonna-whore complex* in women.
   ii. Do you agree or disagree that the traditional masculine gender role demands on men's sexuality are limiting and injurious to sexual relationships with their partners?
   iii. Read and react to the topic of penis size and masculinity in Box 11.1 on pp. 218–219. Do you agree or disagree that there is too much emphasis on organ size among males?
3. Are there only two sexual identities? (Mason, pp. 147–149)
   i. Handout: "The Gender Continuum"
   ii. Handout: "A New Approach in Handling Sexual Ambiguities"
4. The Psychoanalytic View (Mason, pp. 150–152)
5. The Social Constructionist View (Mason, pp. 152–157)
6. The Essentialist View (Mason, pp. 157–162)
7. General Discussion Questions:
   i. Explain the differences between the three viewpoints on sexual identity and their causes.
   ii. Discuss the "gender continuum" and the view that there are a number of varieties of gender expression.
   iii. What questions and / or concerns does the idea that there are multiple sexual identities rather than the traditional two raise for you?

The Gender Continuum
(From Strong et al., *Human Sexuality*, 2002. Used with permission.)

For most of us, there is no question about our gender. We know we are female or male. However, for hermaphrodites and transgendered individuals, "What sex am I?" is a real and painful question. Because our culture views sexual anatomy as a male / female dichotomy, it is difficult for many to accept the more recent view of anatomical sex differentiation as existing on a male / female continuum with several dimensions. Most people still think of genetic sex—XX or XY—as a person's true sex. However, approximately 1.7% of the population has a set of chromosomes other than these. (Blackless et al., 2000)

The concept of gender is viewed as a continuum, with a multitude of possible gender-variant behaviors.

Transgenderism							
Masculine				Feminine			
Female –> Male Trans- sexual	Female trans- vestite / Transgen- derist	Female occasional cross- dresser	Andrrogy- nouse male or female	Male occasional cross- dresser	Male trans- vestite/ transgen- derist	Male –> Female Trans- sexual

Source: From Strong, *Human Sexuality: Diversity in Contemporary America*, 2002. Used with permission.

A New Approach in the Treatment of Sexual Ambiguities
(From Strong, *Human Sexuality: Diversity in Contemporary America*, 2002, pp. 142–143. Used with permission.)

Each year an estimated 1000 babies are born in the U.S. with sex organs that cannot be classified as strictly male or strictly female. These sexually ambiguous infants are typically given a gender assignment (usually female) along with treatment to support the assignment, including surgery and, later, hormones and psychotherapy. Physicians have defended the practice of correcting ambiguous genitals, citing the success of current technology.

Recently, however, this practice has undergone scrutiny by researchers and patients who point to the lack of evidence supporting its long-term success.

The protocol of surgical correction was based on the belief that gender identity is determined not by biological traits but by the way a child is raised and that intersexed children are born psychologically malleable. The American Academy of Pediatrics currently maintains that children born with ambiguous genitals "can be raised successfully as members of either sex" and recommends surgery within the first 15 months of life. The following beliefs are held strongly enough that they might be considered medical protocols: (1) Individuals are psychosexually neutral at birth; (2) healthy psychosexual development is dependent on the appearance of one's genitals; (3) doubt about sex assignment should not be allowed; and (4) sex should not be changed after 2 years of age.

Endocrinologists, physicians, ethicists, and intersex activists have challenged the traditional pediatric postulates for sex assignment / reassignment. This new research suggests that one's sexual identity is not fixed by the gender one is reared in, that atypical as well as typical persons undergo psychosexual development, and that sexual orientation develops independent of rearing. An emerging community of unhappy individuals willing to come out with their medical histories concurs with this response. They consider surgery to be a technology best delayed unless medically urgent (as when a genetic anomaly interferes with urination or creates a risk of infection) or requested by the individual. They believe that letting well enough alone is the better course and that the erotic and reproductive needs of the adult should take precedence over the cosmetic needs of the child. They recommend that the professional community offer support and information to parents and families and empower the intersexed individual to understand his or her status and choose (or reject) medical intervention.

The following chart illustrates the two opposing models of treatment:

Key Issues	Surgery-Centered Model	Psychology-Centered Model
What is intersex?	An anatomical abnormality that is likely to lead to distress for the intersexed person and the family.	An anatomical variation from the standard male and female types.
Is gender determined by nature or nurture?	Nurture. By constructing the genitals as male or female and nurturing that identity, a child's gender can be formed.	Both. Respect for autonomy and self-determination occur along with truth about one's body and life.
Are intersexed genitals a medical problem?	Yes. Untreated intersex is likely to result in psychological problems. These problems can be avoided if genitals are normalized.	No. Intersexed genitals may be a sign of an underlying metabolic concern, but they are not diseased; they just look different. Medical problems should be treated.
What should be the medical response?	"Normalize" the genitals by using cosmetic surgical procedures, hormone treatment, and so on.	The family should secure psychological support and obtain information. True medical problems should be treated medically, but cosmetic treatments should be withheld until the patient can give consent.
When should cosmetic "normalizing" be done?	As soon as possible. The longer the wait, the greater the trauma.	Only when the intersexed person requests it, and only after he or she has been fully informed about the risks and outcomes.
Why should intersex be treated this way?	Because society cannot deal with sexual ambiguity or variation. If the genitals are not fixed, the intersexed child will be ostracized.	Because the intersexed child has the right to self-determination. Performing surgery early interferes with that right, an many treatments are not reversible and may involve risk.

Appendix 269

Key Issues	Surgery-Centered Model	Psychology-Centered Model
How do you decide what gender to assign an intersexed child?	The doctors decide after doing genetic and other testing. If a child has a Y chromosome and an adequate (1 inch or longer) penis, the child will be assigned a male gender. If the child has a Y chromosome and an inadequate penis, the child will be assigned a female gender and be surgically reconstructed as such. If the child has no Y chromosomes, the child will be assigned a female gender. The genitals will be surgically altered to include a clitoral reduction, construction of a vagina, and so on.	The doctors in consultation with the family decide after doing genetic and other testing. Then, given what is known about the child and about the histories of intersexed people with various conditions, they will assign the gender most likely to be accepted by the family and child. The doctors and parents recognize that this gender assignment is preliminary; the child may decide later to change it. (That is why medically unnecessary surgeries should not be done without the child's consent.)
What should the intersexed child be told when he or she is old enough to understand?	Very little, because discussing intersex will lead to gender confusion.	Everything that is known about the condition. The intersexed child has the right and responsibility to know as much about his or her condition as the doctor does.
What is the ideal future of intersex?	Elimination via improved scientific and medical technologies.	Social acceptance and the recognition that sexual categories are socially constructed.

Male Sexual Scripts
(From Strong, *Human Sexuality: Diversity in Contemporary America, 2002,*
pp. 133–134. Used with permission)

Scripts refer to the acts, rules, and expectations associated with a particular role, much like the script an actor uses in a play. Unlike dramatic scripts, social scripts allow for considerable improvisation within their general boundaries. Sexual scripts outline how we are to behave sexually within our gender roles. According to Zilbergeld (1992) male sexual scripts include the following elements:

1. *Males should not have (or at least should not express) certain feelings.* Males should not express doubts; they should be assertive, confident, and aggressive. Tenderness and compassion are not masculine feelings.
2. *Performance is the thing that counts.* Sex is something to be achieved. Sex is not for intimacy but for orgasm.
3. *The man is in charge.* The man is the leader, the person who knows what is best. The man initiates sex and gives the woman her orgasm. A real man does not need a woman to tell him what women like; he already knows.
4. *A man always wants sex and is ready for it.* No matter what else is going on, a man wants sex; he is always able to become erect. He is a machine.
5. *All physical contact leads to sex.* Because men are basically sexual machines, any physical contact is a sign for sex. Touching is seen as the first step toward sexual intercourse, not an end in itself. There is no physical pleasure other than sexual pleasure.
6. *Sex equals intercourse.* All erotic contact leads to sexual intercourse. Foreplay is just that: warming up, getting one's partner excited for penetration. Kissing, hugging, erotic touching, and oral sex are only preliminaries to intercourse.
7. *Sexual intercourse leads to orgasm.* The orgasm is the "proof of the pudding." The more orgasms, the better the sex. If a woman does not have an orgasm, she is not sexual. The male feels he is a failure because he was not good enough to give her an orgasm.

Common to all these myths is a separation of sex from love and attachment. Sex is seen as performance.

Female Sexual Scripts
(From Strong, *Human Sexuality: Diversity in Contemporary America*, 2002,
pp. 134–136. Used with permission.)

Barbach (1982) includes the following elements:

1. *Sex is good and bad.* What makes sex good? Sex in marriage or
   a committed relationship. What makes sex bad? Sex in a casual or
   uncommitted relationship.
   Sex is so good that a woman needs to save it for her husband. Sex is
   bad if it is not sanctioned by love or marriage, a woman will get a bad
   reputation.
2. *It is not okay to touch themselves "down there."* Girls are taught not
   to look at their genitals, not to touch them, especially not to explore
   them. As a result, women know very little about their genitals. They
   are often concerned about vaginal odors, making them uncomfortable
   about cunnilingus.
3. *Sex is for men.* Men want sex; women want love. Women are sexually
   passive, waiting to be aroused. Sex is not a pleasurable activity as an
   end in itself; it is something performed by women *for* men.
4. *Men should know what women want.* This script tells women that men
   know what they want, even if women don't tell them. The woman is
   supposed to remain pure and sexually innocent. It is up to the man to
   arouse the woman, even if he doesn't know what a particular woman
   finds arousing. To keep her image of sexual innocence, she does not
   tell him what she wants.
5. *Women should not talk about sex.* Many women cannot talk about
   sex easily because they are not expected to have strong sexual feelings.
   Some women may know their partners well enough to have sex with
   them but not well enough to communicate their needs to them.
6. *Women should look like models.* The media present ideally attractive
   women as beautiful models with slender hips, supple breasts, and
   no fat or cellulite; they are always young, with never a pimple, wrin-
   kle, or gray hair in sight. As a result of these cultural images, many
   women are self-conscious about their physical appearance. They worry

that they are too fat, too plain, or too old. They often feel awkward without their clothes on to hide their imagined flaws.

7. *Women are nurturers.* Women give; men receive. Women give themselves, their bodies, and their pleasures to men. Everyone else's needs come first: his desire over hers, his orgasm over hers.

8. *There is only one right way to have an orgasm.* Women often learn there is only one right way to have an orgasm: during sexual intercourse as a result of penile stimulation.

Contemporary Sexual Scripts
(From Strong, *Human Sexuality: Diversity in Contemporary America,* 2002, p. 137. Used with permission.)

Contemporary sexual scripts give increasing recognition to female sexuality. They are increasingly relationship-centered rather than male-centered. Women, however, are still not granted full sexual equality with males.

Contemporary sexual scripts include the following elements for both sexes (Gagnon and Simon, 1987; Reed and Weinberg, 1984; Rubin, 1990; Seidman, 1989)

1. Sexual expression is positive.
2. Sexual activities involve a mutual exchange of erotic pleasure.
3. Sexuality is equally involving, and both partners are equally responsible.
4. Legitimate sexual activities are not limited to sexual intercourse but also include masturbation and oral-genital sex.
5. Sexual activities may be initiated by either partner.
6. Both partners have a right to experience orgasm, whether through intercourse, oral-genital sex, or manual stimulation.
7. Nonmarital sex is acceptable within a relationship context.

XI. DIVERSE MASCULINITIES

Objectives:

- To understand and articulate the concept of masculinities.
- To understand, articulate, and apply the concept of hegemonic masculinity as it relates to women and other subordinate masculinities.

- To understand and apply the concepts associated with the social construction of homosexual masculinities.
- To understand and apply the concepts associated with the social construction of African American masculinities.
- To understand and articulate the dynamics that comprise one's own expression of masculine identity.

1. Read Mason, pp. 175–192
2. The Social Construction of Masculinities (Mason, pp. 175–178; *The Masculine Self*, pp. 263–273)
3. Homosexual Masculinities (Mason, pp. 178–186; *The Masculine Self*, pp. 220–230
    i. Activity: Box 11.4: Are You Homophobic, *The Masculine Self*, p. 229
4. African American Masculinities (Mason, pp. 186–191)
5. Read Hooks, *We Real Cool: Black Men and Masculinity* with 11 homework assignments
6. General Discussion Questions:
    i. Explain the key concepts of the social constructionist view of masculinities.
    ii. React to the idea of "masculinities" rather than "Masculinity." Explain in detail.
    iii. How has the information on homosexual masculinities modified or changed your view of homosexual males? Explain.
    iv. How has the information on African American masculinities modified or changed your view of African American males? Explain.
    v. Write an analysis of your masculinity using the social constructionist methodology.

We Real Cool: Black Men and Masculinity Pages ix–xvii

1. Why does Hooks say that "this is a culture that does not love black males?" Do you agree or disagree? (p. ix-xii)

2. Do you agree with Hooks' characterization of American culture as "imperialist white-supremacist capitalist patriarchy?" (p. xi)
3. List some images that Hooks utilizes to describe black males. (p. xii)
4. Explain why "patriarchal masculinity" is the "primary genocidal threat that endangers black male life." (p. xiv)

We Real Cool: Black Men and Masculinity Pages 1–14

1. How were African men different when they first came to America than their white counterparts regarding masculinity? (pp. 2–3)
2. Who was Rudolph Byrd? Summarize his contribution to the masculinity debate on black men. (p. 5)
3. Who was Frederick Douglas? Summarize his contribution to the gender question. (p. 6)

We Real Cool: Black Men and Masculinity Pages 15–32

1. Summarize Hooks' critique of "black assimilation into whiteness and striving to get money by any means." (pp. 18–19)
2. Explain how playing professional sports was a way for black men to assert patriarchal manhood. (p. 22)
3. According to Hooks, how is the everyday world demoralizing to black men? (p. 24)
4. List some teachings of "gangsta culture" that are conveyed to young black men. (p. 27)

We Real Cool: Black Men and Masculinity Pages 33–45

1. Describe the stereotypical view of black males' intellectual skills. (p. 33)
2. According to Hooks, what have black males been socialized to believe? (p. 34)
3. Read McCall's autobiographical passage about being a lone black student in a predominantly white school. Do you agree or disagree with his assessment? (p. 37)
4. Describe Grier and Cobbs' paradigmatic Blackman. (p. 42)

5. Describe Hooks' solution to the question of education for black males. (pp. 44–45)

We Real Cool: Black Men and Masculinity Pages 47–66

1. Describe Western culture's image of black males and its effects. (pp. 48–49)
2. According to Hooks, why do black men assume the persona and behavior of violence? (pp. 55–57)
3. What explanations does Hooks offer for black-on-black violence? (pp. 62–64)
4. What solution does Hooks call for to end black male violence? (pp. 65–66)

We Real Cool: Black Men and Masculinity Pages 67–84

1. According to Hooks, what images have historically been associated with the black male and what effects has it justified? (pp. 67–69) Describe how black males have considered sex based on patriarchal notions of manhood? (pp. 70–73)
2. Summarize Orlando Patterson's characterization black male sexuality. (p. 79)
3. Explain "signifying" as a form of emotional abuse of young black males. (pp. 80–81)
4. What is Hooks' solution for black males' healthy erotic agency. (pp. 83–84)

We Real Cool: Black Men and Masculinity Pages 85–100

1. What socializing techniques of young black boys does Hooks describe as "soul murder?" (pp. 86–89)
2. How do black males deal with shame? (pp. 91–92)
3. How does sports participation function as a strategy for shielding black boys from shame? (pp. 94–95)

4. React to and expand upon Hooks' statement: "Emotionally abused black boys are filled with rage. Primed to act out they become adults who are rageoholics." (pp. 95–98)

5. What is the solution for healing of black men's wounds, according to Hooks? (pp. 99–100)

We Real Cool: Black Men and Masculinity Pages 101–114

1. What reasons are given to explain that "many black children are emotionally neglected and / or abandoned by biological fathers?" (pp. 103–109)

2. Name and explain five self-skills that constitute adult maturity. (pp. 110–111)

3. Why don't fathers know how to parent, according to Hooks? (p. 113)

4. What do black males need to learn about fatherhood? (p. 114)

We Real Cool: Black Men and Masculinity Pages 115–132

1. What is the effect of dysfunctional families on intimacy between couples? (pp. 116–117)

2. According to Hooks, what kind of woman are most black males looking for in a relationship? (pp. 120–122)

3. Describe the romantic bonds between black males and females, according to Hooks / (pp. 126–127)

4. Describe Hooks opinion about lying and withholding truth. (pp. 128–129)

We Real Cool: Black Men and Masculinity Pages 133–145

1. Describe "the crisis in the black male spirit." (p. 134)

2. React and expand upon this statement: "The imperialist white-supremacist capitalist patriarchal society we are living in is to blame for much of the horrors black men must face. However, black males are responsible for the manner in which they confront these horrors or

fail to do so. Black males must be held accountable when they betray themselves, when they choose self-destructive paths." (p. 137)
3. What does Hooks mean by "savior searching?" What forms does it take? What is the true solution? (pp. 141–142)

We Real Cool: Black Men and Masculinity Pages 147–162

1. Explain Hooks' insight about "cool." (p. 149)
2. Contrast hip-hop culture with cool. (pp. 151–153)
3. Explain the difference between healthy and dysfunctional cool. (p. 155)
4. Explain the myth of Isis and Osiris and tell how it applies to black healing. (pp. 160–162)

XII. MASCULINE HEALTH AND SPIRITUALITY

Objectives:

- To understand, articulate, and apply the concepts of masculine gender role stress syndrome and gender scripting.
- To understand articulate and apply how modern culture socializes males to handle pain.
- To understand and articulate the components of a holistic, healthy spirituality.

1. Read Mason, pp. 165–174
2. *The Masculine Self*, pp. 173–189
3. Masculine Gender Role Stress Syndrome (Mason, 166–168; *The Masculine Self*, pp. 155–172)
4. How Modern Culture Teaches Males To Handle Pain (Mason, pp. 168–169)
5. Revisioning the Male Body (Mason, pp. 169–170)
6. Toward a Masculine Spirituality (Mason, pp. 170–174)
7. Michael Gurian's, The Ten Integrities (see handouts)
8. Video: **A River Runs Through It**
9. General Discussion Questions:
   i. Analyze Masculine Gender Role Stress Syndrome and identify where it has effects on you and other males.

    ii. Do you think American culture encourages healthy lifestyles in men?

    iii. Explain your personal spirituality and how it affects your lifestyle and decision-making.

10. Essay: Where are you with your spirituality? Identify and explain the key components of your beliefs and how they support your self understanding as a man.

A River Runs Through It Viewing Guide:

This movie uses the sport of fly-fishing as a metaphor about life's meaning. In its happiest moments the movie celebrates the beauty of the natural world and those mystical moments when the boys and their father are at one with each other and the universe. However, the movie also highlights the self-destructive habits of the younger brother and compares him to his Presbyterian minister father and student-teacher brother. Reverend MacLean's sermon is a touching reflection on the tragedy of life and relationships and begs the questions "Why is it that the people who need the most help won't take it?" and "Why do you thinks it is so hard to help those close to us?" Finally, the narrator's words at the end of the movie evoke words and images about a mystical view of life: "Eventually all things merge into one, and a river runs through it. The river was cut by the world's great flood and run over rocks from the basement of time. On some of the rocks are timeless raindrops. Under the rocks are the words, and some of the words are theirs. I am haunted by words." Reflect on and discuss the symbolic and metaphorical meanings of this passage as it relates to the movie's message.

The Ten Integrities
(From Gurian, *A Fine Young Man,* 1999a. Used with permission.)

A boy is not a man unless he has *appropriately mastered the ten integrities.*

1. *Lineal.* He must know himself as the product of his ancestry.
2. *Psychological.* He must have accomplished individuation and gained adult personal identity.

3. *Social.* He must understand society's most important social rules.
4. *Spiritual.* He must have a refined spiritual life, spiritual practice, and vision.
5. *Moral.* He must have accomplished the development of moral character.
6. *Emotional.* He must have developed emotional range and self-discipline.
7. *Sexual.* He must have learned to honor his own and others' sexuality.
8. *Marital.* He must understand the sanctity or romantic, marital, and gender-equal bonds.
9. *Physical.* He must know and respect his own body, and use it for service.
10. *Intellectual.* He must have accomplished the necessary development of his cognitive and intellectual faculties in order to live in the world of adults.

XIII. MEN AND WORK

Objectives:

- To understand, articulate, and apply the concept to patriarchy and its effects on masculinity and work.
- To understand and articulate the effects of industrialization on men.
- To understand and articulate the notion that males are socialized to connect manhood to production.
- To understand, articulate, and apply the damaging effects of masculine gender role in the work place.
- To understand, articulate, and apply the concept of appropriate male-female relationships in the workplace.

1. Patriarchy's effects on masculinity and work (*The Masculine Self*, pp. 191–195)
2. Social Definitions of Manhood at Work (*The Masculine Self*, pp. 195–203)
3. Male-Female Relationships in the Workplace (*The Masculine Self*, pp. 203–209)

4. Changing Roles in the Dual-Earner Home (*The Masculine Self*, pp. 209–210)
5. Video: **For Love of the Game**
6. General Discussion Questions:
   i. Identify the scripts that you see most often operating among men in the work world.
   ii. Do you think that the essence of a man should be defined by his work or by other qualities? Explain.

For Love of the Game Viewing Notes:

This movie examines the relationship between a major league baseball pitcher and his girlfriend over a number of years and through challenges and success. Note the role of women in these men's lives and especially the role of the girlfriend to the star pitcher Billy. Note the dynamics of the "approach-avoidance dance" in their intimate relations. At another level, note Billy's attitude toward his work and how it reflects traditional masculine gender role norms and expectations—good and bad. Note Billy's mental process as he plays his final game, reflects on his life, baseball career, and relationships and makes his choice to retire.

XIV. AND XV. MASCULINE INITIATION AND THE SOLO EXPERIENCE

Objectives:
- To understand and articulate the need for male initiation.
- To understand, articulate, and apply the prerequisites for an initiation experience.
- To understand, articulate, and apply the initiation process to an initiation experience.
- To understand, articulate, and implement a solo initiatory experience.

1. Read Mason, pp. 93–112
2. Video: Desmond Morris' *The Human Sexes* **"Passages of Life"**
3. What is initiation? (Mason, p. 93–94)
4. The Need for Initiation (Mason, pp. 94–96)

5. The Prerequisites of Initiation (Mason, pp. 96–97)
6. The Process of Initiation (Mason, pp. 97–110)
7. Types of Solo Experiences (Mason, pp. 104–110)
8. Planning and Executing a Vision Quest
9. Video: **Lost Borders**

Desmond Morris' *The Human Sexes* **"Passages of Life"** Viewing Guide:

WARNING: THIS VIDEO CONTAINS GRAPHIC NUDITY. This video highlights the variety of rituals that separate and distinguish males from females throughout the life cycle. Morris explains that the rituals are socially constructed but reflect a biological necessity. Use this video to provide a context in which to present masculine rites of passage.

Lost Borders Viewing Guide:

This video depicts the various stages in the planning and execution of a Vision Quest solo experience. This video will assist students in the planning of their own solo experience as well as help to alleviate any anxiety about a solo experience.

REFERENCES

Awkward, M. (1998). A black man's place in black feminist criticism. In T. Digby (Ed.), *Men doing feminism* (pp. 147–167). New York: Routledge.

Baber, A. (1992). Call of the wild. In C. Harding (Ed.), *Wingspan: Inside the men's movement*. New York: St. Martin's Press.

Baldwin, J. (1962). *The fire next time*. New York: Dell.

Barrett, D. C. (2000). Masculinity among working-class gay males. In P. Nardi (Ed.), *Gay masculinities* (pp. 176–205). Thousand Oaks, CA: Sage Publications.

Benjamin, O. (1995). Healing, community and justice in the men's movement: Toward a socially responsible model of masculinity. In M. S. Kimmel (Ed.), *The politics of manhood: Profeminist men respond to the mythopoetic men's movement (and the leaders respond)* (pp. 287–291). Philadelphia: Temple University Press.

Betcher, R. W. & Pollack, W. S. (1993). *In a time of fallen heroes: The re-creation of masculinity*. New York: Guilford Press.

Blankenhorn, D. (1995). *Fatherless America: confronting our most urgent social problem*. New York: HarperCollins.

Blazina, C. (1997). Mythos and men: Toward new paradigms of masculinity. *Journal of Men's Studies. 5*(4), 285+.

Bliss, S. (1995). Mythopoetic men's movements. In M. S. Kimmel (Ed.), *The politics of manhood: Profeminist men respond to the mythopoetic men's movement (and the mythopoetic leaders answer)* (pp. 292–307). Philadelphia: Temple University Press.

Block Lewis, H. (1971). *Shame and guilt in neurosis*. Hillsdale, NJ: Lawrence Erlbaum.

Blum, D. (1998). *Sex on the brain: The biological differences between men and women*. New York: Penguin Books.

Blumenkrantz, David. Retrieved October 9, 2005 from www.bullfrogfilms.com/catalog/lost.html.

Blustain, S. (2000). The new gender wars. *Psychology Today, 33*(6), 42.

Bly, R. (1992). *Iron John: A book about men*. New York: Vintage Books.

Bolen, J. S. (1989). *Gods in everyman: Archetypes that shape men's lives*. New York: Harper Collins.

Bolin, A. (1997). Transforming transvestism and transsexualism: Polarity, politics, and gender. In B. Bullough, V.L. Bullough, & J. Elias (Eds.), *Gender bending*. New York: Prometheus Books.

Brod, H. & Kaufman, M. (Eds.). (1994). *Theorizing masculinities*. Thousand Oaks, CA: Sage Publications.

Brooks, G. R. (1995). *The centerfold syndrome: How men can overcome objectification and achieve intimacy with women*. San Francisco: Josey-Bass.

Bucholtz, M. (1999). You da man: Narrating the racial other in the production of white masculinity. *Journal of Sociolinguistics, 3*(4), 443–460.

Bush, L. V. (1999). "Am i a man?: A literature review engaging the sociohistorical dynamics of black manhood in the united states." *The Western Journal of Black Studies, 23*(1), 49+.

Buss, D. (1999). *Evolutionary psychology: A new science of the mind*. Boston: Allyn & Bacon.

———. (2000). *The dangerous passion: Why jealousy is as necessary as love and sex*. New York: Free Press.

———. (2003). *The evolution of desire: Strategies of human mating*. New York: Basic Books.

———. (2004). In conversation with David Buss. *The Evolutionist*. Retrieved July 29, 2004 from www.1se.ac.uk/Depts/cpnss/darwin/evo/buss.htm.

Buzzard, K. S. F. (2002). The coca cola of self help: The branding of john gray's 'men are from mars, women are from venus. *Journal of Popular Culture, 35*, 89+.

Campbell, J. (1973). *The hero with a thousand faces*. Princeton, NJ: Princeton University Press. (1991). *The power of myth*. New York: Random House.

Canada, G. (1999/2000). Raising better boys. *Educational Leadership, 57*(4), 14–17.

Cantu, L. (2000). Latino masculinities and homosexualities. In P. Nardi (Ed.), *Gay masculinities* (pp. 224–246). Thousand Oaks, CA: Sage Publications.

Center for Democracy Studies [electronic version]. (1996). *The promise keepers are coming*: Retrieved February 27, 2004 from www.cdsresearch.org/nation/nation1.html.

Chodorow, N. *The reproduction of mothering*. (1978). Berkeley: University of California Press.

Cicchetti, D. & Toth, S.L. (Eds.). (1991). *Internalizing and externalizing expressions of dysfunction: Rochester symposium on developmental psychology*. Hillsdale, NJ: Lawrence Erlbaum.

Clare, A. (2000). *On men*, London: Chatto & Windus.

Clatterbaugh, K. (1997). *Contemporary perspectives on masculinity*. Boulder, CO: Westview Press.

Cleaver, E. (1968). *Soul on ice.* New York: Dell Books.

Conderman, G., Heimerl, A. M. & Ketterhagen, B. L. (2002). Longing for a father. *Reclaiming Children and Youth. 10*(3), 140+.

Connell, R.W. (1995). *Masculinities.* Berkeley: University of California Press.

———. (2000). *The men and the boys.* St. Leonards: Allen & Unwin.

———. (2003). Masculinities, change, and conflict in global society: Thinking about the future of men's studies. *The Journal of Men's Studies, 11.*

Cooksey, E. C. (1997). Consequences of young mothers' marital histories for children's cognitive development. *Journal of Marriage and the Family, 59,* 245–261.

Corneau, G. (1991). *Absent fathers, lost sons: The search for masculine identity.* Boston: Shambhala.

Cowlishaw, B. R. (2001) Subjects are from Mars, objects are from Venus: Construction of the self in self-help. *Journal of Popular Culture, 35.*

Daly, J. M., Mosher, R. L. & Youngman, D. J. (Eds.). (1999). *Human development across the life span: Educational and psychological applications.* Westport, CT: Praeger Publishers.

David, D. & Brannon, R. (Eds.). (1976). *The forty-nine percent majority: The male sex role.* Reading, MA: Addison-Wesley.

Dawkins, R. (1989). *The selfish gene.* Oxford: Oxford University Press.

di Berardino, Angelo, O. S. A. (1997). Christian anthropology and homosexuality: Homosexuality in classical antiquity. *L'Osservatore Romano.* [Electronic version]. March 19, 1997.

Dines, G. (1998). King Kong and the white woman. *Violence Against Women, 4,* 291–308.

Dougherty, P. (1995). Men and intimacy. In R. U. Schenck & J. Everingham (Eds.), *Men healing shame: An anthology* (pp. 261–265). New York: Springer Publishing Company.

Doyle, J. A. (1995). *The male experience* (3rd ed.). Dubuque, IA: Wm. C. Brown Communications, Inc.

Doyle, R. (1996). Deaths caused by alcohol. *Scientific American, 275,* 30–31.

Drew, J. M. (2003). *Where were you when i needed you, dad?: A guide for healing your father wound* (2nd ed.) Newport Beach: CA: Tiger Lily Publishing.

Edinger, E. F. (1992). *Ego and archetype.* Boston: Shambhala.

———. (1994). *The eternal drama: The inner meaning of Greek mythology.* Boston: Shambhala.

Eisler, R. M., Skidmore, J. R. & Ward, C. H. (1988). Masculine gender role stress: predictor of anger, anxiety, and health-risk behaviors. *Journal of Personality Assessment, 52,* 133–141.

Eisler, R. M. (1995). The relationship between masculine gender role stress and men's health risk: The validation of a construct. In R. F. Levant & W. S. Pollack (Eds.), *A new psychology of men* (pp. 207–225). New York: Basic Books.

Eisler, R. M. & Hersen, M. (Eds.). (2000). *Handbook of gender, culture, and health.* Mahway, NJ: Lawrence Erlbaum Associates.

Eliade, M. (1958). *Rites and symbols of initiation: The mysteries of birth and rebirth.* (W.R. Trask, Trans.). New York: Harper Torchbooks.

———. (1961). *The sacred and the profane: The nature of religion.* New York: Harper Torchbooks.

Erikson, E. (1950). *Childhood and society.* (2nd ed.). New York: W.W. Norton & Company.

———. (1980). *Identity and the life cycle.* New York: W. W. Norton & Company.

Everingham, J. (1995a). Inadvertent shaming: Family rules and shaming habits. In R. U. Schenck & J. Everingham (Eds.), *Men healing shame: An anthology* (pp. 228–253). New York: Springer Publishing Company.

———. (1995b). Men facing shame: A healing process. In R. U. Schenck & J. Everingham (Eds.), *Men healing shame: An anthology* (pp. 94–119). New York: Springer Publishing Company.

Farrell, W. T. (1987). *Why men are the way they are.* New York: McGraw-Hill.

Federal Interagency Forum on Child and Family Statistics. (1997). *America's children: Key national indicators of well-being.* Washington, D.C.: U.S. Government Printing Office.

Feinberg, L. (1996). *Transgender warriors: making history from joan of arc to rupaul.* Boston: Beacon Press.

Fischer, A. R. & Good, G. E. (1997). Masculine gender roles, recognition of emotions, and interpersonal intimacy. *Psychotherapy, 34,* 160–170.

Foster, S. & Little, M. (1992). *The book of the vision quest: Personal transformation in the wilderness. Revised edition.* New York: Simon & Schuster.

———. (1998). *The four shields: The initiatory seasons of human nature.* Big Pine, CA: Lost Borders Press.

Fox, M. (2000). *Original blessing.* New York: Jeremy P. Tarcher/Putnam.

———. (2005). Some Thoughts on Thomas Berry's Contributions to the Western Spiritual Tradition. Retrieved August 1, 2005 from www.matthewfox.org/sys-tmpl/tberry.

Franklin, C. W. II. (1994). Men's studies, the men's movement, and the study of black masculinities: Further demystification of masculinities in America. In R. D. Majors & J. U. Gordon (Eds.), *The American black male: His present status and his future.* Chicago: Nelson Hall.

Freud, S. (1962). *Three essays on the theory of sexuality.* (J. Strachey, Trans.). New York: Basic. (Original work published 1905).

Fukuyama, F. (1997). Is it all in the genes? *Commentary, 104,* 3.

Fuller, M. & Olsen, G. (2003). *Home-school relations.* Boston: Allyn & Bacon.

Gagnon, J. & Henderson, B. (1975). *Human sexuality: An age of ambiguity.* Boston: Educational Associates.

Garbarino, J. (1999). *Lost boys: Why our sons turn violent and how we can save them.* New York: Free Press.

Gay, P. (Ed.). (1989). *The Freud reader.* New York: W.W. Norton & Company.

Geary, D. (1998). *Male, female: The evolution of human sex differences*: Washington, D.C.: American Psychological Association.

George, M. (1997). Into the eyes of medusa: Beyond testosterone, men, and violence. *The Journal of Men's Studies, 5,* 4.

Giddens, A. (1992). *The transformation of intimacy: Sexuality, love and eroticism in modern societies.* Cambridge: Polity.

Gilmore, D. D. (1990). *Manhood in the making: Cultural concepts of masculinity.* New Haven: Yale University Press.

Goffman, E. (1963). *Stigma: Notes on the management of spoiled identity.* Englewood Cliffs, NJ: Prentice-Hall.

Good, G. E., Dell, D. M. & Mintz, L. B. (1989). Male role and gender role conflict: Relations to help seeking in men. *Journal of Counseling Psychology, 36,* 295–300.

Good, G. E. & Wood, P. K. (1995). Male gender role conflict, depression, and help seeking: Do college men face double jeopardy? *Journal of Counseling and Development, 74,* 70–75.

Good, G. E. & Sherrod, N. (1997). Men's resolution of non-relational sex across the life span. In R. Levant, & G. Brooks (Eds.), *Men and sex: New psychological perspectives* (pp. 182–204). New York: Wiley Publishing.

Gray, J. (1992). *Men are from mars, women are from Venus: A practical guide for improving communication and getting what you want in your relationships.* New York: Harper Collins.

Greenberg, D. F. (1988). *The construction of homosexuality.* Chicago: University of Chicago Press.

Greenwald, Michael P. (1995). Shame, initiation, and the culture of initiated masculinity. In R. U. Schenck & J. Everingham (Eds.), *Men healing shame: An anthology* (pp. 266–278). New York: Springer Publishing Company.

Greer, W. H. & Cobbs, P. M. (1968). *Black rage.* New York: Basic Books.

Gur, R. C., Mozley, L. H., Resnick, S. M., Karp, J. S., Alavi, A., Arnold, S. E. & Gur, R. E. (1995). Sex differences in regional cerebral glucose metabolism during a resting state. *Science, 267* (January 27, 1995), 528–531.

Gurian, Michael Homepage. Retrieved April 9, 2004 from www.michael-gurian.com.

Gurian, M. (1996). *The wonder of boys: What parents, mentors and educators can do to shape boys into exceptional men.* New York: Jeremy P. Tarcher.

———. (1999a). *A fine young man: What parents, mentors, and educators can do to shape adolescent boys into exceptional men.* New York: Jeremy P. Tarcher.

———. (1999b). *The good son: Shaping the moral development of our boys and young men.* New York: Jeremy P. Tarcher.

———. (2003). *What could he be thinking?: How a man's mind really works.* New York: St. Martin's Press.

———. (2003a). *Boys and girls learn differently: A guide for teachers and parents.* San Francisco: Jossey-Bass.

Hall, C. S. & Nordby, V. J. (1999). *A primer of jungian psychology.* New York: Meridian.

Halpern, D. F. (1997). Sex differences in intelligence. *American Psychologist, 52*(10), 1091–1102.

Harding, C. (2001). Introduction: Making sense of sexuality. *Sexuality: Psychoanalytic perspectives.* East Sussex: Brunner-Routledge.

Harper, C. C. & McLanahan, S. S. (1998). Father absence and youth incarceration. Paper presented at the annual meeting of the American Sociological Association, San Francisco, CA. August 1998.

Harris, B. (1996). *The father quest: Rediscovering an elemental psychic force.* Alexander, NC: Alexander Books.

Havlick, M. J., Jr. (Ed.). (2001). *The archetype of initiation: Sacred space, ritual process, and personal transformation: lectures and essays by robert l. moore.* Xlibris Corporation, 2001.

Hearn, J. (1996). Is masculinity dead? A critique of the concept of masculinity / masculinities. In M. Mac an Ghaill (Ed.), *Understanding masculinities: Social relationships and cultural arenas* (pp. 202–217). Buckingham: Open University Press.

Helgeson, V. (1995). Masculinity, men's roles, and coronary heart disease. In D. Sabo & D. F. Gordon (Eds.), *Men's health and illness: Gender, power, and the body* (pp. 68–104). Thousand Oaks, CA: Sage Publications.

Henderson, J. L. (1979). *Thresholds of initiation.* Middletown, CT: Wesleyan University Press.

Heuer, A. (1995). Men and goodness. In R. U. Schenck & J. Everingham (Eds.), *Men healing shame: An anthology* (pp. 254–260). New York: Springer Publishing Company.

Hicks, R. (1993). *The masculine journey: Understanding the six stages of manhood.* Colorado Springs, CO: Navpress.

Hinsch, B. (1992). *Passions of the cut sleeve: The male homosexual tradition in china.* Berkeley: University of California Press.

Hoff, B. (1995). Interview with shepherd bliss. *M.E.N. Magazine.* May 1995. Retrieved June 6, 2004 from www.menweb.org/blissiv.html.

Hoffman, J. P. & Johnson, R. A. (1980). A national portrait of family structure and adolescent drug use. *Journal of Marriage and the Family, 60,* 633–645.

Hollis, J. (1994). *Under saturn's shadow: The wounding and healing of men.* Toronto: Inner City Books.

Homer. (1963). *The odyssey.* (Robert Fitzgerald, Trans.). Garden City, NY: Anchor Books.

Hooks, B. (2004). *We real cool: Black men and masculinity.* London: Routledge.

Horne, A. M. & Kiselica, M. S. (Eds.). (1999). *Handbook of counseling adolescent males: A practitioner's guide.* Thousand Oaks, CA: Sage Publications.

Houston, J. (1992). *The hero and the goddess.* New York: Ballantine Books.

Jacobi, J. (1973). *The psychology of C G Jung.* New Haven: Yale University Press.

Johnson, R. A. (1989). *He: Understanding masculine psychology. Revised edition.* New York: Harper & Row, Publishers.

Jung, C. G. (1959). *Aion: Researches into the phenomenology of the self. Collected works 9.* Princeton: Princeton University Press.

———. (1989). *Mysterium coniunctionis.* Princeton: Princeton University Press.

———. (1991). (R. F. C. Hull, Trans.). *Aspects of the masculine.* Princeton: Princeton University Press.

Kanin, E. (1967). Reference groups and sex conduct norm variations. *Sociological Quarterly, 8,* 495–504.

Kaufman, G. (1995). Men's shame. In R. U. Schenck & J. Everingham (Eds.), *Healing men's shame: An anthology* (pp. 31–49). New York: Springer Publishing Company.

Keen, S. (1992). *Fire in the belly: On being a man.* New York: Bantam Books.

Kernberg, O. (1992). *Aggression in personality disorders and perversions.* New Haven, CT: Yale University Press.

Kimbrell, A. (1995). *The masculine mystique: The politics of masculinity.* New York: Ballantine Books.

Kimmel, M. S. (1994). Masculinity as homophobia: Fear, shame, and silence in the construction of gender identity. In H. Brod & M. Kaufman (Eds.). (1994). *Theorizing masculinities: Research on men and masculinities* (pp. 119–141). Thousand Oaks, CA: Sage Publications.

Kimmel, M. S. & Kaufman, M. (1995). Weekend warriors: The new men's movement. In M. S. Kimmel (Ed.), *The politics of manhood: profeminist men respond to the mythopoetic men's movement and the mythopoetic leaders answer* (pp. 15–43). Philadelphia: Temple University Press.

Kimmel, M. (1997). *Manhood in America: A cultural history.* New York: The Free Press.

Kimmel, M. S. & Messner, M. A. (Eds.). (2004). *Men's lives* (6th ed.). Boston: Pearson.

Kindlon, D. & Thompson, M. (1999). *Raising cain: Protecting the emotional life of boys.* New York: Ballantine Books.

Kinston, W. (1983). A theoretical context for shame. *International Journal of Psychoanalysis, 64,* 213–226.

Kipnis, A. (1999). *Angry young men: How parents, teachers, and counselors can help "bad boys" become good men.* San Francisco: Jossey-Bass.

————. (1991). *Knights without armor: A practical guide for men in quest of masculine soul.* Los Angeles: Jeremy P. Tarcher, Inc.

Komiya, N., Good, G. E. & Sherrod, N. (1999). Emotional openness as a predictor of college students' attitudes toward seeking psychological help. *Journal of Counseling Psychology, 44,* 1–6.

Krugman, S. (1995). Male development and the transformation of shame. In R. F. Levant & W. S. Pollack (Eds.), *A new psychology of men* (pp. 91–126). New York: BasicBooks.

Kupfersmid, J. (1995). Does the Oedipus complex exist? *Journal of Counseling & Development, 32,* 535–547.

Kurtz, S. P. (1999). Butterflies under cover: Cuban and Puerto Rican gay masculinities in Miami. *The Journal of Men's Studies, 7,* 1999.

Lansky, M. R. (1992). *Fathers who fail: Shame and psychopathology in the family system.* Hillsdale, NJ: Analytic Press.

Lawrence, D. H. (1971). Healing. *The complete poems of D. H. Lawrence.* Volume 3. New York: Viking Penguin.

Levinson, D. J., Darrow, C. N., Klein, E. B., Levinson, M. H. & Braxton, M. (1978). *Seasons of a man's life.* New York: Alfred A. Knopf.

Linneman, T. J. (2000). Risk and masculinity in everyday lives. In P. Nardi (Ed.), *Gay masculinities* (pp. 83–100). Thousand Oaks: Sage Publications.

Lorber, J. (1994). *Paradoxes of gender.* New Haven: Yale University Press.

Low, B. (2000). *Why sex matters: A Darwinian look at human behavior.* Princeton, NJ: Princeton University Press.

Mac an Ghaill, M. (Ed.). (1996). *Understanding masculinities: Social relationships and cultural arenas.* Buckingham: Open University Press.

Maccoby, E. E. (1990). Gender and relationships: A developmental account. *American Psychologist, 45,* 513–520.

MacKinnon, C. (1987). *Feminism unmodified.* Cambridge, MA: Harvard University Press.

Madhi, L. (1987). *Betwixt and between: Patterns of masculine and feminine initiation.* LaSalle, IL: Open Court.

Mailer, N. (1968). *Armies of the night.* New York: New American Library.

Marchioro, K. (2001). From sambo to brute: The social construction of African American masculinity. [Electronic version]. *The Edwardsville Journal of Sociology, 1.* Retrieved October 3, 2005 from www.siue.edu/SOCIOLOGY/journal.

McCartney, B. (Ed.). (1992). *What makes a man? Twelve promises that will change your life.* Colorado Springs, CO: Navpress.

McGrath, E. (1998). *Practice opportunities—business coaching: Be strategic, don't take it personally.* Symposium conducted at the 106th annual meeting of the American Psychological Association, San Francisco.

McNab, S. (2004). Center for Sustained Human Development, Men's Studies and Fatherhood Program, Akamai University, Hilo, Hawaii. Retrieved September 16, 2004 from http://www.akamaiuniversity.us/MensStudies.html#1.

Meade, M. (1993). *Men and the water of life: Initiation and the tempering of men.* San Francisco: HarperCollins.

Men's Health/CNN National Men's Health Week Survey-1998. (1998). *Men's Health Magazine.* Emmaus, PA.

Men's Health Facts. Retrieved July 26, 2005 from menshealthnetwork.org/library/ menshealthfacts.pdf.

Messerschmidt, J. (2004). Varieties of "real men." *Men's lives* (6th ed.). Boston: Pearson.

Messner, M. (1997). *Politics of masculinities: Men in movements.* Newbury Park, CA: Sage Publications.

Miller, G. (2000). *The mating mind: How sexual selection shaped the evolution of human nature.* New York: Anchor Books.

Mirande, A. (1997). *Hombres y machos: Masculinity and Latino culture.* Boulder, CO: Westview Press.

——— (2004). Macho: Contemporary conceptions. *Men's lives* (6th ed.). Boston: Pearson.

Monick, E. (1987). *Phallos: Sacred image of the masculine.* Toronto: Inner City Books.

Mondimore, F. M. (1996). *A natural history of homosexuality.* Baltimore: Johns Hopkins University Press.

Moore, Dr. Robert L. Home Web Page. Retrieved April 9, 2004 from www.robert-moore-phd.com/Index.cfm.

Moore, R. & Gillette, D. (1990). *King warrior magician lover: Rediscovering the archetypes of the mature masculine.* San Francisco: HarperCollins.

———. (1992a). *The king within: Accessing the king in the male psyche.* New York: William Morrow and Company.

———. (1992b). *The warrior within: Accessing the knight in the male psyche.* New York: Avon Books.

———. (1993a). *The lover within: Accessing the lover in the male psyche.* New York: Avon Books.

———. (1993b). *The magician within: Accessing the shaman in the male psyche.* New York: William Morrow and Company, Inc.

Morrison, A. P. (1983). Shame, the ideal self, and narcissism. *Contemporary Psycho-analysis, 19,* 295–318.

Mosse, G. L. (1996). *The creation of masculinity.* New York: Oxford University Press.

Nardi, P. M. (2000). Anything for a sis, Mary. In P. Nardi (Ed.), *Gay masculinities* (pp. 1–11). Thousand Oaks, CA: Sage Publications.

National Fatherhood Initiative. Retrieved January 28, 2005, from https://fatherhood.safeserver.com/fatherfacts/intro.htm.

O'Donovan, D. (1988). Femiphobia: Unseen enemy of intellectual freedom. *Men's Studies Review, 5,* 14–16.

O'Neil, J. M., Helms, B. J., Gable, R. K., David, L. & Wrightsman, L. S. (1986). Gender role conflict scale: College men's fear of femininity. *Sex Roles, 14,* 335–350.

Osherson, S. (1986). *Finding our fathers: How a man's life is shaped by his relationship with his father.* New York: Fawcett Columbine.

Pederson, L. E. (1991). D*ark hearts: The unconscious forces that shape men's lives.* Boston: Shambhala.

Paechter, C. (1998). *Educating the other: Gender, power, and schooling.* London: Falmer Press.

Pellegrini, A., Huberty, P. D. & Jones, I. (1995). The effects of recess timing on children's playground and classroom behaviors. *American Educational Research Journal, 32*(4), 845–864.

Peplau, L. A., Rubin, Z. & Hill, C. T. (1977). Sexual intimacy in dating relationships. *Journal of Social Issues, 33*, 86–109.

Peterson, V. (2000). Mars and venus: The rhetoric of sexual planetary alignment. *Journal of Women and Language, 23*(2), 1+.

Pleck, J. H. (1981). *The myth of masculinity.* Cambridge, MA: MIT Press.

Pleck, J. H., Sonenstein, F. L. & Ku, L. C. (1993). Masculine ideology and its correlates. In S. Oskamp & M. Costanzo (Eds.). *Gender issues in contemporary society* (pp. 85–110). Newbury Park, CA: Sage Publications.

Pollack, W. S. (1990). Men's development and psychotherapy: A psychoanalytic perspective. *Psychotherapy, 27*, 316–321.

———. (1995b). No man is an island: Toward a new psychoanalytic psychology of men. In. R. F. Levant & W. Pollock (Eds.). *A new psychology of men* (pp. 33–67). New York: Basic Books.

———. (1999). *Rescuing our sons from the myths of boyhood.* New York: Henry Holt and Company.

Pollack, W. S. & Levant, R. F. (1995a). Coda: A new psychology of men: Where have we been? Where are we going? In R. F. Levant & W. S. Pollack (Eds.), *A new psychology of men* (pp. 383–387). New York: BasicBooks.

Potts, A. (1998). The science / fiction of sex: John gray's mars and venus in the bedroom. *Sexualities, 1*(2), 153–173.

Promise Keepers: Men of Integrity Homepage. Retrieved April 26, 2004 from www.promisekeepers.org.

Pruett, K. D. (2000). *FATHERNEED: Why father care is as essential as mother care for your child.* New York: Broadway Books.

Reichert, M. (1997). On behalf of boys: Lessons from the field. [Electronic version]. *Independent School Magazine.* Retrieved September 12, 2004 from http://www.haverford.org/about/visitors_boys_article.html.

Reid-Pharr, R. (2004). It's raining men: Notes on the million man march. In M. S. Kimmel & M. A. Messner (Eds.), *Men's Lives* (6th ed.) (pp. 580–585). Boston: Pearson.

Ridley, M. (2003). *The red queen: Sex and the evolution of human nature.* New York: Perennial.

Rites of Passage. Retrieved October 5, 2005 from www.pages.drexel.edu/~ages25/pgeneral.htm.

Robertson, J. M. & Fitzgerald, L. E. (1992). Overcoming the masculine mystique: Preferences for alternative forms of assistance among men who avoid counseling. *Journal of Counseling Psychology, 39,* 240–246.

Rodriguez, E. M. & Ouelette, S. C. (1999). Religion and masculinity in latino gay lives. In P. Nardi (Ed.), *Gay masculinities* (pp. 101–129). Thousand Oaks, CA: Sage Publications.

Rohmer, R. P. & Veneziano, R. A. (2001). The importance of father love: History and contemporary evidence. *Review of General Psychology, 5*(4), 382–405.

Rohr, R. (2004). *Adam's return: The five promises of male initiation.* New York: Crossroad Publishing Company.

Rubenstein, A. *Modern day rites of passage as the ultimate form of preventative medicine.* Retrieved October 5, 2004 from www.menshealthandwellbeing.org.au/content/views/83/0.

Rubin, L. B. (2004). The approach-avoidance dance: Men, women, and intimacy. In M. S. Kimmel & M. Messner (Eds.), *Men's Lives* (6th ed.). Boston: Pearson Education, Inc.

Sabo, D. & Gordon, D. E. (1995). Rethinking men's health and illness. *Men's health and illness: Gender, power and the body* (pp. 1–21). Thousand Oaks, CA: Sage Publishing.

Schaller, J. L. (1999). *Rebuilding your father relationship.* New York: Baker Publishing Company.

Schenk, R. & Everingham, J. (Eds.). (1995). *Men healing shame: An anthology.* New York: Springer Publishing Company.

School of Lost Borders. Retrieved January 23, 2005 from www.schooloflostborders.com.

Seidman, S. (2003). *The social construction of sexuality.* New York: W.W. Norton & Company.

Shaywitz, B. A. & Shaywitz, S. E. et al.[d1] (1995). Sex differences in the functional organization of the brain for languages. *Nature, 373,* 607–609.

Sheehy, G. (1998). *Understanding men's passages: Discovering the new map of men's lives.* New York: Random House.

Snodgrass, J. (Ed.). (1977). *A book of readings for men against sexism.* Albion, CA: Times Change Press.

Solomon, K. (1982). The masculine gender role: Description. In K. Solomon, & N. Levy (Eds.), *Men in transition: Theory and therapy.* New York: Plenum.

Sommers, C. H. (2000). *The war against boys: How misguided feminism is harming our young men.* New York: Simon & Schuster.

Stein, M. (1983). *In midlife: A jungian perspective.* Dallas, TX: Spring Publications, Inc.

Steinberg, W. (1993). *Masculinity: Identity conflict and transformation.* Boston: Shambhala.

Stevens, A. (1990). *On jung.* London: Penguin Books.

———. (2003). *Archetype: An updated natural history of the self.* Toronto: Inner City Books.

Stillion, J. (1995). Premature death among males: Extending the bottom line of men's health. In D. Sabo & D. F. Gordon (Eds.), *Men's health and illness: Gender, power, and the body* (pp. 46–67). Thousand Oaks, CA: Sage Publications.

Strong, B., DeVault, C., Sayad, B. W. & Yarber, W. L. (2002). *Human sexuality: Diversity in contemporary America.* Boston: McGraw-Hill.

Tacey, D. J. (1997). *Remaking men: Jung, spirituality, and social change.* New York: Routledge.

———. (2001). *Jung and the new age.* New York: Routledge.

———. (2004). *The spirituality revolution: The emergence of contemporary spirituality.* New York: Brunner-Routledge.

———. The Men's Studies Project. Retrieved October 13, 2005 from www.csbsju.edu/mensstudiesproject/.

Thompson, E. H. & Pleck, J. H. (1995). Masculinity ideologies: A review of research instrumentation on men and masculinities. In R. F. Levant & W. S. Pollack (Eds.), *A new psychology of men* (pp. 129–165). New York: BasicBooks.

Thompson, K. (1986). Myths as souls of the world. [Review of the book *Inner Reaches of Outer Space* by Joseph Campbell]. *Noetic Sciences Review,* Winter 1986.

Tiger, L. & Fox, R. (1972). *The imperial animal.* London: Secker & Warburg.

Troiden, R. R. (1989). The formation of homosexual identities. *Journal of Homosexuality, 17*(1–2), 43–73.

Turner, V. (1969). *The ritual process: Structure and anti-structure.* Chicago: Aldine Publishing Co.

Turner, V. (1982). *From ritual to theater: The human seriousness of play.* New York: PAJ Publications.

Van Gennep, A. (1960). *The rites of passage.* (S. T. Kimball, Trans.). Chicago: University of Chicago Press. First published in French, *Les Rites de Passage* (Paris 1909).

VanScoy, H. (2004). Hot-headed guys? It's all in the brain. *Health on the Net Foundation.* Retrieved August 10, 2004 from www.hon.ch/News/HSN/ 509404.html.

Von Franz, M-L. (1970). *Puer aeternus.* New York: Spring Publications.

Ward, J. (1999). Queer Sexism: Rethinking Gay Men and Masculinity. In P. Nardi (Ed.), *Gay masculinities* (pp. 152–175). Thousand Oaks, CA: Sage Publications, Inc.

Watkins, P. L., Eisler, R. M., Carpenter, L., Schechtman, K. B. & Fischer, E. B. (1991). Psychosocial and physiological correlates of male gender role stress among employed adults. *Behavioral Medicine, 17,* 86–90.

Webb, S. H. (2001). Defending all-male education: A new cultural moment for a renewed debate. *Fordham Urban Law Journal, 29*(2), 601+.

Weisfeld, G. E (1999). *Evolutionary principles of human adolescence.* New York: Basic Books.

White, P. G, Young, K. & McTeer, W. G. (1995). Sport, masculinity, and the injured body. In D. Sabo, & D. F. Gordon (Eds.), *Men's health and illness: Gender, power, and the body* (pp. 158–182). Thousand Oaks, CA: Sage Publications.

Wilkinson, D. Y. (1995). Gender and social inequality: The prevailing significance of race. *Daedalus, 124*(1), 167+.

Williamson, T. (1997) The history of the men's movement [Electronic version]. In F. Baumli (Ed.), *Men freeing men: Exploding the myth of the traditional male.* Jersey City, NJ: New Atlantis Press.

Wilson, E. O. (1975) *Sociobiology: The new synthesis.* Cambridge: Harvard University Press.

Yee, N. *Catching the Phoenix: The Social Construction of Homosexuality.* Retrieved August 18, 1995 from http://www.nickyee.com/ponder/social_construction.html.

Zuck, J. *Biblical Panentheism: The 'Everywhere-ness' of God—God in all things.* Retrieved July 31, 2005 from www.frimmin.com/faith/godinall.html.

INDEX

Printed in the United States
95966LV00002B/229/A

9 781934 043301